GERMANY: A SCIENCE FICTION

D1477134

Germany

A SCIENCE FICTION

LAURENCE A. RICKELS

FORT WAYNE, INDIANA

www.RawDogScreaming.com

Cover Design © 2014 by Rodolfo Reyes
www.roldolforever.com

Layout by D. Harlan Wilson
www.DHarlanWilson.com

Anti-Oedipus Press
Fort Wayne, IN

www.Anti-OedipusPress.com

PRAISE FOR THE WORK OF LAURENCE A. RICKELS

Aberrations of Mourning

"For Rickels, the link between technology and mourning isn't merely Freudian and speculative, but also solidly historically grounded. In his excellent book *Aberrations of Mourning*, he points to the advent in the west of recording devices such as phonographs and gramophones before in fact mortality rates had been reduced by mass inoculation, even among the better off. Many middle-class parents, following the fad for recording their children's voices, found themselves bereaved, and the plate or roll on which little Augustus' or Matilda's voice outlived him or her thus became a tomb. 'Dead children,' Rickels writes, 'inhabit vaults of the technical media which create them.' Bereavement becomes the core of technologies; what communication technology inaugurates is, in effect, a cult of mourning—indeed, Rickels even suggests replacing the word 'mourning' with the phrase 'the audio and video broadcasts of improper burial' . . . Researching my own novel *C*, which takes place during precisely this period of emergence, I found evidence everywhere to support Rickels' claim."

— **Tom McCarthy**

Nazi Psychoanalysis

"He brilliantly traces discourses on the relationship between pilots and their aircraft, spinning out all kinds of associations around men and machines, treating psychoanalysis as a kind of privileged discourse on the 'ongoing technologization of our bodies' that ran through the twentieth century."

— **Paul Lerner, University of Southern California**

"The author's knowledge of his own writing seems to produce a form of textuality that is forever sliding into the category of materiality . . . The author of *Nazi Psychoanalysis* has sought to develop a style that holds the line between a concern for content and a preoccupation with form in order to fight the restrictive nature of the modern symbolic order . . . Rickels' liminal textuality combines the normal position of the analyst and the dislocated situation of the patient in a mode of writing that is always-already becoming coherent/incoherent. This is the mark of what I want to call his post-modern schizo-style . . . Rickels' schizo-style allows us to see how psycho-pathologies emerge from the same hyper-reflexive modern moment that gave birth to psychoanalysis itself."

— **Mark Featherstone, Keele University**

The Case of California

"Rickels has written an important book reading psychoanalysis at the end of our century. His intent is to complete Adorno's refiguring of Mickey Mouse into his own Rickelsian refiguration of Freud's project."
— **Sander Gilman, Emory University**

"Provocative (and often hilarious), *The Case of California* explores the 'bicoastal logic of modernity,' with California as one coast and Germany as the other. . . . Startling and brilliant."
— *San Francisco Bay Guardian*

"Reading from an array of psychoanalysts, theorists, techno-cultists, psychic disturbances and juvenile converts, Rickels frames the dynamic transference of episteme, ectoplasm from Germany to California and its subsequent impact on the survivors of this endopsychic re-location . . . In California, Rickels observes an entire population of unmourned dead (from splatter films' zombies to neo-Christian vegetarians and 'impostor' adolescents) building bodies to house and preserve the perennial youth (unyouth) of their post-paternal and trans-psychoanalytic culture."
— **Akira Mizuta Lippit, University of Southern California**

Ulrike Ottinger: The Autobiography of Art Cinema

"Ottinger's filmic subjects—the marginal, the freak, the exile, or the nomad—find their way into the fabric of Rickels' text; detours into tangential literary evaluations, psychological musings, lengthy quotations, and even interviews with Ottinger herself work together to form a word-montage augmented by Ottinger's own photographic work. For instead of choosing stills from those films being discussed, Rickels intersperses Ottinger's photographs taken before and during filming to underscore his thoughts on the films in each chapter. Paired with his textual journeys into numerous arenas from journalistic history to Freudian psychology to Thomas Edison, these photos remain not static, but instead take on a nomadic quality as they wander among the words. The passion for collecting identified as central to Ottinger's work here has been virally contracted. Additionally, Rickels' language—playful, impish, and at times even joyfully impudent—celebrates the natural artifice present in Ottinger's approach to difference and the marginal."
— **Carrie Smith-Prei, University of Alberta**

The Vampire Lectures

"It's the ultimate book to give to anyone who makes fun of you for liking vampire novels or films."

— **Anne Rice**

"Rickels mines the study of cult phenomena, including vampire attacks, burial rituals, and sexual taboos that are recounted in legends, literature, and folklore. This vigorous contribution to literary and paranormal theory collections will enhance the pursuit of often remote scholarship into mythology and sorcery."

— *Library Journal*

"In the vampire's attempt to come to terms with his own need to kill, he becomes a proto-Übermensch, a material/maternal disrupter of the paternal line of reproduction, a subverter of the Law whose only law is incest. Now, this may not be your cup of tea, philosophically or otherwise, but it's a genuinely intense brew. In fact, it's almost creepy."

— **Erik Davis**

The Devil Notebooks

"Cultural criminologists are likely to be attracted to Rickels' attention to the expressive, aesthetic and emotional qualities of the Devil fictions he examines. Most importantly, his focus on the Devil as a figure of certainty is provocative precisely because it allows for the examination of a subject that has been marginalized in cultural criminology and criminology in general: the law-abiding citizen. As neither criminal nor victim but potentially both, the law-abiding citizen is the taken-for-granted background entity in the imagination of criminologists, particularly if criminology is defined as the study of crime, criminal and the criminal justice system."

— **Anita Lam, York University**

"*The Devil Notebooks* establishes the astonishing extent to which contemporary pop culture has been preoccupied with demons, succubi, possession, aliens, sexuality of all kinds, and the end of the world. The Devil, then, offers up a counter-history of humankind—a history from below as it were—that Rickels deploys with verve in a truly fascinating and important study of how and why the world as we know it has gone to Hell."

— **Michael Dorland, Carleton University**

I Think I Am: Philip K. Dick

"A Deleuzoguattarian rhizome that deterritorializes a wide array of psychic, anthropological and literary assemblages, *I Think I Am: Philip K. Dick* is the most compelling and philosophically creative book in the growing library of PKD Studies."

— *Extrapolation*

"Rickels does not force the fictions into the mold of his mostly psychoanalytic concepts, but rather bounces the concepts off the texts and leaves the reader to work out what they have dislodged."

— *Science Fiction Studies*

"Rickels does not merely invite readers to see Dick's work the way he does; instead, the theoretical framework invites a broader vision that includes and projects outward from science fiction and fantasy."

— *Studies in Popular Culture*

"Aside from its perfect fit of critic and subject, Laurence A. Rickels' book provides the most thorough and exhaustive reading of Philip K. Dick's literary work that exists. He goes through all the novels literally, both the science fiction works and the so-called mainstream novels Dick did not publish in his lifetime. The reader of science fiction should welcome a book like this, which is both knowledgeable of the SF tradition and creatively analytical. I could not put this book down once I began to read it."

— **George Slusser, University of California-Riverside**

"If the purpose of any interpretation is to build a case, then on some level Rickels—though obviously creating a 'corpus' of work whose sole trajectory is to breach the realm of the dead—does the opposite; he unravels, unearths (note the prefix) those universes that lie entombed inside us. What emerges above all are the terrible introjections that are shared across Dick's novels, the I that is abyssal, death that 'indwells' organisms and systems, our 'inevitable grounding—our being ground up—inside the tomb world.' Looking at 'y(our)' work, Dick, Rickels, the cracks that open up dispel whatever borderlines there might be between the living and the (un)dead, or, as it may be, reality and hallucination; writing is urged toward or 'over and über' death, the tomb worlds with which contact is established."

— *parallax*

SPECTRE

"Laurence Rickels offers blazing illumination of the invisible undertow of disquiet and uncanny in our knowledge of culture, consciousness and technology."

— Jonathan Lethem

"In Rickels's work—as, for instance, in Lars von Trier's films—misery is not a problem to be resolved and overcome, but the foundation for future insights, a setting in which new and difficult material will be revealed in a dialectic that often includes disaster."

— Artforum

"Rickels' . . . use of psychoanalysis makes it something like wallpaper on a computer, just the unquestioned background that provides a support for every-thing else to appear."

— Critical Inquiry

"Laurence A. Rickels, the man with the golden pun."

— The Rumpus

"In Rickels's reading, psychosis, as a state of removal from reality, is tied to the integration brought about at the end of mourning, while in psychopathy, which involves more of a removal from society than from reality, 'the failure to empathize and mourn tests the limits of tolerance.' A resistance to mourning is important in that the subject becomes even more shaken than stirred."

— Los Angeles Review of Books

"The provocations of Rickels' genius combustion engine—*Kulturindustrie*, psychoanalysis, deconstruction, German idealism and Shakespeare—lures us into introjection from the mindless mass media projection Sensurround riding Bond's technological wave."

— The Huffington Post

CREDITS

Address rehearsals of segments in this study appeared in the following publications:

Speaking of Monsters: A Teratological Anthology. Ed. Caroline Joan S. Picart and John Edgar Browning. New York: Palgrave Macmillan, 2012.

Stephen G. Rhodes: Apologies. Ed. Raphael Gygax and Heike Munder. Zurich: Migros Museum für Gegenwartskunst & JRP/Ringier, 2013.

Texte zur Kunst. Vol. 20. No. 80. December 2010.

Texte zur Kunst. Vol. 22. No. 85. March 2012.

Unter Vier Augen: Sprachen des Porträts. Ed. Kirsten Voigt. Bielefeld: Kerber Verlag, 2013.

The Whole Earth: California and the Disappearance of the Outside. Ed. Diedrich Diederichsen and Anselm Franke. Berlin: Sternberg Press, 2013.

Woods: On Identification with Lost Causes. Berlin: Archive Books, 2013.

Zeitschrift für Geschlechterforschung und Visuelle Kultur. Issue 53. June 2012.

CONTENTS

Danmed • Germans in *Plan for Chaos* • The death wish is the primal killer who succumbs to identification and brooding • Half knowledge as object of mourning

Conclusion

Baudrillard's charge of simulation: *The Holocaust* on TV • Television goes to the Frankfrurt School • Lyotard's pacific wall, the multiple chosen test, and digital integration • In the digital archive, opposition and democracy return among all the other names, events, or eras of history • Admitting the dead victims as credentials of the heirs to psychopathic violence • The shame of survival and the prospect of collective mourning

PREFACE

That I had moved not to the winter fairytale of Heinrich Heine's itinerary but to a science fiction was brought home by the German disinvestment in nuclear energy following the mishap in Japan. It's not just that the decision was facilitated by the spectacular disownership of its futural trajectory: the Atom bomb was the only technology going into the World Wars not made in Germany. More to the point was the *Gleichschaltung* operative in a decision too sudden and total to be rational, despite the benign content. One government figure disappeared together with his party from the map of German politics because he voiced caution and time out for further reflection. The ability of an entire nation to close ranks—which, as my former colleagues at UC-Santa Barbara confirmed, makes Germans good subjects but not necessarily the best leaders (or chairs)—is a syndication of the German legacy of doubling. The Doppelgänger is the single-minded contribution of German culture to occult literature; all along, it was in the ready position for streamlined re-entry at the high point of German science fiction: Fritz Lang's *Metropolis* (1927) and *Woman in the Moon* (1929). Although this engineering term for wiring AC electric motors to turn at the same speed was first borrowed by the Nazi party to name its coordination of society in all its parts and members, *Gleichschaltung* designates one of modernism's neutral structures, one that is as content-dependent as the double for its ethical tendency. It is doubling's mass-psychological counterpart.

In *The Case of California*, I submitted the (anti)thesis that California and Germany were the two coasts of the twentieth century's traumatic histories. I traced the about-face of émigré writers, theorists, filmmakers and psychoanalysts who saw in California the new frontier of the very symptoms that they had tried to leave behind in Nazi Germany. This double-take was best encapsulated in two equations that go back to the Frankfurt School: both National Socialism and the Californian culture industry constitute "psychoanalysis in reverse." This reversal on two counts and coasts led me inside the project I titled *Nazi Psychoanalysis*. Here, for the first time, I unfolded the endopsychic genealogy of German science fiction, reread and re-spelled "psy-fi." It was a tradition that had been left unattended by our reception of the genre as Cold War borne, although it came to shadow postwar science fiction in the mode of spectrality that won't be ignored.

I returned to psy-fi in response to the kind invitation by the Comparative Literature majors at New York University to deliver their annual lecture. It was to their positive reception of my book *I Think I Am: Philip K. Dick* that I owed the summons—and the consequent pressure to squeeze something new out of my recently concluded reading. But then I could see better that, in order to fix my focus on schizophrenia, I had overlooked the other limit concept in Dick's oeuvre. En route to my new work situation in Germany, I recognized psychopathy as the undeclared diagnosis implied in flunking the empathy test. The switch from psychosis to psychopathy as an organizing limit opened the prospect of a genealogy of the Cold War era. The immediate result was the initial section of this study, a new "close reading" of Dick's *The Simulacra* (1964).

Lang's *Woman in the Moon* was shown in Nazi Germany only in an expurgated version that deleted the camera pans of the rocket designs. It was felt that they already occupied and revealed the planning stage of the V-1 and V-2 rockets. The rockets that subsequently took off were adorned with mascot insignia referring to Lang's film. As a teenager, Wernher von Braun had also worked as an assistant to Germany's leading theorist of space travel, Hermann Oberth, the film's technical advisor. German science fiction was a countdown to a takeoff into techno-realization. No sooner projected, it was enlisted in the Nazi era of realization of science fantasies—which is why it was the prehistory to be forgotten vis-à-vis a genre now identified as a Cold War exclusive.

While my analysis of the James Bond oeuvre, *SPECTRE*, examined the Cold War era from within the adult profile of mourning that Ian Fleming gave his own Bond with modern German history, this study works through the preliminaries of repair that must be met in a world devastated by psychopathic violence before mourning can even be a need. *I Think I Am* was the endopsychic allegory of Dick's corpus. *Germany: A Science Fiction* makes the corpus a point of context—of onset and of return—for my endopsychic genealogy of the post-WWII containment and integration of psychopathy.

Philip K. Dick is my spirit guide in this genealogy. His work in the 1960s connected all the dots regarding the shift in perspective or repression that coincided with his death. Neither his reception (as psychedelic surrealist, for example, or political mystic) nor the extent of his influence on fellow authors fully registered the content of his California-Germany amalgamation—the genealogical foresight this study hopes to reclaim. Dick's projection of the change in direction and onset at the returning point in the 1980s was without precursor or peer. The forecasts of postwar worlds comprising Cold War science fiction were waylaid by aberration and error; I will argue that they were important contributions to the staggering of the onset of return so crucial to the developments after 1980 that made possible the recognition of the direct hit of Dick's vision.

Before recognizable science fiction entered his works as a recurring strand among split-off sections of a few words, right from the start—already in his first novel, which was identified as science fiction—Kurt Vonnegut was a satirist. In *Slaughterhouse-Five* (1969), a conceivable candidate for inclusion in this genealogy, the protagonist, Billy Pilgrim, is introduced to science fiction by his fellow inmate in the mental ward at the local veterans' hospital, Eliot Rosewater, who proclaims that A-literature "isn't *enough* any more" (101). Only science fiction can aid them in reinventing themselves and their universe. In the sparse topography that folds out of Vonnegut's oeuvre, there are references or coordinates that resonate with turns that this genealogy will take. Ilium, the Roman name for Troy, is the first name on Vonnegut's map, an invention to protect the innocent addresses. However, *Slaughterhouse-Five* deploys science fiction as an escape fantasy in the traumatic reckoning of the good war being not so good. To this end, time travel does not so much reinvent as rename the flashbacks symptomatic of Pilgrim's posttraumatic stress disorder with psychotic features. He carries the narrative forward by escaping or splitting, but each split is traumatically fixated on the author's own sojourn as a POW in Dresden at the time of the firebombing. This fixated splitting becomes the medium of recall of moments in Pilgrim's history, which alternate with stopovers in his psy-fi delusion of alien abduction. Pilgrim's loopy progress toward and away from Dresden, which brings him into contact with US protectors of the good war's reputation, mounts a satire of the home front during the Vietnam War.

Not as an introjected device displaced with regard to the truth in a protagonist's history (and occluded by topical reckoning and treatment), but on its own,
science fiction registered the steps in a larger process of integration that this study
follows out in the span of jump-cuts through postwar histories.

I will be rereading Thomas Pynchon's *Gravity's Rainbow* in terms of the
itinerary of integration. At first, the novel left itself behind by the dead weight of
its misconstruction of psychoanalysis in terms of a symptomatic yet forgettable
turn to the occult; just the same, the novel was engaged by its rewiring of behaviorism in the preliminary work of inside-out repair. Hans Jürgen Syberberg's
1977 *Our Hitler: A Film from Germany* (*Hitler: Ein Film aus Deutschland*) falls
short in anticipation of the work of integration. The reparation dynamic, which
addresses a wrong turn taken in Late Romanticism (and from which Syberberg
notably excludes Wagner), remains exclusive to the relationship between "Hitler"
and "Germany." In both Susan Sontag's enabling reception of *Our Hitler* and in
the film itself, "Hitler" is the tainted cultural artefact that assumes the status of an
object to be mourned. This scenario, compelling in a genealogy of fantasy, flunks
Dick's empathy test on a global scale. As the protagonist of the movie *American
Psycho* (2000) allows in his case: this is empathy with oneself.

On average, the haunting of identification, the draw of fiction, refers not to
missing people (or lost objects) but to the withholding of affect at the moment of
separation or withdrawal with which the consumer of literature catches up through
the catharsis offered by the fiction of identification. Freud insisted that affect,
always available and triggered in realtime, was never the content of repression.
What is repressed is the ideational content that cannot be allowed. This content of
repression is analogous to the object relation in mourning and melancholia. While
the mourner can grieve as readily over objects as over causes or ideals, the fixity
of the object relation skewers the lost causes and ideals also retained in melancholia. It is through melancholia, which draws a limit of relationality or legibility
through narcissism, that genealogy can address our biggest symptom. Philip K.
Dick showed us the way.

In 1997, the film *Contact* advertised that contact with German science fiction
was available again by flushing out the rocket's content of Nazi realization with
value-free science and melancholia. First there was the contact of a message from
an alien species, which was carried by German science fiction, or rather by one of its
realizations: the 1936 live TV coverage of the Olympic Games in Berlin. Encoded

in the copy of the transmission that the aliens sent back are the plans for building a rocket to take contact to the next level: communication in person with alien intelligence. Rocket, television, magnetic tape and the monitors of digital computation are uncanny-proofed as continuity shots, which now reach to the stars.

The protagonist, Ellie, is a father's daughter raised by the guardian of the tomb of the mother between them. As with Christine and her father in Gaston Leroux's *The Phantom of the Opera* (1910), they projected a communications network for contact with the other side, which the father's departure could then carry forward. One young woman's opera singing career under the missing father's aegis is another woman's professional commitment to the exploration of Outer Space. Ellie projects the death cult she maintained since childhood into the cosmos, which doubles as her inner world of lost love objects. To make the encounter as benign as possible, the alien mind meets her indirectly via the double of her dead father. In *Contact*, three histories of science fiction are conjoined full circle for our overview: the emergence of science fiction out of the discursive spread of modern Spiritualism, the rise of German science fiction in a countdown to realization, and postwar American science fiction, which, by 1997, can look past Cold War denial and do the aftermath. The contact in Outer Space with the alien mind in the father's ghostly drag leaves the tape recording blank, but for eighteen hours—the alleged duration of the encounter. This blank overlaps with the empty space inside the woman whose apprenticeship to contacting the departed was in the media of radio transmission and recording. The alien species made first contact through the noise and static between stations or off the radar. The ghost messages of the postwar chapter of modern Spiritualism known as the Voice Phenomenon also had to be extracted upon endless replaying and rerecording from noise on tape.

By its intrapsychic elaboration of the *Metropolis* test labyrinth and its mad scientists, Nosferatu lookalikes from Outer Space mediated by one Earthling, "Dr. Daniel P. Schreber," Alex Proyas's film *Dark City* (1998) completed the posttraumatically delayed contact the following year by adding the doubling momentum to the foreground of its confirmation of German science fiction's return. While eighteenth and nineteenth century English and French literature gave quality time to the representation of the vampire, for example, the creature of the night did not enter German letters, even though he could be considered native to the German backwoods. The Doppelgänger alone was given a place in German Romanticism. Murnau's *Nosferatu* (1922), the first film adaptation of Stoker's *Dracula* (1897), reclaimed the literary advantage for the medium of projection. Divorced from his own mirror image, the vampire Count would qualify as a Doppelgänger, but his doubling is not caught between the literal and the literary. Not until the advent of the film medium does the vampire arise in the form of a sheer image without copy. Murnau's revalorization of the vampire for cinema as a new Doppelgänger made the jump cut from German Romanticism to film, establishing itself—now in the guise of a robot, now of a rocket—as the continuity shot of German science fiction.

Friedrich Kittler spelled out that the double left letters to enter both film and psychoanalysis. Even before "The Uncanny," in his "Introduction to *Psychoanalysis and the War Neuroses*," Freud committed to theorization a splitting of the ego into "Doppelgänger"—in one corner the peace ego, in the other its "parasitical" double, the war ego (209). Freud's analysis of the doubling disorder led him to remap the topography of his theory and served as a blueprint for a series of applications in German military psychology; ultimately it became Nazi psychological warfare and mass psychology. The divisions of doubles that emerged from the experience-mutating changes brought about by WWI projected a new standard of survival of the fittest: *the fit with technologization*, a psychic fit now thought best secured through the unbalancing acts of dissociation, the new internal frontier of doubling. Dissociation was the mindset required of the modern pilot according to the German psycho-technical manuals plotting his course since the 1920s. His merger with the machine in flight rendered him an "auto-pilot" not only akin to the Maria double in *Metropolis* but even, after the fact, a missing link in the evolution of the self-steering rocket. Because Nazi Germany appeared so closely associated with specific science fictions as their realization, after WWII the genre had to delete the recent past and begin again within the new Cold War opposition. Certainly the ancestral prehistory was still intact (Jules Verne and H. G. Wells). But at the bulk rate of its generic line of production, science fiction would henceforth be native to the Cold War habitat. Nothing that was so much fun (before traumatization took over) ever really goes away. This study addresses the syndications of the missing era in the science fiction mainstream, the phantasmagoria of its returns, and the extent of the integration of all the above since some point in the 1980s.

It turns out that my collected work on group psychology and its media settings can be seen to offer in situ testimony and commentary to this era of return and reparation. In time, I entered upon a quasi-ethnographic aspect of my work. In the course of publishing on genres with strong and long B-lists, I came into contact with fan communities. Time to remember that the prize for hospitality goes to the vampire-heads. One recollection in lieu of many: at the Museum of Death in Hollywood, a family of vampires—and I don't mean the Manson kind, but father, mother, and two children—politely and decorously attended my book signing. The award for provincialism goes to the science fiction fans. You'd think their exposure to the adaptation industry would have installed some appreciation for the inevitability of interpretation. Instead, one of Dick's widows judged that the abundance of citations in *I Think I Am* amounted to plagiarism. Given Dick's extraordinary interest in the clinical literature, you'd think that his base would tolerate reading along psychoanalytic lines, but no: Dick-heads prefer to find their support in the arcane philosophies and theologies Dick, too, knew largely via encyclopedic paraphrase, unlike the case studies he read verbatim, up close and personal. But fans are the in-group portraits of larger tendencies. That my book's appearance coincided with the onset of academic interest in Dick's oeuvre didn't help matters. A junior highlight in American studies observed that my reading of Dick's relationship to melancholia represented the worst tendency in psychoanalytic criticism. But his characterization of my readings of discrete works as plot summaries meant he didn't even know what a case study looks like. From the widow to the dunce, the amazement that whole sections of *I Think I Am* don't refer directly to Dick (or that I make recourse to repetition throughout the book) betrays an allergy to formal mediations of thought (like literature) as profound as the ignorance of psychoanalysis. Literature is lodged in "the underworld of psychoanalysis"—as Freud named the source of the resistance to his science in the closing line of "The History of the Psychoanalytic Movement." And the academic suburbs of intelligent life, literature department by literature department, are crowded with the unwashed . . . I mean, the unshrunk.

Is it only because the recent past that my endopsychic genealogy would address is emplaced within my mortal loop that this work was harder to hold than to pull together? Certainly the genre of genealogy is the most trying task for your basic miniaturist. I give thanks to D. Harlan Wilson for his editing, which helped get across my transfer of endopsychic insights into a narrative ranging society-wide and history-long. I am grateful for the opportunities I had to present trial runs of my thought experiments in the course of several teaching assignments at the Academy of Fine Arts Karlsruhe and the European Graduate School in Switzerland. In the place of my signature, I acknowledge Jacques Derrida. In

Spectres de Marx he supplied the rebus (the return that returns) that I kept turning around and re-turning to in my thoughts until, coincident with my decision to switch coasts, I began to turn out this case study.

FROM HERE TO CALIFORNIA

1

Future worlds made in Germany were left unattended during the Cold War reception of science fiction. Then, beginning in the 1980s, the *Metropolis* look was in our faces in films, music videos, and the redesign of Disneyland's Tomorrowland. It is this watershed of return, rather than the decade or so that lies between them, which gives divergent styles to the first movies made of the American superheroes. In Richard Donner's *Superman: The Movie* (1978), the city called Metropolis is as modern as 1970s New York and the hero's secret bachelor pad from Krypton is of the same era, but befitting a Las Vegas wedding chapel. While Gotham City in Tim Burton's *Batman* (1989) belongs by its gadgets to the present, even the future, to look at it is to pass through a relay of Lang's film sets. The return of German science fiction left a fork in the look of the future between 1950s modernism with futurama accents (the original style of Tomorrowland) and the art-deco future in the past, a souvenir of New York made in Germany. Even the 2010 film *Inception*, ostensibly free to dream up alternate realities, was stuck in the turnstile of alternation between two choices: James Bond or *Metropolis*.

It is no surprise that *Blade Runner* (1982), Ridley Scott's adaptation of Philip K. Dick's *Do Androids Dream of Electric Sheep?* (1968), belonged to the avant-garde of this blast from the past. Dick's collected work inherited the metabolization of "Germany" in science fiction, from the establishment of "German" science fiction—as the transformation of the wound of gravity and grave into the wonder or miracle of takeoff—to "Germany" as the problem and object of integration in the postwar future worlds of the genre. In his 1964 novel *The Simulacra*, Dick confronts us with a new entity, the USEA, the future state of cohabitation of the United States or California with Germany. If there is a bicoastal dialectic whereby symptoms of Nazi German provenance wash up onto the Coast, then Dick brings it to its crisis point with the prospect of Germany's postwar integration so close to home. In *Do Androids Dream of Electric Sheep?* and *Ubik* (1968), the difficulty of this integration was carried forward as the ongoing social problem of psychopathy in which the failure to empathize and mourn tests the limits of tolerance.

    Martian Time-Slip (1964) and *The Simulacra* offered two perspectives on one future world seen now from Mars, now from Earth. The future belongs to America or California but with Germany and Israel as its most proximate, overlapping, even internal neighbors. The first Californian co-op housing unit to be built on Mars bears the name AMWEB, an acronym standing, in lieu of translation, for *Alle Menschen werden Brüder*. While the theory behind the therapy is immersed in German, the treatment of schizophrenia on Mars is conducted in American at hospitals in New Israel. In the off-world, which faces incipient psychosis as the greatest risk and chronic psychosis as a new social contingency, the autistic-schizophrenic ten-year-old Manfred, whose family emigrated from West Germany, is the one to watch and rehabilitate. The Californian settler Jack Bohlen, a repairman and recovering schizophrenic charged with building a delay chamber for the translation of Manfred's perceptions, undergoes the task of society's project of integration as a painful proximity to the youth, especially on the inside. Working to add a lapse in time to the boy's sensorium, he begins to undergo a relapse. Like Melanie Klein's patient Dick (in her 1930 study "The Importance of Symbol Formation in the Development of the Ego"), Manfred suffers from a premature onset of empathy and capacity for grief. The condition that amounts to a paradoxical intervention in Dick's regimen of testing leaves Manfred wide open to every unconscious thought crossing the minds around him. But what he sees via the fast-forwarding of his time sense is the tomb world: the ongoing prospect of entropy's omnipresence.

    Whereas on Mars schizophrenia is rampant, on Earth psychosis retains an endopsychic privilege held by one figure at a time. In *The Simulacra*, Kongrosian is the identified psychotic whose symptomatology coextends with Rollo May's *Existence: A New Dimension in Psychiatry and Psychology* (1958). This collection of studies by practitioners of existential analysis first made available to the English-only readership Ludwig Binswanger's "The Case of Ellen West," Dick's source for the image of the tomb world, which he used over and again as an interface between psychotic delusional states and the relationship to mourning. Kongrosian, himself a close reader of the literature on psychosis, cites Minkowski, Kuhn, and Binswanger as being among the few who could help him if they were still around (63). The obsessive compulsive disorder he presents is modeled on Minkowski's essay in May's collection, but the diagnosis "anakastic," which Kongrosian applies to fit his case (60), shows that he knows von Gebsattel's contribution as well. What seems not to be represented at all in the case of Kongrosian is Roland Kuhn's study of Rudolf, who was hospitalized in Switzerland following the attempted murder of a prostitute. In his introduction, May singles out Kuhn's study as the best demo of the existential-analytic reconstruction of a patient's complete world, which, for Rudolf, conjoins psychopathic violence, arrested mourning, and fetishism. Lost in the translation of Kuhn's title in May's collection is the specification of the case-subject up front as "depressive fetishist." When he lost his mother at age three, Rudolf applied activity in the missing place of affect. He found his dead mother and talked to and touched the corpse he did not take for dead. When this body was taken away, he searched for his living mother. Thus begins the section "Everyday Life" that Kuhn won from the static in the course of reconstructing Rudolf's history. "A small boy is searching the house looking for his dead mother. After having found the body he speaks to it and touches it. Later, after the body is lost to him through the funeral, he rummages through the entire house . . . In all these instances Rudolf is acting, behaving in a peculiarly active fashion which already reveals a certain industry. There is nothing contemplative to be found in his early memories" (397). In the beginning was activity, productivity, even industry in lieu of the recognition of loss.

When his father died, what returned was the dead body that Rudolf, now a young man, could again manipulate, searching for signs of the life sustained by his looking. Kuhn concludes that "it is certain that in the night during his bizarre activities" with the father's corpse, Rudolf "did not feel like mourning" (403). Back next day, though, as he witnessed the coffin being removed from the interior of the home, was the loss of the dead body. Whereas, according to Kuhn, absence of the body tends to stabilize the initial mourning affect, for Rudolf "the affect emerged precisely because of the loss of the body" (411). Kuhn searches for Rudolf's motivation: "Since to him the matter of the body represents its essence

. . . living man and dead body are not so very different, in certain conditions"
(414). In fact, "the materiality of man is more fully represented by the dead body,
since in man, alive, other factors disturbingly interfere" (ibid.). Stopped in the
tracks of his first murder attempt following the double loss of his father in 1938,
Rudolf spent the war years under Kuhn's care reclaiming his history of delayed
mourning from the narcissism of his chaos. In time, he could get out of the tight
spot he was in with the dead bodies of his parents by projecting the machinery of
repair upon his relationship to all the bodies that mattered. "[I]n various dreams
. . . he occupied himself, mostly with the help of complicated machines, with the
body of his father or of people unknown to him, predominantly of the female sex.
In most of these dreams he succeeded in bringing the dead back to life, a result
that gave him the feeling of indescribable happiness" (373). As preliminary and
prerequisite to a happy treatment outcome, one that begins to feel like mourning,
Kuhn separates out the violence from Rudolf's psychopathic industry, which he
reapplies toward recovery. Ellen West gets bogged down in the tomb world of her
schizophrenia, but "Rudolf stays productive and alive" (424).

Kuhn was Binswanger's disciple; he also inadvertently introduced outpatient
psychopharmacology when he discovered that an anti-psychotic medication they
were trying out in the hospital was useless in its prescribed purpose but seemed
to be effective in relieving depression. The drug in question, Imipramine, is
offered for Kongrosian's treatment by a representative of one of the Berlin-based
chemical cartels that recently pushed through the prohibition of psychoanalysis
in the USEA. Throughout society, everyone's expertise is called on to deliver
Kongrosian from his incapacitating symptoms. A psychokinetic virtuoso who
plays piano without hands, Kongrosian alone raises the middlebrow of official
entertainment, which otherwise shows (live from the White House) selected acts
from the amateur hours, talent shows, or auditions taking place nonstop in every
cooperative housing unit. Since, as the star of White House TV, he is inside the
hub of the USEA's government, Kongrosian's psychic ability—which represents
an acausal factor, one that even time travel-enhanced surveillance cannot control
or predict—poses a threat to the best-laid plans of political intrigue. Pembroke,
the head of police plotting to become dictator, allows one psychoanalyst, Dr.
Superb, who was treating Kongrosian, to remain in business, ultimately in order
to help anticipate and somehow bind this wild card in the pack. The sessions of the
last psychoanalyst connect up all the subplots in the novel. But it is Kongrosian's

paranoid refusal of drug treatment that leads to the first manifestation of his psychokinetic tendencies outside the concert setting. Pembroke, the one it takes to know one, identifies this new series of Kongrosian's violent removals of organs from bodies and of bodies to places far away as a political act (167). Following the drug to swallow, Kuhn's study emerges as the subtext of Kongrosian's switch from identified psychotic to society's everyman, who politically activates the psychopathic violence that the USEA aims to contain even as its sole content.

During the long term of Kuhn's treatment of Rudolf, D. W. Winnicott was beginning to retrofit what he would rename a neurotic analysis to admit the psychopath. Under wartime conditions, juvenile delinquency in the UK was treated as mental illness for the first time. Winnicott worked out his initial approach to treating the new ailment by improvising group therapeutic support for the children and teens who, evacuated from cities under air attack, were under evaluation for disorders first modeled by shell-shocked soldiers. During the postwar era, Winnicott sought to nip the budding psychopath by intervening early in the antisocial tendencies of children; the disturbances he thus addressed were developmentally earlier than the advent of the capacity for mourning toward which he, in theory, was ushering his clients. "Mourning in itself," Winnicott advises and admits, "indicates maturity in the individual," while "the immature ego cannot mourn" ("The Psychology of Separation" 132). But Winnicott himself was uncomfortable with mourning, which he handed over to his precursors Freud and Klein for theorization. He situated his psychopathic analysis within the corridors of an institutional approach to the containment of acting out that he was reclaiming and revalorizing for analytic understanding. To the role of long-term analyst, Winnicott preferred that of on-call consultant, who, with one opening interview, established the teamwork of therapy for which the child's family was commandeered as a site of recovery. Once consolidated and rationalized for secondary gain, the antisocial tendencies in young children can spawn the psychopath, and they symptomatize a deprivation in what Winnicott termed the holding environment prior to the egoic maturity set for mourning, but at an age old enough to be beyond a fateful internalization of this environmental fault line. In Winnicott's estimation, there are certain advantages to the industry of the psychopath over the psychotic's playing dead or the neurotic's endless involution of dependency.

According to Winnicott, the child, whose grounds for stealing or acting destructively are as yet unconscious, signals both the importance of the environment and the return of hope with each delinquent act ("The Antisocial

Tendency" 123). These two senses or directions of delinquency must be met halfway and contained by analyst and family if testing for love in all the wrong places is to be reversed and the child replaced on the path toward integration and mourning. In "Delinquency as a Sign of Hope," Winnicott identified the hope that begins to emerge as the "hope of a return of security" (95). What returns, in other words, is an environment the child can reality-test for its capacity to endure and contain inner turbulence. "Lack of hope is the basic feature of the deprived child who, of course, is not all the time being antisocial. In the period of hope the child manifests an antisocial tendency" ("The Antisocial Tendency" 309).

Winnicott argued that when the stealing or destructive child replaces his unconscious objective with a denial of the deprivation or loss, that which he steals or destroys becomes a thing with dangerous properties of its own that the child must master over and again. At this turning point, the act no longer communicates hope. Instead, "the secondary gains that arise out of the skill that develops whenever an object has to be handled in order to be mastered" support fetishism, which Winnicott sees as heading hope off at the impasse of denial ("Transitional Objects and Transitional Phenomena" 19). But Winnicott's criteria for treating or scheduling the treatment of antisocial patients cannot cancel the new legibility he at the same time extended to the limit. His attribution of hope's expression to the antisocial child's first delinquencies resonates with a sense of hope to which the history of the word tracks back; this is especially the case given the importance of the environment that these acts illuminate. Preserved to this day as the cognate *verhoffen* in the German language of hunters, hope originally designated the startle response that allows you to consider—in pulling back before a blockage in the intended path—the alternate directions to take within a suddenly altered environment. The moment of hope thus gives pause for thought or reality testing. Within this extended sense of hope inherent in delinquency, the development of a fetish can be considered not only as blockage but also as the very transit center for a deferral process that renders the onset of integration an act of gainful maintenance and repair.

Freud saw the fetish incorporate the last and lasting memory at the border of traumatic amnesia, which it supports ("Fetishism" 155). But according to the non-sexological examples he cites of two sons who both know their fathers to be dead and don't acknowledge that they're gone (155-156), Freud discovered, in lieu of psychotic foreclosure, fetishistic dissociation as the new functioning in a world shaped by traumatic histories. The unstuck momentum or oscillation in this border zone between neurosis and psychosis inspired Walter Benjamin in his media essays to identify the sensorium of dissociation as gadget love, the new reality testing. In the twittering occupation with push buttons and switches, Benjamin recognized fetishism to be protective of function, which administered shocks or shots of inoculation against the otherwise psychoticizing direct impact of technologization and massification. According to Benjamin, with each click the camera imparts a posthumous shock to the moment taken; hence the protective loop of delay is specific to this immunizing relationship to and through gadgets ("On Some Motifs in Baudelaire" 328).

2

In *The Simulacra*, German is not the USEA's second language but the sacred one that supplies all key terms governing society. For this postwar state that contains Californians and Germans in strained cooperation and includes representatives of Israel in foreign policy deliberations internal to this cohabitation, the split-level social division is between the Ges and the Bes, the *Geheimnistraeger* (those privy to the secret or, literally, those who carry the secret) and the *Befehlstraeger* (those who carry out commands). The Ges know or carry a double secret. The two leaders of the USEA, *der Alte*, as Konrad Adenauer was known, and First Lady Nicole Thibodeaux, who is modeled on Jackie Kennedy, are not only mere figureheads but also fakes. *Der Alte* is an android whose replacement with each new election upsets the whole balance of power in the ensuing rivalry over the commission to build the next one. Nicole Thibodeaux, long dead, has since been played by actresses selected for their resemblance to the original. The USEA incorporates two date marks, then: the opening season of the German Federal Republic under Adenauer's direction; and the Kennedy presidency, famous for the stamp of identification accorded West Germany on the occasion of a wounding division but nonetheless the high point of the era of the economic miracle or *Wirtschaftswunder*.

In name, the postwar miracle resonated with the earlier transformations of lack or loss into the wonders of German science fiction, which underwent realization as the *Wunderwaffen*, the miracle weapons of WWII. In the 1950s, when these miracles were reclaimed in name for the onset of the repair of wounds inflicted during the Nazi era, the science factional track of the once projected exploration of the outer limits was to be continued by the Space Race and the Californian culture industry. Both syndications first came together in 1955 in two Disneyland TV shows starring Wernher von Braun and dedicated to the Tomor-rowland of interplanetary travel. NASA was founded in the late 1950s after the US was back in the race following setbacks that were reversed under von Braun's new direction. Responding to US taunts that Soviet advances in rocket technology rode on the backs of captured Nazi scientists, Krushchev declared that Americans had no excuse for their space impotence since the mastermind behind the Nazi V-2 rockets was at their disposal. Unstuck by this doubling of the negative, von Braun's postwar career began to take off until he could be found sharing photo ops with President Kennedy, who gave NASA the direction and funding to land on the Moon in the immediate future.

In 1958, von Braun's successful satellite launch was the first proof positive that the US was still in the Space Race. The acceptance that the launch automatically brought with it led the rocket scientist into two excursions through fictionalization. In *First Men to the Moon* (1960), von Braun gave himself license to the writing of passage through Outer Space. An earlier science fiction, *Project Mars*, also largely conveyed real-time science of the day that already counted down to takeoff, but there was still that stretch of fictionalization required for the flight to Mars, which implied a future past of successful Moon landings and an intervening history of satellite weaponry and final world war. *First Men to the Moon* is launched in the present while the fiction of the two astronauts interpersonalizes the scientific forecast of a roundtrip to the Moon as NASA's next step, which is presented by a layout of fact-driven "pop ups" surrounding the narrative. The fiction von Braun intro-duces into the demo largely conjugates out of human frailty a succession (almost a sitcom) of mishaps that the team of two survives. The smell of the fish one astronaut savors makes the other one sick; but there's a fish bowl-like gadget handy that was specially designed for this among other items on the list of what's hard-to-do under gravity-less conditions. Double duty is served: while he's throwing up, he remains out of range of the bullet-size meteor that suddenly cuts through the craft.

Von Braun's other exercise in fiction or propaganda was a wrap: the film *I Aim at the Stars* (1960) was about him. His proximity to Nazi war crimes—the involvement with the exhaustion of "human material" in post-Peenemünde rocket production at the underground Mittelwerk plant—was edited out. The history of his V-2 rocket career ends with the British raid on Peenemünde; his decision to surrender to the victorious US forces follows. A charge from his past must be admitted, however, ultimately as an immunological part of the whole to be excluded. Curd Jürgens as von Braun is pursued by a wandering witness, but it is an American GI turned journalist who lost wife and child in a rocket attack on London. Preferable by millions is the witness who gratingly interrupts von Braun's assimilation to US interests—until even the witness must accept the American hero following the successful launching of the satellite. The administration of this inoculation consists in the repeated hard-to-prosecute charge of von Braun's criminal responsibility for specific casualties among the collateral damage of warfare. His invention of the rocket as an infraction is negotiable, especially if war is conceded to be a flawed but implacable standard of moral behavior. The British director, J. Lee Thompson, would go on to make the Hollywood film *Cape Fear* (1963) about the relentless pursuit of upstanding US citizens by a homegrown psycho. Whereas the horror symptomatizes the earlier assimilation-cum-disappearing act of the Nazi past, the decision at the end not to kill but to imprison the psycho for life reflects the postwar concession to integration.

The launching of von Braun's American career as a pop culture star internalized turbulence—so often the case in acts of idealization—although the volatility that his case for mascot status had to pack away was historically unique. The founder of the self-esteem support franchise EST, for example, would base the new motivational therapy on his own name change in 1960 from John Rosenberg to Werner Erhard, the first name a tribute to von Braun, the second to Ludwig Erhard, Adenauer's minister of finance during the economic miracle. In Werner Erhard's words: "Freudians would say this was a rejection of Jewishness and a seizure of strength" ("Werner Erhard"). The attempt to reverse the taboo bust through subsequent revisionism turns up the volume on the original breach: Erhard would later claim that his first name, which he had happily misspelled in the original appropriation, always referred to Heisenberg instead.

On the Disney shows in the early 1950s, von Braun's stagefright played to a double audience. In the studio's recent past, Walt Disney alone received Leni Riefenstahl in 1938 on her state visit to Hollywood to show and promote *Olympia*, but his own technical staff refused to project her film. Nervous, as though he at least felt he was getting away with something or leaving something unaddressed, von Braun nevertheless worked hard to help establish in and with the Disney shows a continuous, upbeat history of invention. Throughout his career, von Braun demonstrated highly focused industry in turning over vast sums of debt into the prospect of Outer Space exploration, which promised the unification of peoples and promoted his own integration inside and out. As soon as von Braun arrived, he recognized that, in the United States, a space program could be funded only upon becoming part of popular culture. He tried his hand at science fiction, conceiving and commencing what he called his "technical tale" in 1946. He packed into the fiction of a mission to Mars endless mathematical and technical calculations as the testimony given by experts to governmental agencies from which support for the Mars voyage had to be obtained. When his novel was rejected, von Braun turned to popular science, a genre in which he published numerous projections of future voyages based on the science and technology of the day. The Disney shows animate text and illustrations of some of these books that von Braun used to advertise the possibility of space travel and its funding in the first place.

The second Disney show starring von Braun folded Kurd Laßwitz's 1897 novel *Two Planets*, the ancestral work of German science fiction, into its official timeline of imaginative projections of travel to Mars. Whether this was under his direction or brought about by one of the émigrés on the staff, von Braun gave an endorsement of the continuity passing through them for the first English language edition of Laßwitz's novel in 1971: "I shall never forget how I devoured this novel with curiosity and excitement as a young man. . . . From this book the reader can obtain an inkling of that richness of ideas at the twilight of the nineteenth century upon which the technological and scientific progress of the twentieth is based."

Laßwitz's *Two Planets* projected Martians as benign figures who, like friendly ghosts from an idealized cultural past, bring to Earth the news that the foundation for limitless cultural and intellectual innovation constitutes a transformation of the struggle for survival of the fittest into an acceptance of the fit with technology. Because Earthlings can't rise above the brutal view of survival, their instructors from Mars suffer from the prolonged contact and then contract Earth fever, which makes them short-tempered, arrogant, corrupt, even violent, and in desperate need of treatment back home. The Martian view of techno leisure-time as the setting for perfectibility of our evolutionary legacy of intelligent life is unique in early science fiction. The tradition that prevailed, beginning with H. G. Wells's *The War of the Worlds* in 1898, sees technological progress, via the Martians, as a calamitous agency of evolutionary regression.

In Laßwitz's fiction, the rarefied Martians select the Germans as the most advanced Earthlings for the experiment of elevating humankind to Martian or Kantian standards. Wells imagines that the Earthlings, who can't defeat the technologically advanced vampire brains from Outer Space, will nevertheless prevail by dint of their own mortality, the evolutionary milieu that guarantees survival of what Wells names an ordinary brain in the title of his autobiography. The microbial organisms that attack human bodies when they lapse into lifelessness take the Martians for dead and set about disposing of them as corpses while yet alive. "But by virtue of . . . natural selection of our kind we have developed resisting power; to no germs do we succumb without a struggle, and to many—those that cause putrefaction in dead matter, for instance—our living frames are altogether immune. . . . By the toll of a billion deaths man has bought his birthright of the earth" (380). To be taken for dead while alive (and yet to survive) is the closing image of the ordinary human bond of relationality that Wells's narrator submits in the last line of the book: "And strangest of all is it to hold my wife's hand again, and to think that I have counted her, and that she has counted me, among the dead." This surviving acknowledgment of the death wish at close quarters as the intrapsychic counterpart to the victory over the Martians did not make it into the narrative's conscription for total psychological warfare. Already in 1938, when Orson Welles broadcast his radio adaptation of *The War of the Worlds* in the guise of breaking news, the Outer Space narrative was pulled through the passing comment by H. G. Wells's narrator that the public reacted to the reports of the Martian landing with less excitement than they would to news of an ultimatum to Germany. That ordinary people miraculously triumph over the unbeatable foe against all odds would become the organizing injunction of US Propaganda. Only the Death Star foe threatens to win out of mastery; those gathered together into a slapdash crew on the good side must win, but as potential victims and losers, never as outright winners. Roland Emmerich, the highly successful Hollywood genre filmmaker, switched at film school in Germany from production to direction when he saw *Star Wars* and was able to recognize the true formula for success, which its second nature for Americans concealed from them. In the States, the success formula behind *Star Wars* was attributed to Joseph Campbell's 1949 book *The Hero with a Thousand Faces*. But Emmerich's *Independence Day* (1996) proved the rule by its consummate redevelopment of the Allied propaganda pattern that Lucas had perhaps unwittingly hitched to fantasy heroism in 1977. Emmerich's later

skirmish over the transfer in *The Patriot* (2000) of an incident of Nazi atrocity to
the account of the British in his rendition of the American Revolution—a score
his 2011 film about Shakespeare not being Shakespeare (*Anonymous*) was still
settling—fits the PR profile of Wernher von Braun's US assimilation. To this day,
the preservation of the good war—in which every foe of Anglo-America is again
the Third Reich, but as an intact and unexamined threat—is a hideout for war
profiteers who can get off only via evil. But the fantasy derived from WWII propaganda also keeps a secret and holds in store an object of repair as the good that
comes with mourning.

What remained largely unaddressed in post-WWII science fiction was the
Holocaust, just as it went unaddressed in the public sphere at large until some
turning point in the 1980s, an absence the nervous von Braun on Disney TV tries
to pass beyond in the pitch and toss for space exploration. In his 2003 foreword
to George Orwell's *Nineteen Eighty-Four* (1949), Thomas Pynchon identifies the
place of this absence in the work written in 1948, the date mark that the title
preserves by metathesis. "There is some felt reticence, as if, with so many other
deep issues to worry about, Orwell would have preferred that the world not be
presented the added inconvenience of having to think much about the Holocaust.
The novel may even have been his way of redefining a world in which the Holocaust did not happen" (xvii).

If *Nineteen Eighty-Four* passes over the Holocaust, then this motivates a
reading of the doomed future world of Newspeak as a kind of natural history
exhibit of the extinct possibility of a victorious postwar Nazi world. The import
of the protagonist's decision to begin keeping a journal lies in the past tense of
the closing appendix on Newspeak: the project of Big Brother is struck out in
the turning of the diary page. Reframed as alternate history and Bardo delusion,
Philip K. Dick's *The Man in the High Castle* (1962) installed another display
case in the wonder room of false forecasts; for all its dead weight, the novel's
prospect of a Nazi victory securing a postwar world was vulnerable to the
deregulation of history to which it owed its fictional account. More than the pen,
what is mightier than the delusional world in *Nineteen Eighty Four* is the word
given in adolescence. The salient feature of Newspeak, the amalgamation of
abbreviations and acronyms, is at the same time the very essence of linguistic
metabolization before which the ideological goal of language's neutralization
pulls up short and surrenders. Big Brother's death sentence is issued in or by

adolescence as the original occupation or cathexis of language in the mix of the buffering metabolization of the techno-massificatory pressures that are upon us. The original authorial upsurge of personalized language in adolescence isn't a phase or phrase that passes. Its essence continues as jargon in scientific and theoretical work or as the punning of news-speak.

Winnicott argued that Nazi Germany sought to harness adolescent energy to its project of total warfare by establishing the teen as superego. By thus skipping the personalization of the death of parental guidance, a process otherwise developmentally constitutive of adolescence, the Nazis placed the teen in the position of Big Brother. "Rebellion no longer makes sense, and the adolescent who wins too early is caught in his own trap, must turn dictator, and must stand up waiting to be killed—to be killed not by a new generation of his own children, but by siblings. Naturally, he seeks to control them" ("Contemporary Concepts of Adolescent Development" 146). Once total war is taken out of the equation and replaced by chronic conflict pulling up short before the prospect of nuclear destruction, the now less likely scenario of the Nazi socius no longer speaks to teens. According to Winnicott, the atom bomb was dropped on war as we knew it. If war once extended via prep work into the training and containing of adolescent energy, then without the ideology or rationale of future total war, adolescence was deregulated and, following the introduction of effective contraception, here to serve as the metabolic site of sex and violence. As Winnicott concluded in 1963, "Adolescence now has to contain itself, to contain itself in a way it has never had to do before. . . . So adolescence has come to stay, and along with it the violence and sex that is inherent in it" ("Struggling through the Doldrums" 151).

In containing itself, adolescence reaches to the border it shares with psychopathy. Winnicott comments: "[T]here is nothing more difficult than to decide whether one is seeing a healthy boy or girl who is in the throes of adolescence or a person who happens to be ill, psychiatrically speaking, in the puberty age" ("Deductions Drawn" 326). Only time will tell, just as the passage of time or maturation is the "only one real cure for adolescence" ("Struggling through the Doldrums" 145). At the group level, the one who begins to fit a psycho profile reduces the pressure on the other group members to act out: "[I]n a group of adolescents the various extreme tendencies tend to be represented by the more ill members of the group. . . . Behind the ill individual whose extreme symptom has impinged on society . . . are grouped a band of adolescent isolates. . . . The ill one had to act for the others" (153). Adolescence and psychopathy inhere in one another now as inoculum and expiration date, now by proxy and antibody.

In the science fiction horror movie *The Blob* (1958), basic assimilation of adolescence for realigning the socius in the face of psychopathic violence is demonstrated in good breast/bad breast alternation by the local cops. The good cop enters into a tentative alliance with "the kids" over and against the protests of the bad cop. "He acts like he was still fighting the war." But "it's not a crime to be seventeen-years-old." Later the bad cop will counter the excuse that "they're just kids" with: "Every criminal in the world was a kid once."

In the beginning, the protagonist played by Steve McQueen and his date take care of the first casualty of the menace from Outer Space, an old man who touched the stuff, which, clinging to him, progressively absorbs him. Following the instructions of the doctor (to whom they brought the ailing man), they go back to the setting to find out more about what in fact happened to the victim. On the way, the protagonist and his wondrous date, who by her voice alone mediates, moderates, and modulates the tension between group and couple, are held up by a car race to which three friends in a truck challenge them. This detour through the short attention span of adolescence introduces the good cop who referees the traffic violation but then decides to give McQueen, who is after all trying out a two-seater relationship, another chance. Remembering his doctor-prescribed duty, McQueen enlists the three friends to join in the search for evidence. In what looks like a point of impact, they find the cracked sphere out of which the goo first flowed. They also find the old man's house: the date decides to bring along and care for his "doggie."

Because the good cop is not always on duty and is anyway biding his time in the face of the bad cop's dissenting opinion, McQueen and his date are on their own. The three friends have hooked up with a larger group to watch a midnight screening of "spook" films. The vigilant duo shows up to enlist the greater group for help in warning the community that the monster of mass murder is at large. The kids don't jump to; they wanted to see the movie. But then, after all, they do rally. Their attempts to raise consciousness in the community, however, meet only with midlife criticism/crisis. When the first door opens, partying midlifers want to absorb the teen fun and play along with the "Paul Revere" gag. Another try annoys an adult bar tender, who deals all the time with "monsters" and tells them to "beat it!" But the group-warning expedition also disturbs a couple of young people necking behind the foliage and withdraws from this limit internal to its own dynamic.

McQueen and his date enter the curiously abandoned store of his dad and for the first time both see the blob, which claims the doggie, whose loss elicits the first show of grief. They rally their posse of friends, but again can't get past the on-duty bad cop's dismissal of their call for help as a prank. So they make a ruckus that we first overhear and identify together with one adult couple as "air raid sirens." When we join the town gathered around the source of the noise, however, it's just the kids in their cars honking. In the meantime, the blob has left the store and targeted the packed movie theater (it looks like no one there heard the sirens). Like an undeveloped analogy, it first seeps through vents into the projection booth. After the projectionist is absorbed, the projector stops and the film is reduced to its own blob-like celluloid stuff. But when the annoyed moviegoers look up to see what's going on, they recognize the blob oozing down into the theater. That's why, when the cops and the witnesses turn away from the store (which, empty of evidence, looks like another false alarm), the unstoppable testimony of an incalculable number of people fleeing the theater and screaming out the warning of the blob's ongoing menace undoes the bad cop's aversion, just as it was verging on paranoia. Shortly beforehand, in the police office, he announced that the kids were out to test him, to get him: "They heard about my war record. . . . They're trying to break me down, figure out how I tick."

The blob is revealed where the teens breed in groups. An available association from the lexicon of postwar science fiction lies between the gelatinous organic blob and the collected protoplasm of the race or species from which future generations are engineered or replicated rather than reproduced. The replicational bonding of the teen group is thus lifted out of its frame—on one side, the off-limits and out-of-it parental couple; on the other, the future couple that is ambivalently stamped out of the group—to represent the dystopian prospect of a totalitarian alternative history. The cop with the war record learns to distinguish between the unframed youth of Nazi ideology and the family-next-door teens.

McQueen and his date are trapped in the path of the blob's advance. A newly coordinated response ensues. The good cop phones the small group inside the diner, which the blob has entirely enwrapped, counselling them to go down into the basement. Once the group has cleared out of the diner, the converted cop applies his artillery skill to sever one of the overhead electrical wires and electrocute the blob. It doesn't work. In fact, it only starts a fire, a problem subsumed by the greater problem of the diner's diminishing oxygen content. While the good cop faces the prospect of the loss of the good kids, the converted cop pats his shoulder in empathic recognition of the man's grief. Then the diner's owner automatically applies his extinguisher to the fire—and the blob retreats. It can't stand the cold of the CO_2 extinguisher, a specific brand that is in short supply. The father of McQueen's date, the otherwise wooden principal of the local high school, remembers that his institution is stocked with this particular brand. He goes there with the kids to obtain the extinguishers; when he can't find his keys, he lifts the first stone to break into school. The reconfigured social group contains the menace. Now the military can be summoned in recognition of the threat, and the frozen blob is transported to the North Pole. The blob can't be killed but only stopped—"as long as the Arctic stays cold." The classic science fiction closing line from this period is pronounced by McQueen. The bad cop's paranoia gives way to the teen's good paranoia, nice as ice. As long as the Cold War was the only greater container available, the problem of psychopathic violence could be integrated only up to a point by the postwar adolescent or group psychological response to it. The spookshow movie theater of teen projection and socialization made the problem manifest, but then it had to be surrendered to the Cold War opposition—until, beginning at some point in the 1980s, its containment came in from the cold.

In von Braun's science fiction novel *Project Mars: A Technical Tale*, completed and translated into English by 1948 but not published until 2006, the preparations for the voyage are staged in amusement-park-like settings that already project the Disney TV show's simulation of a voyage to Mars. "Even a Martian landscape was portrayed on the rolling carpet that passed before the eyes of the pilot as he synthetically flew along" (104). In German science fiction, rocket flight, which takes over where the pilot takes off as an auto-pilot merged with his machine in flight, is the ultimate android double, wheras in post-WWII science fiction, as already in von Braun's technical tale, a new android interface begins to fold out of the onboard computers that, when supplied with the right tape for the emergency scenario, can steer the spaceship clear.

In *2001: A Space Odyssey* (1968), Hal's psychopathic forwarding of deprivation twists free, internally, from the psychotic techno-doubling of Hel, the missing mother preserved in or as *Metropolis*. As one side of a defensive split, the android in German science fiction always introduced metabolic representation of the to-be-excluded (in the first place woman, in the same place reproduction and death) as the objective of technologization. What the postwar shift in reception adds to the mass-psychological transmission of the android passing through it is adolescence in the family setting. Adolescence, the time-based version of psychopathy, is the container in which we must face the psycho as our double at close quarters: *there but for the grace of the good object go I.* The android comes to draw the distinction we hold fast to in this tight corner between psychopathy and empathy. The prospect of what psychoanalysis considers as integration crosses the mind of the protagonist, tester, and android hunter in *Do Androids Dream of Electric Sheep?* when he concludes that, in future tests for empathy or its absence (which would continue, just the same, to be used to identify the difference between androids and humans), questions should be included that would test for the ability to empathize with androids, too.

Although it is in fact Dick's third android novel, *We Can Build You* (1972) was most likely written first but certainly sets itself up as an opening installment by its origin story, which re-stages the other two android novels in the form of a genealogy. Androids or simulacra are invented and two demos built in anticipation of Civil War reenactments using replicants as the future of mass entertainment. Dick's origin of the android and the Disney development of Audio-Animatronics, which premiered in 1964 with the simulation of President Lincoln, coincided with the 1961-65 Centennial season of commemorative Civil War battle reenactments in the US. In *We Can Build You*, the investor, who is otherwise in the business of Outer Space colonization, reroutes the invention of simulacra for the production of simulated settings of stability to offset the psychoticizing effects of the isolation. This is how androids are marketed in *The Simulacra*: Colonists on Mars can expect to share a property line with a "famnexdo," a family of androids who live next door.

In *Do Androids Dream of Electric Sheep?*, the rebound from this outer rim of containment introduces the problem android who, subjected as a famnexdo member to the very loneliness and boredom that androids were built to deflect, grows up adolescent going on psychopathic. On Mars, alienated androids take drugs, consume pre-science-factual science fiction, drop out of their family settings, and follow their psycho-visionary leaders. German science fiction explored psychotic Outer Space via the android dyad. Postwar science fiction that introjects

Germany, on the other hand, evaluates psychopathic violence in the family and group settings of androids as teens.

It is possible to link the victory of the Allies over Nazi Germany (as well as their follow-up success in winning the immediate peace) to the promotion of differentiating group or in-group formats in lieu of mass psychology. In Nazi Germany, television was installed in public places that admitted up to three hundred viewers. In the US, however, the direction was taken from TV to introduce as a group-psychological format the circle of family and friends that comfortably wraps around the set for optimal interaction. Hence the world according to Nazi German victory—in Dick's *The Man in the High Castle* (1962)—never really makes it to TV land. "I wonder what it's like to sit home in your living room and see the whole world on a little gray glass tube. If those Nazis can fly back and forth between here and Mars, why can't they get television going?" (77). This cultural difference came to be reflected in publications by US psychoanalysts and military psychologists toward the end of the war advising what were the best conditions for the successful return home of the soldiers, which in time would also be the conditions to be met by civilians undergoing family systems therapy.

Wernher von Braun got the message that the related format of teamwork could draw his Faustian striving onward. Arnold Schwarzenegger and Jürgen Klinsmann followed Wernher von Braun into the Californian Valhalla of team spirits. I have already analyzed the Governator's rise to power out of his bodywork from Austria to Munich to world prestige (in California this time) and his follow-up prep work onscreen. As an update, I can quickly add that Schwarzenegger lost his emissary status on the coast, the synthetic position he long occupied between Freud and Hitler, when he confused his film therapy with the politics of his elected position. Still following the direction of his films to implant the good maternal object or breast and thus transform the paternal substitute running on empty, Schwarzenegger took on two powerful step-institutions early on in his term of office: the teachers' and nurses' unions. And then he was history. Klinsmann's career, between California and Germany, is still open (in 2011 he was placed in charge of the US—really, the Californian—soccer team). The German soccer team was in a rut in 2006 when Klinsmann was brought out of his retirement in California to coach and manage it. In California, Klinsmann became a convert to the lifestyle, which he studied and packaged as the team-spirit model he subsequently imported: the German team made third place in the World Cup. Klinsmann returned to California, delegating his second in command, Joachim Löw, as the new manager. According to the model made in California, Löw kept the team in a finals position until winning first place in 2014. Even this cumulative victory is imbued with the team model of momentum, which builds to victory out of losses or near-misses. I remember sitting in the tea room associated with Heinrich Heine on the North-Sea German island Norderney, watching with other vacationers the Moon landing on TV. I picked up the muttering among the assembled guests that this was their doing, too, their triumph, Wernher von Braun, etc. Even though Klinsmann did not lead the US team to victory in 2014, he brought the team into the World Cup semi-finals, a first, in which the German TV audience claimed a share: the double victory of 2014.

Von Braun understood that a total effort is realizable by linking the different agencies in the US that would cooperate in the event of space travel. In the Introduction to his 1952 *The Mars Project*, which contained the projected science and math separated out from his abandoned science fiction novel, von Braun summarized the difference between space flight as entertained in science fiction and space flight as obtainable now. "The central figure in these stories was usually the heroic inventor. Surrounded by a little band of faithful followers, he secretly built a mysteriously streamlined space vessel in a remote back yard. Then, at the hour of midnight, he and his crew soared into the solar system to brave untold perils—successfully of course" (1). Von Braun considers Fritz Lang and Thea von Harbou's *Woman in the Moon* the acme of these developments. Here the symptomatic picture of German science fiction is complete: the central figures are joined together by various aberrant mental states (from traumatic neurosis to psychosis) and they leave behind no one to mourn them. What the future holds is teamwork. "Since the actual development of the long-range liquid rocket, it has been apparent that true space travel . . . can only be achieved by the coordinated might of scientists, technicians, and organizers belonging to very nearly every branch of modern science and industry" (ibid.).

Von Braun's *Project Mars: A Technical Tale* commences in 1980 California, which is now part of a global government established after the third and final war. Not the atom bomb itself but its launching from a satellite orbiting the moon put an end to warfare. Because of the satellite's role in the war, the peace on Earth was at the same time "the symbol of the final victory of man over space" (ibid.). For his fictional encounter between Earthlings and Martians, von Braun brings together the two receptions of our future projected upon Outer Space (i.e., those of Laßwitz and Wells) as the precondition for the future world's integration. Whether it is the early 1980s or the late 1940s, the postwar era gives up war for space exploration. On Mars, the explorers encounter and acquire a "refined technology" that prompted Martians long ago to abandon "all regional concepts," including racial prejudice, national or local patriotism, and nostalgia (178). "So integrated had their economy become that any trouble afflicting one locality was immediately painful to the entire planet" (ibid.). Earth has only begun to benefit from peace. On Mars, the Earthlings learn that a long burgeoning of culture will follow, but that in time the "inner urge to action" responsible for invention will grow lethargic under global conditions of standardization (177). But the cultural pessimism of one Martian host gives way before evidence that the lassitude on Mars has been shaken up by contact with Earth. Now another brand of advice can be given in response to an Earthbound pessimism that the Earthling commander cites from recent terrestrial history. In the final war, mankind had come "so close to the abyss of universal cultural suicide" that "many Earthling thinkers . . . proclaimed that technology bore an eternal curse and that naught but a return to a simple bucolic existence of self-determination could preserve humanity from utter self-destruction" (203). But a Martian sage warns against the very thought of a return to Nature. "There can . . . be no turning back for any civilization which has once pinned its faith to the advance of technology" (ibid.).

3

"Germany is Our Problem" is the title of Henry Morgenthau's 1945 book version of his proposal from the year before that postwar Germany be pastoralized to insure world peace. Carrying forward the sense of defenselessness in the face of unstoppable psychopathy, the book opens with Corporal Adolf Hitler weeping with hysterical rage on his hospital bed the day Germany signs the armistice. Then it's the next sentence and it's twenty-two years later—it's Hitler again, this time beaming and strutting for the newsreels, jump cutting his sense of loss with its reversal. "What had happened to the world's high hopes of peace?" Morgenthau asks. "So many precautions had been taken to prevent the Germans from breaking out again! But something must have been omitted" (1).

In *Stimmen der Nacht* (*Voices of the Night*), Thomas Ziegler implements the Morgenthau plan as an alternate historicization of WWII. The excess population that Germany's pastoralization could no longer support moved to South America, with Nazi leaders in charge of this migration and movement. Unrepentant Germany reestablishes its might and mission in exile while Germany proper is a jungle chaos of fragmented rogue movements. The electronic bugs that spread advertising in *The Simulacra*—it was a persistent Nitz commercial on the topic of body odor that drove Kongrosian to a renewed manifestation of his psychotic break, ultimately as psycho—convey the voices of the dead in *Stimmen der Nacht*. But the audio devices are now electric *Kletten*, burrs still clinging from the German forest but as typical "Nazi-invention. Paranoia crystallized in technology" (12). They start out besetting only Jakob Gulf as his wife Elisabeth's static clinging. She planned her death on his live TV show as a preliminary gesture to her comeback. By now, in parallel realtime, the dead Nazi leadership is transmitting on the line that one man's dead wife opened up. This is the deep reversal or alteration in Ziegler's alternate history. What was heard on the postwar tapes of the Voice Phenomenon was a true underworld in which all the dead were clamoring for contact, their communication no longer regulated by opposition. In the postwar world of Germany's punitive regression and split-off unity as continuous with the Nazi past, only the White Night harangues and broadcasts of the Nazi murderers press for transmission. Now that the talking dead of the Reich are on the air, the aged surviving leaders, preserved on ice and cocaine in bunkers deep inside the Andes, are ready to let the Teutonic plates blow nihilism high. In Ziegler's 1993 revision of his 1984 novel as a dream from which the new conclusion awakens to welcome the reunification of Germany, the change or typo that renders the original *vergoß* (169) *vergaß* (182) takes back the therapeutic termination. When Mengele, still alive in South America, hears the Führer's live transmission, he sheds all the tears he denied the dead of Auschwitz. His shedding or *vergießen* of tears slips on the altered past tense, *vergaß*, and issues the verdict that he "forgot" all the tears.

Morgenthau's proposed intervention proved short-lived, however, once the problem it solved became part of the proposal. Critics in the States calculated that the aftermath of Morgenthau's plan was that at least twenty million Germans would have to go. It is this prospect of mass murder's renewal through sentencing of Germany (more than the immediate shift of the total war fronts to the new dividing line of the Cold War) that led to the project of Germany's integration in the postwar Western world, although it was indeed the Cold War that diverted the attention of the victors from the conditions Jewish survivors brought to the peace. Under no pressure from the Allies, Konrad Adenauer pushed through the policy of restitution that the German Federal Republic negotiated in the early 1950s with Israel. It counts as the premier and most lasting foreign policy of the postwar world. From within its perspective of restitution, the continued existence of the two postwar states could only be projected in tandem.

It was as traumatic neurotics that a line of reception awaited survivors of the Holocaust who qualified. This specialized area of evaluation was up and running on a massive scale since the WWI epidemic of shell shock. In both world wars, it was soldiers first, then women, children, and teens in the air war. Survivors of Nazi persecution were summoned to undergo a screening process administered according to insurance standards of suspicion. This gave rise to a rejection of the restitution policy as retraumatization. The search for an adequate relationship of and to restitution had to find alternatives to preexisting models (e.g., pension evaluation for psychological casualties of war or war reparations between states). When an interruption of professional development (considered, that is, as a developmental problem under duress) was added to categories for compensation, the alternative notion of "good" productivity was introduced, not as an injunction to be productive, but as a measure of deprivation, the other's as one's own. In this way, restitution inadvertently but inevitably provided a language of valuation that former perpetrators of and heirs to psychopathic violence could recognize and use to address deprivation and loss without laying claim to ethical cleansing. With its introduction, restitution delivered the family value of adolescent promise from Nazi mass-psychologization to the victims to be integrated as applicants for the correction of the recent past. Inequities in the protection of productivity could be corrected (symbolically, Adenauer stressed), which allowed postwar Germany to inherit German history as the history of this inalienable right. If it is true, as is generally claimed, that the policy of restitution was intrinsic to the *Wirtschaftswunder*, then the recovery at the foundation of the German Federal Republic happened not in spite of but because of the commitment to productivity as standard of deprivation's measure and repair.

In 1960, her first year out of art school, Eva Hesse produced a body of work that E. Luanne McKinnon dubbed "the spectre paintings." Hesse saw herself as an artist and a painter already in adolescence; at the appropriate age, she allowed herself to be represented as such with her paintings reproduced in the magazine *Seventeen*. But in 1960 she decided to paint herself out, through and through (McKinnon 7). Several of the "spectre paintings" are identified as self-portraits. Hesse took two of these paintings to sessions with her psychiatrist at this time, a strong sign of their breakthrough status. The look of the work reaches back through Willem de Kooning to Edvard Munch (the trajectory most often noted), but it also bounces off the saturated elegance of Milton Avery's art as well as making contact with paintings by German Expressionists like Ludwig Kirchner. While she was thus not working through the most contemporary influences in 1960, they do follow the summons of the Doppelgänger, the motif that occupies or cathects the foreground of this early work as its recognition value. In particular, the double portrait of the monstrous ghoul and the ethereal bride is resonant with many Gothic narratives of couplification shadowed by the unfinished business of haunting. But the double occupancy of these paintings is rarely quite so literal or literary. At times a figure appears alone, but stands off to the side, displaced by the felt blank that sets the place and pace of the unidentified double. When we discern a trio, the middle figure, like a substitute (or a stepparent), marks the loss or divide that just takes two.

At the first showing of the "spectre paintings," one's viewing was inscribed within a progress toward abstraction that would then have been the outcome of this season of painting. But there was also a thread of continuity to pull in Hesse's use of line, which contributes to the compositional and thematic dynamic of doubling pursued throughout this work. In time, Hesse would regularly claim to be producing "non-art," even "nothing" (Godfrey 48). She also struggled to reclaim this sweet nothing from another tendency in her art making. Hesse was often wary that her work strayed into the court of the beautiful. When one sculptural piece, "Right After," proved too beautiful in her estimation, she in a sense remade it—without, however, tossing the prior version (Godfrey 32). Instead her 1970 "Untitled (Rope Piece)" doubled but diverged from "Right After" largely through an immersion of the material in visceral-seeming latex, giving us the inside view of a body of work, only for zombies.

In German, the word most commonly associated with that which isn't beautiful, but ugly, "hässlich," seems to carry forward the artist's own patronymic as modifier; in this capacity, it subsumes all the doubles it summons, gathers them in a space not of resolution or annihilation but of legibility. If the "spectre paintings" work through a past steeped in Germanicity, then it was another contact with "Germany" that allowed Hesse to find an outlet for external innovation and to restart as a contemporary artist. Joseph Beuys, whose work came out of a German reception different from her own but turning on the same era, came to stand for a cluster of renewals that she, too, reclaimed from the returns. As a stowaway in her husband Tom Doyle's 1964 residency in Düsseldorf, a sense of secret or spectral agency came to attend this first contact with her native land since her rescue by the *Kindertransport* in 1938.

For Hesse's 1964 return, her father entrusted her with gathering materials for the family's restitution claims, specifically for losses her mother's family had to pack away. The father's reckoning of reparation for the Nazi undermining of a German family's productivity, however, came after the mother was gone. The father separated from her, took a new wife, and received custody of the children. Then his forlorn ex marking the spot (she was in with survival) committed suicide when Eva was ten. In sync with the restitution policies that made it possible for Germany to continue in history, Eva's father followed out a larger structure of righting wrongs that did not subsume (though for the time being did contain) the insupportable responsibility to and for the dead. He inoculated his daughter with the task of reparation, which Eva Hesse in Germany went to great pains to fulfill meticulously on her father's account.

In the West German factory studio where she spent over a year pursuing what she would come to characterize as "non-work" (Sussman 9), Hesse followed her husband's recommendation that she experiment with the material lying around. As Doyle remembered it, "It was the string that got her going" (Danto). In the case of a boy studied by Winnicott who tied up everything with string, this symptomatic overuse revealed in his case that it was the interruption of his transitional bond with the maternal environment that sent him spinning around within an orbit of near-missing contact. In "Transitional Objects and Transitional Phenomena," then, Winnicott distinguished between the use of string as communication (of separation and deprivation) and its use as denial of separation. On the one hand: "String can be looked upon as an extension of all other techniques of communication. String joins, just as it also helps in the wrapping up of objects and in the holding of unintegrated material" (19). On the other: "As a denial of separation string becomes a thing in itself, something that has dangerous properties and must be mastered. . . . In this case the mother seems to have been able to deal with the boy's use of string just before it was too late, when the use of it still contained hope" (19). We learn in the postscript that it was too late after all; the boy didn't fill the blank of his depressed mother and the rest is the history of his drug addiction beginning in adolescence. The mother and the analyst were able to string the boy along until he fell through the gaps, proving that the string medium itself is not limited to the framing conditions of the case study, namely communication or its failure, denial.

Between the lines of her drawing and painting, Hesse's sculpture began to fold out as the translation of line into string. The externalizable line was the residual charge of doubling, which she was able to wrap around a new period of non-work. For her signature sculptural works after 1966, Hesse temporalized the translation of line into string by re-projecting doubling as repetition. This was reflected both in the serial composition of the sculptures and in the imperative she heeded during this period to remake several of her earlier works as *hässlich*.

While one door opened in Germany for her future art, another door closed upon her past. The most telling re-encounter with her background during the residency in West Germany was her visit to what had been the Hesse family's home in Hamburg. When she introduced herself as a former occupant, perhaps as an opener to gain entry for a tour, the new inhabitant slammed the door in her face. The door opened and shut on the many lives that were allowed to proceed unprosecuted from the Third Reich unto natural death in West Germany. Set before her, however, is the uncanny yet inevitable prospect of the postwar integration of "Germany." Given its forever untenable placement, wasn't the place of "Germany" (in the sum of experience or even history) a true underworld where the dead could no longer be organized according to any opposition of belief systems or precept of successful mourning?

Unconsciously on purpose, McKinnon gave to Hesse's 1960 paintings the same name, British spelling intact, that Ian Fleming gave the underworld organization he introduced into the Cold War setting of James Bond in 1960 while preparing his narratives for projection into the new medium of film. Up against the screen, Fleming stood an outside chance of assuaging the spectral figures returning by name and background (as victims and perpetrators) from the traumatic recent past. Eva Hesse's spectre paintings gave the foundation for her own explorations of the underworld, initially as the place of past losses and separations, then as the site of her innovative and Hesse-lich assembly of lines, the formal counterpart to the uncanny work of integration that alone renews our relationship to history as contemporary.

The capacity for mourning, the undeclared but pressing objective of the industry of Outer Space transport (which is overshot by the rocket's unimpeded progress through continuous history), is brought closer in *The Simulacra* through time travel. By its trailblazing exploration and construction of alternate realities, time travel is science fiction's own internal simulacrum. Time travel is the inner world of space exploration, and space exploration is the external reality in which time travel studies and contains itself. Time travel moves in the orbit of testing and mourning where Melanie Klein situated our all-important relationship to the inner world. As the safety zone of internalized good objects, this inner world must take the brunt of the impact of the traumatic loss that, before it can be individually addressed or redressed, awaits the shoring up of the very foundations of this after-life. The external world is good for providing a less phantasy-muddled version of reality that the inner world can use as a control in the testing and re-securing of its reserve of posthumous relations.

In *The Simulacra*, then, time travel takes over where the fetish function of Outer Space transport leaves off. Before it recognizes itself as science fiction, time travel functions as the essence of Christian and Oedipal fantasies. The over-riding daydream wish that time travel would appear to fulfill is the circumvention of the present tense of ongoing tensions through the more perfect union between the idealized past and the future. Fantasies of attending one's own development from conception onward rehearse and repeat the ultimate fantasy: the death of death. Projected upon history, time travel could reenact the Civil War or WWII to bring about one's own private happy ending. But these illusions of time travel are ultimately not supported in *The Simulacra*. Bertold Goltz, an Israeli who hides out in the counterculture (although all along he is the behind-the-scenes head of the USEA's government), is the media Meister of time travel. "He was long since back there, at the time of his birth and onward into childhood. Guarding himself, training himself, crooning over his child self . . . Bertold Goltz had become, in effect, his own parent" (152). When an assassin takes aim in the present and fires—Goltz simply drops dead. And when the First Lady and the Israeli foreign minister try negotiating with Göring a separate peace for the Jews in exchange for a Nazi German victory, the *Reichsmarschall*, who has been brought back from the past on a time trip, is unable to think outside the box that claims him. His execution in the future does not even produce a ripple of change in the present. Indeed, von Lessinger, who invented time travel technology during the foundation of the

German-Californian state, warned that there were two exceptions to the enhanced surveillance that his technology provided: one, any psychic or psycho medium like Kongrosian, and two, the Third Reich. "I think that von Lessinger was right in his final summation: no one should go near the Third Reich. When you deal with psychotics you're drawn in; you become mentally ill yourself" (43). (In the 1978 German edition, the "psychotics" are translated as "Psychopathen.")

And yet unceasing industry goes into the attempted manipulation of boundary concept Nazi Germany via von Lessinger's time travel technology. Hitler's assassination is attempted many times over and, on one occasion, Hitler even receives twenty-first century psychiatric treatment. In their attempts to remove the Holocaust and lose the losses, time travelers, who cannot but run up against the limit built into the technology, would appear to be in reality-training to abandon redemptive fantasy and recognize the limits of reparation and integration. In time, the responsibility to and for the dead, mourning's ethical imperative, comes up from behind the limitation von Lessinger programmed into the very time travel that turns the denial.

Hawthorne Abendsen is the fictional author in *The Man in the High Castle* whose internal novel reintroduces a version of our reality into the external narrative's alternate history of Axis triumph. In a 1978 letter to Joseph Milicia dated August 7, Dick identified Abendsen as *Geheimnistraeger*, "a carrier (knower I mean) of a secret, and it is a secret which frightens him" (*Selected Letters: 1977-1979* 181). If the ability to mourn means, bottom line, that there's a place in your psychic reality for absence, then Dick's opening exploration of the legacy of WWII in or as California could only initiate an approximation to the secret via the introductory offer of alternate histories. Two years prior to his exploration of the outer limits of reparation and integration in *The Simulacra*, Dick began with the construction of an alternate history in which the "loss" of California reserves a place for absence.

It all came back, full circle, with the onset of mystical or psychotic revelations in 1974. *VALIS* (1981), the science fiction novel that folded out of this breaking experience, was originally projected as a sequel to *The Man in the High Castle*. During the time of revelations, Dick suddenly woke up and saw a figure standing by his bed. He recognized himself—as did his wife beside him, who started screaming. "I trying to soothe her kept saying over and over, 'Ich bin's,' which the next day I looked up in my German dictionary. It is the idiom for 'It is I,' but I didn't know that. Later on, up to now even, in fact more and more, under abrupt duress, I can only speak in German" (*Selected Letters: 1974* 101). While Dick couldn't be sure what or who it was speaking through or to him when he spoke German, in the science fiction it is up to his namesake by translation, Horselover Fat, to recognize in the UFO a computer-like teaching machine, which projected reality "as a sort of mirror of itself, so that it can obtain thereby an objective standpoint to comprehend its own self" (*Selected Letters: 1977-1979* 136). The loopy outreach of the *VALIS* trilogy added computing to the tighter testing situation in *The Simulacra*, where the rocket-and-Doppelgänger history of German science fiction gave the objective standard for the reality test by which the postwar inner world of time travel came to and through the past.

Dick never intended to deconstruct, as he puts it, WWII history (*Selected Letters: 1977-1979* 183). The historical fact Abendsen introduces after the fact must join a relay of variations on the history he reclaims from blank denial. In *The Simulacra*, the secret has been submitted to time traveling reenactment, which does not change history but folds out of what-history-shows alternate present realities that multiply or deconstruct the finite recording surface of remembrance.

Klein always addressed hope in conjunction with reparation in the span of their joint intervention or definition: hope *is* hope of making reparation. When less overwhelmed by destructiveness, reparation becomes possible and the all-important process of integration takes place. And yet, in what would be her final but never finished essay, "On the Sense of Loneliness," Klein showed how integration must pull up short before a "feeling of irretrievable loss" (301). The sense or direction of loneliness, which guarantees the incompletion of the analytic work of integration, harbors mourning, but as the final frontier.

At the height of the Nazi German threat to the UK, Klein undertook the analysis of the ten-year-old Richard. Although it was condensed to fit the span of evacuation from the air war, the analysis ended up, in Klein's estimation, becoming the best demo of her diagnostic innovations. *Narrative of a Child Analysis*, as she titled the document, is also her final completed work, prepared for publication on her death bed. Here the work of integration, reduced to its essential incompletion, requires that at least the two wars be brought into some kind of relationship. Debt or guilt must be expended on the work of repair, which is brought back as hopefulness, even happiness. As "the wish to restore" came more and more "to the fore" (50 n1), the patient "became gradually able to face and integrate his destructive impulses" while "greater tolerance towards other people as well as towards his own shortcomings developed. . . . He no longer felt compelled to turn away from destroyed objects but could experience compassion for them" (466).

The war little Richard brought to session and reenacted as primal scenes was also the external war he followed and studied in the radio news broadcasts and three daily newspapers. He was Jewish and knew that for him there could be only one outcome to the war. But that didn't stop him from goosestepping up and down the office and giving the Hitler salute (164). It didn't stop Klein from interpreting the bad Hitler Daddy Penis inside him (158). Far more difficult and consequential than identification with Hitler was Richard's consideration of sharing the work of repair with the destroyed enemy. "This was shown, for instance, when he regretted the damage done to Berlin and Munich and, at another occasion, when he became identified with the sunk *Prinz Eugen*" (466). Even as the untimely deadline of the analysis was approaching, Richard remained hopeful, which Klein reasoned (together with his conduct of the war inside and outside him) was proof that his relationship to the good internal object had been re-secured.

Inadvertently, the word chosen for the West German restitution policy, *Wiedergutmachung*, over and above its horribly banal promise of making it literally all better again, and in accordance with Klein's Nietzschean understanding of the noble valuation of the internal object, spells out the making good again of objects of repair as preliminary to the onset of the capacity for mourning. Those who lose as winners would turn gravity or the grave around by the industry of their crypto-fetishism. But like Philip K. Dick, who decided to major in German in high school shortly after the United States entered WWII (*Selected Letters: 1977-1979* 117), Richard also takes mourning like a victim to the next level. Both tendencies are shaped toward mourning in *The Simulacra* by a double exposure to the links and limits of time travel, the inner world as science fiction.

SIMULATIONS

1

Part documentary of the V-2 rocket and part adaptation of Thomas Pynchon's *Gravity's Rainbow* (1973), Robert Bramkamp's 2002 film *Prüfstand 7* (*Test Stand 7*) relied in both parts on the expertise of Friedrich Kittler, who appeared twice in person in the film. What I learned as late as 2012 while reading Bramkamp's book on his film—watching the film doesn't give this away—was that the director's impetus or license for making *Test Stand 7* came out of his reading of *The Case of California*. For the documentary book, Bramkamp conducted an extensive interview with Kittler that goes off purpose when the filmmaker raises the question of the technobody as object or objective of the psy-fi impulse.

> I believe it is true that every cyborg or cyberspace film and all techno fantasy, techno philosophy, including Laurence Rickels, that they all refer to and affirm the conceptual, hoped-for, and feared fusion of human bodies with nonorganic materials—today that would be silicon. I am, I believe, the only skeptic on this score. For the simple reason that I believe that technology is far too good to knock around forever with us humans. (116)

When Bramkamp next brings up Pynchon's provenance of the rocket as "won" from the "feminine dark" to bring it into association with the internal feminine of mourning that I entered into my compilation of group or adolescent psychology,

Kittler elides the mourning and identifies Pynchon's "feminine dark" as mother earth, the rocket's point of departure. It was technology that thus left the earth behind at takeoff, Kittler underscores. He adds that it is incidental to the significance of this rupture whether a rocket is manned or not (122).

> Rickels draws a very strict parallel between psychoanalysis as, he thinks, the most formative science or theorization of the twentieth century, on the one hand, and technology on the other hand. I'm not so sure and would argue instead that Freud was simply mistaken in his analysis of the essence of technology in *Civilization and its Discontents*. Where all machines are always only prostheses of humans. They are only reading glasses, better eyes, better ears, and so on. As I said before that is a very, very narcissistic view of technology. It could be described in far more inhuman terms, such as the way a coral branch grows. . . . Technology is more likely to accept such anorganic principles than orient itself to lung and muscles. That is precisely the trick of technology—that it can't and really doesn't want to do that. (125)

When the disagreement was more interpersonal and current, back in the 1980s during Kittler's two quarters as guest professor at UC-Santa Barbara, I offered what I thought was a good boundary. Granted that technology has auto-accelerated beyond corporeal analogues or prostheses, just the same a Freudian consumerist perspective on media is back when it comes time to bury the dead, and the mass media perform the service. In *Grammophon Film Typewriter*, Kittler had in fact made room, to my mind, for this proviso by identifying the site of every new generation of spooks as the latest new border or outer limit of the sensorium's media extension (24). That one man's technology is another man's mass psychology apparently isn't a compromise. It's a trigger.

I offer the interview souvenir I came upon after Friedrich Kittler's death as an epigraph to the reading that follows. It comes from Outer Space and espies in behaviorism a test pattern or blank that the impasse of simulation opens up. We begin to follow Pynchon's bouncing rocket.

After the publication in 1945 of his essay "The Space-Station: Its Radio Applications," which contributed to the launching of the first satellite, Arthur C. Clarke introduced the precondition upon which his science fiction depended in his 1951 short story "The Sentinel": the ability to view the Earth from Outer Space has to be in place before contact between Earthlings and sentient species from other planets can commence. Science fiction (as the positing of hypotheses in advance of their possible realization) had already come to an end with the takeoff of the V-2 rocket, which drew a Before and After line through science fiction reckoning. At this border, Clarke and Stanley Kubrick drew a blank in *2001: A Space Odyssey*, signaling contact with the alien mind.

The *Whole Earth Catalog* was the consequence of or afterthought to a photograph of Earth taken from a satellite, which was then used as the publication's first iconic cover. Before proceeding with his catalog project, Stewart Brand mounted a public campaign in 1966 to get NASA to confirm the rumor of this science-factual POV and release the photo. It is said that the encyclopedic *Whole Earth Catalog*, in its pitch for holism in thought and consumerism, looked forward to the Web. But did it also project a half-empty frontier zone, presumably post-apocalyptic, in which pioneers were starting over from scratch ecologically but with the help of a handbook? Was the catalog a container for the bric-a-brac that would remain after the nuclear apocalypse, addressing not only the survivor who had to re-start but also the survivor as a Benjaminian allegorist sorting through and reading the ruins? Did the photograph show the Earth as a vulnerable object for our protection or was it already the parting shot taken by colonists bound for Mars? The Phildickian reception would confirm that the *Whole Earth Catalog*'s product placement of ecological consumerism was a new mode of adaptation to the alternate prospect of the end of the world.

In her 1963 essay "The Conquest of Space and the Stature of Man," Hannah Arendt identified the POV from Outer Space. Space exploration was filling in the blank opened up by "our new ability to handle nature from a point in the universe outside the earth" (273). However, Arendt argued, man cannot reclaim the Archimedean point of his universal science by way of Outer Space transport (272). She also discounted a special effect of this vanishing point—the trust in man's mutation within a large-scale biological process of which technology would be a part. It is just the same essential for the understanding of this trajectory that the spacecraft is considered to be occupied by or prosthetically attached to a human. For example:

The astronaut, who is shot into Outer Space and imprisoned in his instrument ridden capsule where each actual physical encounter with his

surroundings would spell immediate death, might well be taken as the
symbolic incarnation of Heisenberg's man—the man who will be less
likely ever to meet anything but himself and man-made things the more
ardently he wishes to eliminate all anthropocentric considerations from
his encounter with the non-human world around him. (272)

At close quarters, this external view is the import of what's already down to earth.

If we look down from this point upon what is going on on Earth and upon
the various activities of men . . . then these activities will indeed appear to
ourselves as "overt behavior" . . . Under these circumstances, speech and
everyday language would indeed be no longer a meaningful utterance that
transcends behavior even if it only expresses it, and it would much better
be replaced by the extreme and in itself meaningless formalism of mathematical signs. (273-74)

In his 1988 essay, "Media and Drugs in Pynchon's Second World War,"
Kittler summarized the amalgam that rises up before the rocket POV of *Gravity's
Rainbow*: "When technologies take the upper hand over science and aesthetics,
information alone counts. And after all, semiotics and the behaviorist techniques
Pynchon analyzes as strategies of war share certain roots" (56). Kittler is right that
it indeed takes behaviorism and film to recognize the time traveling effects of the
rocket in *Gravity's Rainbow*.

Imagine a missile one hears approaching only after it explodes. The
reversal! A piece of time neatly snipped out . . . a few feet of film run
backwards . . . Pavlov was fascinated with "ideas of the opposite" . . . you
weaken this idea of the opposite, and here all at once is the paranoid patient
who would be master yet now feels himself a slave. (48)

At the end of what's dubbed a "Pavlovian's Progress" (169), the protagonist,
Tyrone Slothrop, becomes an everyman signaling conditions of paranoia that, in
the meantime, are as pervasive as information, which has "come to be the only real
medium of exchange" (258). While information is the plain text of technology, it
circulates among men shot through with explanation, as Walter Benjamin advised

in "The Storyteller" (147). In other words, it functions as opinion, the basis for the behavioral administration of mass psychology.

What Arendt looks down on (both explicitly and by absence or implication) are the two tendencies in the organization and comprehension of mass media society, the behavioral and the psychoanalytic, which, in science fiction, are the reigning orders of simulation. These orders can also be characterized as the Public Relations trajectory of adaptation to information or opinion and the advertising aspect of identification. In Aldous Huxley's *Brave New World* (1932), they keep company in one belief system. The future divinity of behavioral and biological adaptation is addressed as Our Ford, although he prefers to be called Our Freud when psychological issues are raised (39). Otherwise the trend assigned by Huxley to Fordism in 1932 hosts tendencies that have been kept distinct from Freud's name. It is possible to derive one more paranoid proverb out of Pynchon's reduction of psychoanalysis to occult hobbyism in *Gravity's Rainbow*. In the foregrounding of the amalgam of Pavlovian behaviorism, film, and rocket, we might also recognize "another story" or allegory of a joint delegation (e.g., the belief system Ford/Freud). To make the line of separation legible as an adhesive strip, we turn to science fiction, the genre in which Pynchon initially tested his decision to write.

Dick's first published novel, *The Man Who Japed* (1956), is set apart as his sole representation of a Public Relations model of mass psychology. Throughout his science fiction proper, which commenced the following year with the publication of *Time Out of Joint*, Dick focused on advertising as an object or trigger of identification and projection. But in *The Man Who Japed* society is held together by a culture industry of mediatized packets issued by Research Agencies to promote a "Morec," a message or moral. Protagonist Purcell runs one of the agencies trying to "anticipate future trends" (5). "Remember the packet we did on Goethe? The business about lens-grinding? . . . The optics angle made a good Morec—Goethe saw his real job. Prisms before poetry" (8).

Morec society mediatizes adolescence as a line of informant-robots called "Juveniles," which penetrate every space and convey the audio and video surveillance to the guardians of the status quo. And yet the novel tarries with the actual adolescents, who hang out near the launching pads to watch the rocket traffic with colony planets and imagine the prospect of escape. Something like "individualism" is Purcell's guilty assumption in identification with the teens.

Otherwise the so-called unique individual is the concern of the therapy business alone, which treats the outsiders at occupational-therapy resorts on other planets. That the therapy client counts as the treating therapist's "obsession" encircles each client in a "noose," the "derisive term contracted from *neuro-psychiatric*" (21). It is a loop that extends through the other outside world to the term "psycho." Because the wife of this society's founding father had a predilection for analytic psychotherapy, the "Psych Front left over from the war" was allowed to institute itself as part of the new order (54).

WWI was the ultimate setting for the departure of one model of mass media society from the other one. While Freud's nephew Edward Bernays won the war for his theory of Public Relations, which found a successful application in the propaganda of the Entente, Freud himself won the postwar period for psychoanalysis over the symptomatizing bodies of war-neurotic soldiers. Freud's inside view of the shell-shocked soldier (a subject incapacitated by a conflict inside his ego between the peace-ego and war-ego) issued the owner's manual to the psyche's protection and projection. When the defeated German command conceded that the Central Powers had succumbed to the propaganda savvy of the enemy and had lost on psychological grounds alone, the direction was given for the new German investment in military psychology and the development of what the Germans would rename psychological warfare. By the end of WWI, psychoanalysis became the treatment of choice for war neurosis, giving the ultimate stamp of approval to Freud's concise grasp of where self-esteem goes under conditions of traumatic duress. It was the open sesame that introduced Freud's science into all institutions of psychological understanding, treatment, and application. The Nazi authorities could not forego the counsel of Freud's science, even though the founder's name was a *Geheimnis* carried by insiders of the new German psychotherapy.

2

In *The Man Who Japed*, Purcell is placed in charge of Telemedia, the government's own PR control tower of opinion. He sets in motion a campaign that is at once an adolescent prank and the marketing rehearsal of Dick's later interest in alternate history. First he circulates the hot topic of "active assimilation" until everyone needs to know all about it; then he releases the explanation—a surprising prehistory about the founding father's predilection for cannibalism—into the awaiting sensoria. PR creates a more general need to be filled before pitching a specific product as the filler. In the fourth chapter of his 1928 study *Propaganda*, Bernays recalls the example of pianos for sale. Rather than extol the attractiveness of pianos, for example, which would be mere advertising, the PR strategy was to publicize the hottest new accessory of the home, the music room or corner, via miscellaneous reports, interviews and editorials. Once the need for such a space or displacement was instilled, it followed that pianos would meet the need to complete the installation as recognizable (77-78). The gist of the anecdote is that simulation is another word for the PR organization of blanks that advertising and consumerism proceed to fill.

Before the identifiably new can appear, there must be a place for absence, an emptiness or blank. In her 1929 essay on the artistic process, "Infantile Anxiety Situations Reflected in a Work of Art and in the Creative Impulse," Melanie Klein considered the artwork as filling or fulfilling a space inside, at once the setting of dread anxiety (for example, the idea that one will be left alone and unloved in consequence of the devastation inflicted by one's early sexual research) and the placeholder for the work of reparation that must follow. Thus Klein concludes her interpretation of the pictorial art of Ruth Kjär: "It is obvious that the desire to make reparation, to make good the injury psychologically done to the mother and also to restore herself was at the bottom of the compelling urge to paint these portraits" (218). Kjär's breakthrough came about when another's painting was removed from her meticulous interior decoration and revealed the melancholic lack at its core. Rather than find, select and collect another filler for this blank, she painted directly onto the wall in the missing place her own first painting, the life-size portrait of a naked Negress. "In the analyses of children, when the representation of destructive wishes is succeeded by an expression of reactive tendencies, we constantly find that drawing and painting are used as means to restore people" (218). The empty spaces had come to be aligned. The work of reparation for the spoiling, inside and out, of her mother as herself assumed the guise of a global target displaced from the paternal force of destruction.

In Georg Scholz's 1926 "Selbtsbildnis vor Litfaßsäule" ("Self Portrait in front of an Advertising Column"), we see that the city street in the backdrop is one surface inscription and that the surface, the canvas as a whole, could be rolled up into and folded out of the advertising column. In Scholz's earlier work, all signs were legible or cut off metonymically to include a whole. Here individual names appear, but anything longer than a name is a fragment that's hard to read. Is the *retrait* of letters as the column turns a reference to the film medium? But as the column slows it shows levels and edges of former wraps of advertising. The memory traces of inscription are really only visible when a brand new ad layer is about to be applied.

In the beginning, before there could be advertising, the surface on which it was to be pasted or projected had to be invented, fabricated, or secured. One early ad agency, Volney Palmer of Philadelphia, which opened in 1841, was essentially a space brokerage, buying up surface in newspapers and selling it in sections to advertisers. Circulation increased in 1836 when La Presse introduced paid advertising into its pages in Paris. It is a longstanding *pointe* that what we watch for in the media is the advertising.

In 1855, a new dance song, the "Annoncier Polka," was introduced at the opening ceremony for the installation of the first advertising columns ("Annoncier-Säulen") in Berlin. Ernst Litfaß had commissioned the piece just for this event; it was what Bernays would identify, almost a century later, as a "tie-in." In 1845, when Litfaß at last joined the printing and publishing firm of his stepfather, L. W. Krause, which he had put off through the detour of his other career as the actor and poet Flodo-ardo, he introduced his first advertising innovation within that inaugural year: pages or posters for announcements ("Annoncier-Zettel"). Litfaß's father, another book dealer and printer, died shortly after Ernst's birth, whereupon his mother married the next best man in the business. As a proper heir to two fathers, then, Litfaß extended the book business into a highly profitable brokerage of new surfaces for advertising and information, even the news. *Avant la lettre*, he let loose the letters of the old hierarchy and let them roll as mass media.

Fatherless, Scholz became a foster son in the home of Julius Elster. This was also home to a research laboratory. All Elster's work in physics (which resulted in the invention of the first photocell) was pursued in collaboration with his best friend from childhood, Hans Geitel, who kept a room of his own in the Elster household and never married. As occupational therapy for Elster's depressed wife, who was on her own, Scholz was taken in. They didn't get along. Upon admission to the Academy of Fine Arts in Karlsruhe, he left never to return. The war no doubt deepened his insight and alienation, but on its own it didn't bring about a change of art. The military was one institution Scholz could later count on. Contacts from his military service arranged the commissions that supported his inner emigration during the Third Reich after he lost his teaching position for being a "decadent artist."

As his main inspiration, Scholz carried forward the primal scene of the two men, his foster parents and co-workers in the lab, which he had been kept from joining. Scholz would pursue alternatives to inheritance for his art, such as the teamwork constituting a group or in-group structure. A member of artist groups like the Gruppe Rih in Karlsruhe, Scholz alternated between his art work and work in advertising and packaging design. His career came to be organized around two art exhibitions that succeeded as PR campaigns for new lines of production and coincided each time with a change in the direction of his art, which it helped launch. In 1920, at the "Erste internationale Dada-Messe" ("The First International Dada-Fair") in Berlin, he presented his polemical caricature style. It was distinct from his earlier brand of Expressionism and identified with the work of Otto Dix and Georg Grosz. The 1925 "Neue Sachlichkeit" exhibition in Mannheim wasn't called a fair or *Messe*. It was called by the title that named and inaugurated the new art movement. At this time, Scholz was appointed professor at his alma mater, the Karlsruhe Academy. He painted "Selbtsbildnis vor Litfaßsäule" within a year. In this work, his success is measured by the ability to stand with his back to the sinuous force of media like a snake charmer. Scholz's work in the new style recognizably belonged to the "Neue Sachlickheit" movement, as did the other member works, but it was a group signature whereby each work was identified. There was no identification that referred and deferred to a precursor, original, or proper heir.

S. H. Foulkes, the British exponent of psychoanalytic group therapy, who hailed originally from Karlsruhe, published his first clinical paper in 1930. "Observation on the Significance of the Name in a Schizophrenic" documents a schizophrenic patient's delusional relations with a father who split for America never to be heard from again when the boy was six. The delusional system of this relationship to the father can be read off the back of the patronymic. The outbreak of the patient's schizophrenia, the cutting loose of the surname Tieger, was triggered in the course of a lecture.

At the start the lecturer spoke about the countries of India and had an atlas just like the one the patient's father had owned. . . . Then the talk was about the tigers in India, that there were three kinds of tigers—some were wild and malicious, then there were tame ones and finally those who attacked small children. This caused the patient to laugh. . . . The lecturer also showed a picture of a tiger snake which was said to wind itself round the tiger's neck and throttle him. At this the patient felt that a snake was winding itself around his own neck. (33)

He started visiting the zoo, looking closely at the lions, tigers, and snakes. From the start, he had felt hypnotized by the lecturer and then heard voices—first two voices that he couldn't really keep apart and follow, in time voices that rebuked him for old crimes. In bed, he saw moving pictures on the wall "as at the cinema" (34). The pictures showed men and women stripping, dancing, fighting, copulating, or licking each other between the legs.

In the course of treatment, Foulkes's patient related a memory that was already ensconced in its delusional elaboration. His father had given him a small toy tiger as a gift. But when the boy slipped on ice, the toy bounced up (leapt up) and scratched his upper lip, which led to blood poisoning. Father blasted the little tiger with his rifle. That's the disconnection between them that is transmitted: "he himself, once married, would perhaps kill the little tigers, his children" (34). Out of this disconnection, the patient derived "a number of conceptions which at times reproduce, as it were, literally what is reported of primitive peoples" (ibid.). Three thousand years ago (but in the span of only ten years) mankind descended from different animals whose characteristics were retained. His missing father was a wild American tiger, while he was, being European, a more tame variety.

The tigers swarm around the name, but the snakes bear the phallic significance of the stare that penetrates. "Language, in the expression 'fascination,' also points to a phallic conception of the snake's stare" (36). All his departed died of snake bites, but he also imagined "that he had been injected with snake blood to make him more nimble, more like a snake" (ibid.). The look of castration as "fascination" is the bottom line of this case, which Foulkes presented at the end of his training on the old continent, in the former language. Fascination (resonating not only with the etymons Foulkes gathered together in a footnote but also with fascism) was the line that would be drawn through the author's life, Before and After. "The patient believed his illness to be due to the Indian's influence, having been hypnotized by his look. This gave him a kind of insight into his delusions which, like his physical symptoms, appeared as a kind of punishment and penance, leading to death and rebirth in India. The illness prepared the final objective—to put himself in the father's place" (ibid.). It's not that he inherits this place. Literalizing the legacy of Tieger, he exceeds the inheritance, circumscribing it as an empty place, as a blank to be filled by something new.

For his new life in Britain beginning in 1933, Tieger's treating clinician gave his own surname, Fuchs, the phonetic transcription Foulkes. Unlike his schizophrenic patient, he didn't focus on its literal meaning, which he could have preserved as "Fox." Instead he adjusted his name to his new social group, the echo chamber in which its mispronunciation would be, as "Fucks," a curse upon sociality, announcing always with his first name his engagement in the illicit act. Ignoring the semantic content and anticipating instead its homonymic misapprehension, the name change signifies the determining power not of the father's name but of its reception in the group. By attending in the first place to the group, Foulkes circumscribed the father or the patronymic in a structural blank. His innovative work in psychoanalysis as S. H. Foulkes would be set on the group, and he would attend to what he called "resonance" in contrast to transference.

3

Because the public is readymade while its adaptation to opinion is ongoing, the PR campaign must be in a position to project or forecast consumerism via sampling opinions and taking polls and surveys. In Daniel Galouye's *Simulacron 3* (1964), the business of polls and surveys has impinged on everyday life. An electronic simulation of consumer society offers an alternative: the changes that pollsters can only ask about can be directly introduced into the simulacron and the reactions of the simulated figures observed in double realtime. The world to which we are introduced through the protagonist, Hall, one of the programmers of "Simulacron 3," turns out to be yet another simulation. And yet this simulated world reacted to stimuli by preparing to launch the very simulacron project that subsumes its own reality.

During the trial runs and installation of "Simulacron 3," the denizens of both worlds begin to wonder if they are real, if their world is reality. Hall searches for the point or unit of contact between the two worlds to settle the philosophical or psychotic questioning of reality, which is the only hypothesis among "all the metaphysical concepts . . . open to final verification" (91). That the infinite regress of PR simulation could pull up short before one original world symptomatizes the denial of depression basic to the worlds of *Simulacron 3*. At one point, Hall is dismayed over the grief of Jinx, his deceased employer's daughter. He calls it a

> striking throwback to the mid-twentieth century . . . before enlightenment had . . . swept away the vicious cruelty of the funeral convention. In those days, proof of death had to be established on a practical plane. Those who attended wakes and funeral services saw and believed. And they went away convinced that the loved one was actually beyond this life and that there would be no complications arising from a supposedly dead person showing up again. That the close ones also went away nursing traumatic wounds made little difference. (41)

In the future according to *Simulacron 3*, the news of a loved one's passing means that the body has already been removed.

The science fiction forecast is a 1936 diagnosis in Benjamin's "The Story-teller." The removal of the dying and the dead from all living quarters circumscribes the encapsulation and internalization of an inoculation we began taking in with the novel. The protagonist's death scene at the end of the novel is a reclamation of the whole life as meaningful, rendering that life at every moment the life of one who died thus and then—this is what the readership swallowed. The inoculation service was accelerated with the advent of information, which guaranteed the demise of history, counsel, even experience itself. At the same time, Benjamin singles out the psychic impact of WWI (traumatic enough to forego a history) as alone responsible for the autoimmune crisis otherwise informed by the novel's Happy Ending in death.

In *Simulacron 3*, it is jolting to witness the sudden disappearance of your neighbor, swiftly followed by the erasure of his trace in the environment. This new shock is specific to the electronically simulated nature of its setting and is thematized in Fassbinder's 1973 TV-movie adaptation, *World on a Wire*. It introduces the onset of mourning according to the logic of a PR campaign. "Watching a man disappear isn't something you simply shrug off and forget" (9). PR campaigns must get around the consumer's ability to shrug off advertisements of new products. The display of electronic erasure simulates a change that remembrance supplies and supports. The evidence of utter disappearance like a blip from the screen promotes the inside view that reality is an infinite regress of simulacra. But each inner world is now a place for absence.

The simulation lab was designed to penetrate "the core of our basic drives, fears, aspirations" and "dissect the very soul itself" (62). Beyond the shaping of opinion out of information, the lab can follow or even direct what develops out of the instinctual core. "By prodding those analog units, we can observe not only the beginning, but also every step in the development of undesirable, antisocial tendencies" (ibid.). The psychopathic violence that develops out of antisocial tendencies is the boundary concept of all the worlds in *Simulacron 3* that depend upon the philosophical "peephole" between the real world and its simulated copy. To observe the reactions in the simulacron, the operators can either rotoscope themselves directly into the faux setting or borrow a simulated person's POV ("empathy coupling"). For regular functioning, however, the system requires that one artificial denizen, a so-called Contact Unit, know that he is a figment in a simulated environment serving real operators in the real world. Hall diagnoses the symptom: "Somehow I couldn't shake off the conviction that permitting a Contact Unit to know he is nothing more than an electronically simulated entity was the height of ruthlessness" (46). It is the detail into which Hall's operator lodges his "perverted gratification" (128) when, by a technique of "faulty" or psychopathic coupling, he makes Hall feel the pain of being his electronic dupe and hear the echo of his operator's derisive laughter. "I knew now that the Operator was a sadist. Perhaps, in that Higher Existence, everybody was" (110). The fact that Hall prevails only by replacing the Operator, who then really disappears, underscores how psychopathic violence remains the flaw in the appointment that *Simulacron 3* otherwise tries to keep with mourning.

The future world associated with German science fiction (which a proximity to psychosis built) struggles in its postwar incarnation and revaluation to contain and integrate both historical and actual psychopathy. We can follow this tendency in the simulated worlds of science fiction into a real one via Theodor Adorno's 1959 "Was bedeutet: Aufarbeitung der Vergangenheit" ("The Meaning of Working Through the Past"). This essay set the trend Alexander and Margarete Mitscherlich misappropriated in 1967 for their outright dismissal of the West German policy of restitution as retraumatization. There is a particularly overdetermined aside that belongs to this delegation of symptoms. Adorno belittles the tendency of West Germans to shrug off the possibility of change simply because they are too immature for democracy, like the juvenile delinquent who says he's only a teenager and can't help himself (559-60).

But where did all the Siegfrieds go? Following elevation to the position of cultural superego in Nazi Germany, the adolescent was largely missing from the postwar reopening of Germany, at least from the mirrors of the mass media. The economic miracle cannot be separated from the policy of restitution twinning West Germany and Israel as the two quintessentially postwar states. And yet the very industry of that miracle was adolescent. The new notion of the teen, whose main task of finding a job to occupy or cathect begins to keep the promise of childhood, is one of the overriding continuity shots uniting the culture of *Bildung*, psychoanalysis, and the Western World. On the road to the Teen Age on the Coast, Jack Kerouac's narrator extols those "who . . . burn, burn, burn like fabulous yellow roman candles exploding like spiders across the stars and in the middle you see the blue centerlight pop and everybody goes 'Awww!' What did they call such young people in Goethe's Germany?" (7). The energy or industry of application and misapplication associated with adolescence since Werther's sorrows got separated out from the psychopathy that was its outlet in Nazi Germany and reapplied to the prospect of repair. In turn, the deprivation that applicants for reparation had endured could be assessed in terms of the promise not kept, a potential productivity that had been curtailed. The centrality of teen industry to this economy of recovery was not, however, personalized. There were exceptions, like the fantasy movies starring Romy Schneider as Sissy, but they tended to underscore on average a general absence, which in other syndications of mass culture almost proved generic. First shown on West German TV in 1966, the science fiction series *Raumpatrouille* (*Space Patrol*) demonstrates how the vitality of youth belongs to the middle-aged hero. And whenever he's in crisis, it is not identified as midlife in contrast to an adolescence to be envied, identified with, or criticized, which is how we encounter the paradigm of youthfulness in the mass cultural productions of the former Allies.

World on a Wire adapted a work that, since it was most successful in its German translation, had already been adopted by the culture prepared to watch it or itself on TV. The PR model of mass psychology in *Simulacron 3* (introjected by the postwar German public) reflects the propaganda savvy that defeated the second Reich, and not, precisely, the application and reversal of psychoanalysis that went into Nazi psychological warfare or mass psychology. Germany was still too close for closure. As Allied propaganda "confirmed," the Nazis only lost because they didn't know when to stop winning. That Fassbinder wrapped his projection of the PR science fiction model around a full frontal absence of adolescence applied the date mark to the German fantasy. Sex appeal in *World on a Wire* belongs to the buffed, polished midlifers who do not in any way depend on teenagers as though, like the cat the canary, they had swallowed them. German science fiction—notably Lang's *Metropolis* and *Woman in the Moon* in which the Outer Space of psychosis underwent colonization for the survival of the species—went under following its season of realization in Nazi Germany. Postwar science fiction introjected Germany inside California (the secret identity of most future worlds) as the problem of the containment and integration of the prospect of psychopathic violence (à la Dick's android testing). Identified as the time-based enactment of a psychopathy one grows out of, adolescence modeled the android problem in Dick's science fiction, which cannot be solved by termination but only by that testing for empathy that approximates integration. At once stand-in and go-between, adolescence in the postwar mass cultures of the former Allies became the medium for immunization against the troubling, doubling prospect of going psycho. In postwar Germany, adolescence was swallowed whole. Teen industry was split off from the ruthless violence in the recent past and applied to economic recovery and restitution while the midlife carriers of youth smacked the lips of their recent repast.

4

According to Kittler, Pynchon advances a relay of plain texts that fit technically. Cinematic projection of the illusion of continuously moving images does the same math that enables the V-2 rocket to attain velocity and stay on course. The rocket's strike precedes its screaming across the sky, leaving a blank that the "time axis manipulation" basic to behaviorism and film can fulfill. The reversibility readily available on film can make legible the ways in which the technical processes of warfare (as in an RAF bombardment of a V-2 station) can regress a truck, for example, to its blueprints. The reversal attributed to aerial bombardment in *Gravity's Rainbow* makes room for the technical view of Gestell as always being laid bare for new and improved construction/destruction.

But in the allegorical realm of machine objects, there cannot be a regression or reversibility without end. The devolution of technical objects in Dick's *Ubik* that ensues from the introduction of half-life (the influence of the dead in the midst of life and of psychopathy or adolescence in undeath) stops at the year 1939. Pynchon draws the line through allegory when he addresses Europe as home to the technoculture of death. In the interview with Bramkamp, Kittler gives the death defying explanation of this charge. Pynchon is ultimately addressing a realism of numbers that corresponds to the Lacanian Real. The other candidate for this correspondence that Kittler identifies is the dust of the moon. What alone counts, then, is information and dust.

> What Pynchon is referring to is calculus, which he reckons the same in spirit as the rocket. I would argue somewhat more generally that calculus is magic with real numbers. And I can think of no other culture that based its knowledge on real numbers, on the decimal breaks after the point, and which thus leapt out of the realm of the Symbolic . . . into contingency, the final incalculability of the real physical world, which one can approximate only with the infinite number of positions that follow the decimal point, for which approximation we have our computers. (119)

Using Pavlov, Pynchon conjoins the themes of time modification and paranoia largely in step with the overall comedy routine that begins with the substitution of the infant Slothrop's erections for canine salivation as a most elegant binary. Dismissal of psychoanalysis also belongs to this routine. The interpretation of Slothrop's psychokinesis by the "most Freudian of psychical researchers" is deadpan laughable and yet, seriously, the only instance of interpretative involvement with the outhouse humor rampant in the novel (85). "He subconsciously needs to abolish all trace of the sexual Other, whom he symbolizes on his map, most significantly, as a star, that anal-sadistic emblem of classroom success which so permeates elementary education in America" (ibid.).

Freudian theory is belittled to a knee-jerk norm in Dick's future worlds—the very measure of the immersion of those worlds and works in psychoanalysis. Pynchon consigns the psychoanalysts within the Allied war effort to the occult department while the behaviorists lead the psy war. It's time to follow Heidegger's words of caution (this time as an advertisement) that psychoanalysis, if not the philosophy of technology's essence, is the owner's manual to our ongoing technologization. The mobilization of psychological theories and therapies between the wars in Germany sought to reverse the outline of psychic breakdown that Freud sketched in the shadow of the Doppelgänger. Following the trajectory of Freud's forecast of the implications that the encounter with shell shock held for his theory and therapy, Germany would find new stability at the border to psychotic states through the prosthetic fit between dissociation and the novelty of a merger with, say, the machine in flight. It is possible that the Germans didn't lose on psychological grounds the second time around. On such grounds, loss would not be an impediment to winning.

Psychoanalysis was sent to the front of emergency treatment of the soldiers suffering war neurosis during WWI. Then, in time for the second coming of the war under the more aggrandized aegis of psychological warfare, psychoanalysis (or what I prefer to call "greater psychoanalysis") became the eclecticized and reunified amalgam of all the therapies that took their departure from Freud's science or otherwise shared a border, including behaviorism. In the essays comprising *Psychoanalysis and the War Neuroses*, for which Freud composed his hallmark introduction, we observe the bona fide analysts opening up within psychoanalysis a concession stand and understanding of treatment options taken from the whole milieu of psychological treatment. In *V.* and *Gravity's Rainbow*, Pynchon assigns the historical influence of Freud's science together with the former homoeroticism among pilots to the WWI period where he draws the line and no further. To date, this history is recapitulated (but with a functional difference) by the profiling function of psychoanalysis in non-analytic psychiatry as a kind of fact-finding, history-taking preliminary to choosing the other subsequent treatments. Stripped down for the purpose of interrogation rather than treatment, the alien test subject in Walter Tevis's *The Man Who Fell to Earth* (1963) also undergoes this "history."

> The reason we've been asking foolish questions of you for two months has been to conduct a kind of psychoanalysis. We've had cameras in here, recording eye-blink rates and things like that. We've already concluded that torture wouldn't work on you. You'd go insane too easily under pain: and we just can't learn enough about your psychology—guilt and anxieties and things like that—to do any kind of brainwashing on you. We've also loaded you with drugs—hypnotics, narcotics—and they don't work. (180)

In *Gravity's Rainbow*, the general consensus is that nothing will remain of the psychoanalytic specialization in the Psi Section, namely the "search for some measurable basis for the common experience of being haunted by the dead" (276). And yet the search for some measurable basis of this experience aligns the project with Pavlov's own move into the study of psychopathology. The immediate context for this move was a mishap that befell the dogs. Traumatization came into focus as a factor in conditioning or deconditioning after a flood that nearly wiped out the entire test population. The surviving dogs were manifestly changed by the ordeal. All their conditioned reflexes were gone, they simply wouldn't eat regardless of stimuli, and the excessive fear they showed no longer fit the grid of response. In the course of reconditioning the animals at considerable effort, Pavlov saw the connection between their aberrancy and traumatized human behavior. The give and take of the stimulus/response model of adaptation didn't bring about profound change. However, once the breakdown of psychic reality was factored in, a working model was secured for opening up the depth of the field of adaptation for far-reaching alteration.

Pavlov's breaking insight seems delayed or denied in the setting of research dedicated to obtaining, through animals, a so-called mechanistic explanation of human behavior. This is the form of tribute paid to the unspoken connection between the hub of human psychic aberration and the wheel of animal fatality or behavior. Pavlov's mother withdrew into psychosomatic illness never to return when he was too young to hate her but old enough to blame the environment rather than internalize the deprivation as his fault line. The influence of this absence, which the test dogs put into Pavlov's scientific perspective, is picked up in *Gravity's Rainbow* as the prospect of deconditioning or extinguishing a reflex to zero or beyond. What computes here is that we are doing the aftermath of early trauma. "Not only must we speak of partial or of complete extinction of a conditioned reflex, but we must also realize that extinction can proceed beyond the point of reducing a reflex to zero. We cannot therefore judge the degree of extinction only by the magnitude of the reflex or its absence, since there can still be a silent extinction beyond the zero" (84-85).

IDENTIFICATION WITH LOST CAUSES

1

Kittler underscored that, for the *Pax Americana*, the rocket and the atom bomb could be combined in nuclear missiles. This functional merger of the effects of Europe's phantom wars could go through displacement into a continuous history of innovation only by their uncanny-proofing. In real or trauma time, however, the rocket took off as a byproduct of the air war, which the Germans had already lost. From the phantasmagoria of the Axis to the extensive psycho-technical research and training that made the German pilot into an "auto-pilot" ever in the ready position to merge with the machine in flight, the investment in air power as the ultimate total war front was all along, without knowing it, building up to the crypto-fetish of rocket flight. Following the loss of WWI and flying into the loss of the second one, the crypto-fetish of rocket flight carried forward the end as a "final victory."

The premier lost cause was that of Troy and the miracle weapon of its over-turning the wooden horse. Lest we not see the *hylē* for the woods: the same word for matter/energy in Aristotle was exclusively *hylē* = wood in Homer. With the Trojan horse, we entered the ultimate ready position for a machine age, an after-the-fact origin that the Western history of its metabolization and fabulation supports. Mass psychology placed its art before the wooden hearse of techno-history. The reversal of Troy's lost cause—skewered upon one weapon, ruse, or fetish—was basic to the poetic historiography of Rome.

The Trojan horse continues to circulate in the digital archive as a type of malware: while carrying out the helpful function it advertises, it in fact opens access to the user's computer system. The sense in the borrowing runs deeper in the nomination of Trojan for the leading brand of condoms and its identification by a wooden horse icon. It was in the course of WWI that the German monopoly on the continent was busted and replaced by the US brand of rubber contraceptives. Can we stop short of the "safe" penetration of the stronghold by the Greeks? Or mustn't we admit what lies beyond, the prospect of the rubber tearing or otherwise leaking the carriers of impregnation or HIV? Something like truth in advertising (sponsored moreover by the death drive) subsumes the Trojan War as a primal scene. By its deception or secret cargo, the Trojan horse breached the impasse or no-man's land of the stuck war. But the victory obtained by the Greeks introduced the Trojan cause—a lost object of identification, reversal, and preservation carried out defeat first.

In 1968, Stanley Kubrick projected *2001: A Space Odyssey* onto and out of the unidentified signifying object from Arthur C. Clarke's 1951 story "The Sentinel." In his own novelization of the screenplay that he coauthored with Kubrick, Clarke described this object before according it the rocket-test-and-countdown-designation TMA-1: "slab or monolith of hard, black material" (159). It sends or summons into space Homer's *Odyssey*, which can stand the updating because of all books it alone transmits "most vividly across the gulfs of time" (100) the prospect of "ruins a thousand times older than Troy" (162). The science fiction Odyssey identifies with a more ancient loss than Troy, which childhood harbors. We run up against the blank of the alien and new only to encounter our own limit concept, the problem of psychopathic violence. Regression as the other means of recording (and, at the same time, erasing) holds in store the prospect of rebirth, which is less the problem's solution than its extension.

Whereas in Clarke's novelization, the slab is introduced as a televisual monitor giving instruction in the use of tools, onscreen the monolith remains a blank that Kubrick's cinematography fills with delegations of violence. The camera follows the arc of the tool turned weapon that prehistoric man hurls upward along the slab's vertical axis. Editing allows the tool from primal time to intersect the future flight trajectory of the spaceship. Clarke lays the blame on Hal's creators for the computer's violent proclivities: "The fact that Hal's builders had failed fully to understand the psychology of their own creation showed how difficult it might be to establish communication with truly alien beings" (169). Onscreen we enter Hal's "psychology." We are inside Hal's POV watching the talking heads of the astronauts in secret consultation through the sound-proofed enclosure's window. We read their lips and compute their doom.

The fulfillment of contact that awaits the sole-surviving astronaut on Saturn follows a double movement of regression and uplifting metamorphosis or merger. This final stop in the Odyssey that the blank obelisk set in motion is station identification: the "hosts" who set up the Saturn station "had based their ideas of terrestrial living upon TV programs" (ibid.). The distillate of information was gathered from the TV shows, which are replaying on the TV set in the station. "All the programs were about two years old. That was around the time TMA-1 had been discovered" (215). But beyond the details of his containment, off in the "labyrinthine complexity" of the vista, the astronaut recognizes "the operation of some gigantic mind" (217). The Saturn habitat, "not intended to deceive but rather—he hoped—to reassure" (211), acts as a cradle for speeding up evolution. "Mind would eventually free itself from matter. The robot body . . . would be no more than a stepping-stone to something which, long ago, men had called 'spirit'" (174). The astronaut's mutation follows in the steps of memory and self-observation in close proximity to (analogues with) media technologies. Like Hal's memory lane to which his unplugging reduces or returns him, the life that flashes before the astronaut's eyes is mediatic. "His life was unreeling like a tape recording playing back at ever-increasing speed. . . . He was retrogressing down the corridors of time, being drained of knowledge and experience as he swept back toward his childhood" (217). Childhood as end, at once conclusion and purpose, was Clarke's metaphysical frame of reference. The film belongs rather to the Teen Age and embarks instead upon another "trip" through the psychedelic special effects.

In Orson Scott Card's *Ender's Game,* childhood and early adolescence are up against the containment, instrumentalization, and integration of psychopathic violence. The eponymous hero is tricked by his long season of video game training to cross over into real battle with the Buggers, mankind's mortal enemy. In the end, he plays for keeps, still thinking that he's engaged in yet another round of hypothetical battle. By the end of this session, Ender and the pre-teen recruits under his leadership have in fact exterminated the alien species. "I didn't want to kill them all. I didn't want to kill anybody! I'm not the killer. You didn't want me, you bastards, you wanted Peter, but you made me do it, you tricked me into it" (297-98). Peter is the older brother who is regularly portrayed to be an outright psychopath and likened to Hitler. One of the adults in charge replies: "We had to have a commander with so much empathy that he would think like the Buggers, understand them and anticipate them. . . . But somebody with that much compassion could never be the killer we needed" (298). Hence the total war had to be waged as a game for pre-teens.

By the time of the First Gulf War, the conceit basic to *Ender's Game* entered realization: video games played by teens and pre-teens were continuous (in group psychology as in technology) with the war that was being run by midlifers seated before consoles and screens. But the continuity describes the inoculum from the inside. What counts is the strategic calibration of violence between psychopathy and empathy in select psyches now that all-out war outside the socius is in such short supply. Since Kant erected an RIP over perpetual peace, we have remained, as we say in California, self-aware that the violence in life cannot be readily separated out. Anthony Burgess's *A Clockwork Orange* (1962) encysts the German legacy of WWII violence within the background setting of the Cold War. Teen-psychologization in the pidgin English-Russian of the containing culture jettisons the music (i.e., Beethoven's music) into the foreground of failure to treat a violent psychopath. This results in the following liberal consensus by midlifers: "Delimitation is always difficult. The world is one, life is one. The sweetest and most heavenly of activities partake in some measure of violence—the act of love, for instance; music, for instance" (131).

In *Ender's Game*, the android test is to be used to select efficient soldiers by their high empathy scores. That every soldier was sent to war with a license to kill is as old as history. It was an initiation ritual left behind in another place, a limited edition of gender identification. The Third Reich introduced a socialization process (not in the army now) of adaptation to psychopathy for which violence without restraint or compromise was a duty. Only in this way was it out in the open as problem. In the US, the movies comprising the opening season of slasher and splatter entertainment bear discrete connections with the German history of psychopathy, which, in its proper place, was the content filling the doubling range of *Gleichschaltung*. In unsuspected US heartlands, it irrupted onscreen, but as psycho-terror fitting profiles.

The screenplay for the 2013 film adaptation adds a note of saving grace to the empathy formula: in getting to know his enemy to the point of being able to anticipate his every move and destroy him, Ender must also love him, but just as this foe loves himself. The kill is thus not anaclitic but narcissistic, melancholic (i.e., without object relation) rather than mournful, and any backfire is contained in a self-relation more reminiscent of suicide than of grief. Ender's identification with the Buggers folds out of yet another video game, one that draws on Ender's unconscious, which it guides and directs, as seen in his own dreams. Out of the dream series emerges the bond with the Buggers—a bond that outlives them. That the innocent agent of the biggest crime in history comes to bear endless testimony to the annihilated species as Speaker of the Dead is a redemptive fantasy that skips the present tensions of history. In the movie, Ender makes contact not in the reservation of his dreaming but in person with a dying Bugger queen, who (in a reversal of Siegfried's initiation) drinks his tears and is thus able to understand him. The dying survivor entrusts the egg of the future to Ender for safekeeping. Ender accepts the task as his work of reparation for the US foreign policy of humanity.

2

Shakespeare, our first man on the scene of modernity's spectral transmissions, called the new delegation of the horse, the miracle weapon out in the harbor of world domination, Birnam Wood, the immobility of which was the guarantee the witches gave Macbeth that he would remain inviolate—save for the impossible prospect of the woods advancing. The battle lines that the woods cross draw together in Shakespeare's day (like two sides of concluded sibling conflict) Scotland and England before the new horizon of the island's far-flung interests. The Stuarts came from Scotland to hold the throne of the United Kingdom, which ultimately displaced the historical rivalry through colonization of the new and third worlds. The American writer Edgar Rice Burroughs, whose identification with Virginia, with the losing side of the American Civil War, ran deep, projected his first protagonist, John Carter, an unreconstructed veteran of the Confederacy, to Mars. By all accounts, he subsequently introduced the first American superhero: the African-born Tarzan, son to a shipwrecked Scottish Lord and Lady.

Considering himself a descendent of Banquo, James I inherited the throne from Queen Elizabeth, who was responsible for his mother's execution. But the succession did not contradict the accounting for history that became the official position. That Mary Stuart's sentencing was justified knows only one allied position outside the world community or consensus: the officially unrepentant US support for the atom bombings of Japan. According to Carl Schmitt, the taboo upon the disambiguation of Gertrude's responsibility in *Hamlet* refers to the earlier history of Mary's intrigue and remarriage. In the setting of succession, the civil peace, the two women, the two sides, had to get off the opposition scot-free. The German royal families that later succeeded to Great Britain's throne advertised their relationship to James I.

In time for the unification of Germany, Heinrich Schliemann followed out the identification with the loss of the Trojan War, but from both sides. Already in childhood at the time of his mother's death, he conceived, as he later claimed or recalled, the goal of Troy's excavation. He was not aided by his father, whose embezzlement of church funds made it impossible for the son to complete an academic approach to his goal. He had to fast-forward through the selfmade-man test in order to retire early from the import/export business and apply the fortune he had amassed to his childhood investment in burial and exhumation.

Before getting down to business in Russia as a supplier of raw materials needed for the Crimean War, the news of his brother's presumed death in California brought him to the gold rush where he ended up devising cans to keep former food safe for the prospectors and pioneers. At that time, California became a state and citizenship was automatically conferred on Schliemann. Convinced that the epic accounts of Homer and Vergil were historical fact, the retired Californian located Troy's site using the evidence of *The Iliad* remediated by stopwatch. When he excavated what he took to be the graves of Priam and Hecuba, he had to watch the perfectly preserved Trojans turn to dust.

The destructiveness of archaeology is harder to admit than the desecration. During an elaboration of the meaning of the unconscious for his crypt-carrying patient (the so-called Ratman) while using the archeological finds cluttering his desk as show-and-tell, Freud pointed out that the contents of Pompeii—which, entombed, were preserved against time like unconscious thought—only now began to disintegrate upon being raised up into consciousness (or light and air). Freud recognized that he had to rush to retract or deny the destruction and give his obsessional neurotic patient reassurance that everything was being done at the excavation site to contain and even restore the damage (outside and inside the heir) (176-77). The focus of Schliemann's archaeology never shifted away from the loss of the Trojan War, the mother of all that followed. He was also caught in a balancing act of commemoration between Priam's Treasure and the Mask of Agamemnon, as though the fall of Troy had concluded a war of sibling unrest and rivalry.

While the English crowd symbol is the sea, the German crowd symbol is the army, but as another *Macbeth* citation, the mobilization of the woods against all odds. Elias Canetti writes:

> The mass symbol of the Germans was the army. But the army was always more than the army: it was the marching forest. . . . In a forest in which trees of many of the same species are found, the bark of the trees, which may at first seem like armor, in fact resembles the uniforms of an army regiment. Army and forest were for the German, without his being aware of it, in every way merged together. What might appear to others stark and bleak in the army has for the German the life and radiance of the forest. (202)

Canetti's army contains the spark of panic exemplified in its uncontained state by the out-of-control crowd trying to exit the burning theater. Freud and Bachelard attribute this panic content to the same-sexual, onanistic, or perverse origin of fire that is reignited each time two sticks of wood are rubbed together. For Bachelard, this is the dotted line of repression that turned fire into the biggest obstacle to its scientific understanding.

There was a legend associated with Paris, the second son of Priam and Hecuba, which, according to Otto Rank, belongs to one genre of myths of the birth of the hero, cycling through dire prophecy, consequent exposure of the baby, restoration of his birth right, and ultimate realization of the forecast. When Hecuba was about to give birth to Paris, she had a dream: "that she brought forth a burning log of wood, which set fire to the entire city" (23). Where there is wood there is fire. Birnam Wood carries in its name the injunction to "burn them!" The mobility of the army of timber contains and ignites the spark of this command. It is by his theory of the open and closed crowds that Canetti inscribes the inimical advance of the wooden army within the passage of conflagration. Only "Fire!" can immediately bring "to a head" the pent-up "crowd feeling" of an audience assembled in a theater (26). "It is strange to observe how strongly for the person struggling with it the crowd assumes the character of fire . . . That emphatic trampling on people, so often observed in panics and apparently so senseless, is nothing but the stamping out of fire" (27).

Bachelard invokes death in the flames as the least lonely way to go (28). "Burn'em" is indeed a funeral direction. Fire destroys but also preserves. The phantasm of cremation reflects its genealogical introduction: preservation from desecration of the complete contents of a mummy's tomb. Like the hollow reed of Prometheus, the wooden horse already carried the violent ignition that set fire to the towers of Ilium and preserved Troy's lost cause.

According to Bachelard, animism imagines every forest fire as a sacrifice offered now to the fire, now to the woods (46-47). Fire not only destroys and preserves but also, Bachelard underscores, cleanses. In his account, the cleansing aspect of fire is the variation on preservation that undoes the safe deposit. The flames of purgatory cleanse the souls of their ghostly unfinished business. In the primitive society of Schreber's delusional system, the souls of the departed bore the wrong identification to let the disposal service of cleansing pass over them: the so-called purified souls were the souls not yet purified or redeemed. Bachelard affirms the "brutal death" by fire, which leaves behind not a trace, as the "guarantee" of bodily entry into the Beyond (26). The inclusion of the body in this all-is-nothing scenario shows that Bachelard would have his pagan preservation and erase it, too. He generates a Jungian appreciation of the reception and application of fire. This culminates in cleansing, not out of the unconscious of night dreams, but out of daydream fantasy, which, like its incarnation in the redemptive fantasy genre, remains within the loop of its ultimate "realization" as the Christian death of death.

Fire purifies also to the extent that it consumes the excremental side effects of the fateful proximity between food and death. This applies as well to alcohol by the fermentation it both instills and distills. "The roasting of meat signifies victory over rot. Together with the fermented drink, it is the principle of the festive gathering; which is to say, it is the principle of primitive society" (135). That principle, according to Freud in *Totem and Taboo*, was the control release of murder as the special event of the totem meal whereby the clan could be kept on a schedule of mourning.

When Freud counted the Macbeths among those wrecked by success, he gave the inside view of their other success as among the most identified-with losers in literature. Lady Macbeth's inability to "out" the damn spot confirms an internal reservation about the success of her power couple—a success upon which she is wrecked. Since it is clear (*klar*) that Macbeth must realize he cannot live forever, Freud considers Macduff's outcry that Macbeth has no children the "key" to Macbeth's transformation (299). Freud allows Macduff's outcry to mean that only a man without children could order children to be killed. But Freud overhears the curse of infertility upon success and succession. There could be more to hear along this line. Macbeth asks for male offspring in recognition of his wife's inspiring pledge of her own ruthlessness. In passing, she makes reference to her having had a child; it's the reason she knows of what she speaks. She declares that, if she had vowed to kill her own infant (as Macbeth vowed to kill Duncan), she would and could commit even that murder.

When Freud speculates that poetic justice pays back the Macbeths for their crimes against generation by granting them childlessness, he overlooks the contradiction he himself mentioned in passing, namely that the infertility fulfills Lady Macbeth's express wish that she be unwomaned to steel her and her husband's resolve to proceed to the first act of murder. It was this murder that was to be "the be-all and the end-all" of consequence, the success that trammeled up succession, allowing the Macbeths to "jump the life to come" (1.7.1f).

In the season of Lady Macbeth's resolve, there is one spot of hesitation: she is unable to murder the man who in his sleep resembles her dead father. Often one recognizes a parent's likeness in one's own child. Upon murdering Duncan, her husband heard his crime denounced as the second death that sundered sleep and death: "'Sleep no more! / Macbeth does murther Sleep,' the innocent Sleep, / Sleep that knits up the ravel'd sleave of care, / The death of each day's life, sore labor's bath, / Balm of hurt minds, great nature's second course, / Chief nourisher in life's feast" (2.2.33f). Sleep may look like death but it is the life of life: it is or engenders the next generation, the second course, whereby life is rejuvenated. It's the day's newborn and the life source for the day's recreation and renewal. To murder the life of life is a tall order. But its punch is packed inside the murder of the semblance of death in sleep.

As in *Hamlet*, murder is tied to the second death of the dead. Getting rid of Duncan amounted for Lady Macbeth to losing the loss of her child and giving a wide berth/birth to the afterlife of successful mourning. From start to finish, Lady Macbeth proves unable to put the dead to second death. Her figuration of loss is then carried forward as the identification with it as carried out by King Macbeth.

Even when the safeguards of witchcraft are turned around, his resolution to lose as a winner remains intact. By then the identification with lost causes exceeds the Macbeths, who perpetrated their own wreckage upon their victims at the impasse to mourning. In the multiplication of the divisions of one psychic entity, we detect the intrapsychic connection between the wreckage over the prospect of success in mourning and the identification with lost causes. For all their violence, the Macbeths are not themselves psychopaths. Instead they scoop out the spousal medium of mourning, scrub it down and detonate it. Against their nature, they fill up with the black magic of ruthlessness and destroy forever the very prospect of successful mourning, of succession through substitution. Heroism lies here—in wait for an identification that is untenable, undeclared, but ever so strong.

3

Are the walking trees inheriting the earth in John Wyndham's *The Day of the Triffids* another fulfillment of the prophecy of the witches in *Macbeth*? If it is conceded, it is not by direct citation but by non sequitur. In response to the evidence of the post-apocalyptic spread of untended nature—and in the very place where the development of instant neighborhoods not so long ago was criticized for erasing the natural setting—the protagonist-narrator, William Mason, touches on the notion of revenge and then spills the blood in the *Macbeth* citation, but as an uncanny harbinger of survival, regrowth, and other return engagements. "'The countryside is having its revenge all right,' I said. 'Nature seemed about finished then—"Who would have thought the old man to have had so much blood in him?"'" (202). The vengeful return of defeated, finished nature overflows from the murdered father's unstoppable lifeblood. The walking trees are the advance guard of this development.

Like the Martian tripods in *The War of the Worlds*, a triffid advances by the limping, lurching momentum of its three-pronged root that otherwise rests in the earth but can also move above ground. "When it 'walked' it moved rather like a man on crutches. Two of the blunt 'legs' slid forward, then the whole thing lurched as the rear one drew almost level with them, then the two in front slid forward again" (27). The mobile forest of injured father figures can be stopped, if only for the time being, by electricity or fire. And yet triffids also continuously rub their front twigs together or against the stem, producing not sparks but a kind of communication among them.

A triffid packs a tendril it whips out to sting its victim with a dose of poison. It turns out that triffids belong to the sideshow of plants that eat flesh. They sting not to protect themselves but to hunt their quarry, which you can follow and understand as a consequence of the stinging only if you wait and watch as long as they do around the victims. "The stinging tendril did not have the muscular power to tear firm flesh, but it had strength enough to pull shreds from a decomposing body and lift them to the cup on its stem" (31).

The triffids make short shrift of the evidence of an end that is final, which reaches the narrator as a stench at once unforgettable and indescribable. "When I woke to it that morning it convinced me beyond doubt that the end had come. Death is just the shocking end of animation; it is dissolution that is final" (125). The triffids administer a return to nature that proceeds more swiftly than history to lift the depressive effect from the sites of the end. "And, curiously, as the living things increasingly took charge, the effect of the place became less oppressive. As it passed beyond the scope of any magic wand, most of the ghosts were going with it, withdrawing slowly into history" (192).

Mason was one of the lucky few to survive a triffid's sting, which struck his eyes. He was in the hospital with his eyes covered up for treatment on the night when almost everyone else watched a bright cloud of comet debris fill the sky, the light show that left them blind by the next morning. Mankind is largely wiped out by the consequences of general blindness. The triffids benefit by the evolutionary advantage they now hold. Mason, too, benefits. The catastrophe has turned around his schizoid retirement from life toward a new opening:

> My way of life, my plans, ambitions, every expectation I had had, they were all wiped out at a stroke, along with the conditions that had formed them. I suppose that had I had any relatives or close attachments to mourn I should have felt suicidally derelict at that moment. But what had seemed at times a rather empty existence turned out now to be lucky. My mother and father were dead, my one attempt to marry had miscarried some years before, and there was no particular person dependent upon me. And, curiously, what I found that I did feel—with a consciousness that it was against what I ought to be feeling—was release. (46)

The three dots that follow the "release" introduce the three-pronged advance of the triffids into the open ending or uncontainment of his illicit feeling. But they can also be connected with the other series of reversals leading to the protagonist's own triangulation. In the new world order, Mason finds that he has changed places with everyone else who can still see his way to survival. "Curiously I realized that in all this I had met no other person who was searching for someone else. Every one of them had been . . . snapped clean away from friends or relatives to link them with the past, and was beginning a new life with people who were strangers. Only I, as far as I could see, had promptly formed a new link" (163-64).

Before the end of the world, Mason thought of loneliness as a negative that could be replaced as something temporary, like the absence of company.

> That day I learned that it was much more. It was something which could press and oppress, could distort the ordinary and play tricks with the mind. Something which lurked inimically all around, stretching the nerves and twanging them with alarms, never letting one forget that there was no one to help, no one to care. It showed one as an atom adrift in vastness, and it waited all the time its chance to frighten and frighten horribly. (169-70)

This drifting atom is the bouncing ball to follow in the reception or interpretation of the disaster, which entails a key elision. The speech of hope that another seeing-eye leader delivers to his pack reiterates the survivor ideology that is the consensus by the end of the novel: the catastrophe at least—at last!—spared the earth the ongoing prospect or traumatic history of nuclear warfare. We are invited to a timeline of denial: "From August 6, 1945, the margin of survival has narrowed appallingly. Indeed, two days ago it was narrower than it is at this moment. If you need to dramatize, you could well take for your material the years succeeding 1945, when the path of safety started to shrink to a tightrope along which we had to walk with our eyes deliberately closed to the depths beneath us" (95-96),

In a 1951 novel where the future seems no more remote or timeless than the next day, the evacuation of German science fiction and the history of its realizations in the course of WWII is especially pressing. There is one explicit reference to WWII as part of the novel's prehistory. It is embedded in Mason's one intact souvenir of his own past, specifically of his father: "My father once told me that before Hitler's war he used to go round London with his eyes more widely open than ever before, seeing the beauties of buildings that he had never noticed before—and saying good-by to them" (70). But when he next admits that he has a similar feeling, Mason abruptly interrupts himself and, by the force of the catastrophe upon his world now, subsumes and displaces his father's earlier forecast as premature. "Much more than anyone could have hoped for had survived that war—but this was an enemy they would not survive. It was not wanton smashing and willful burning that they waited for this time: it was simply the long, slow, inevitable course of decay and collapse" (ibid.). The paternal tour of London in anticipation of destruction is revisited and erased by the son's later London visit on a mission to remember the past, which concludes this loop of exclusion of the traumatic history of WWII.

> Once—not that year, not the next, but later on—I stood in Piccadilly Circus again, looking round at the desolation and trying to re-create in my mind's eye the crowds that once swarmed there. I could no longer do it. Even in my memory they lacked reality. There was no tincture of them now. They had become as much a back cloth of history as the audiences in the Roman Colosseum or the army of the Assyrians, and, somehow, just as far removed from me. (192)

The evacuation of the relationship to the recent past, to one's dead, folds inside the back cloth of history a reference not only to the "poor player that struts and frets his hour upon the stage" but to photographic practice. It is a buried reference to the satellites that wield a new, inhuman POV. The *Whole Earth Catalog* promoted the ecological identification with the earth, the rescue of nature from the prospect of earth's nuclear devastation, as an afterthought to the first satellite photo of the "whole earth."

The satellites orbiting the future world on the eve of blindness occupy a highpoint in the evolution of artificial flight that is seen to surpass the rocket's transitional objective: "Sustained research in rocketry had at last succeeded in attaining one of its objectives. It had sent up a missile which stayed up. It was, in fact, possible to fire a rocket far enough up for it to fall into an orbit" (22). That satellites are the future leads to a traffic jamming in the skies of inimical objects and contents that can fall upon the earth at any time, on or off purpose. "It was by no means pleasant to realize that there were an unknown number of menaces up there over your head, quietly circling and circling until someone should arrange for them to drop" (ibid.). The satellite firmament is an unseen host to rumors or reports "that as well as satellites with atomic heads there were others with such things as crop diseases, cattle diseases, radioactive dusts, viruses, and infections not only of familiar kinds but brand-new sorts recently thought up in laboratories" (ibid.). Mason looks to these skies, then, for the origin of the triffids, "the outcome of a series of ingenious biological meddlings—and very likely accidental, at that" (20).

The temporal paradox of future worlds in science fiction alters the historical past, too. The first successfully launched satellite, *Sputnik 1*, escalated the Space Race as a Cold War exclusive. That only the rocket to the moon qualified as the ultimate victory goes back to the prehistory of the Nazi realization of German science fiction. The rocket is a fetish, a monument to an overcoming of unidentified losses, the history of which can be forgotten; it occupies the border to that very history's condemned site and guards its future excavation. The interception of the rocket by the satellite in *The Day of the Triffids*, which reroutes the evil in human history, blocks reception of the Nazi era as decisively as the foregrounding of atomic power.

The 1962 film adaptation of *The Day of the Triffids* keeps WWII close: survival is secured through an alliance between a French woman and the American protagonist, Bill Masen, who has to abandon London to get to the turning point. He addresses his French partner's depressed mood following the loss of her fellow survivors. Yes, he knows: "You survive. Why?" He knows all about it "from the war." For Masen, an American Naval officer—who, by the end, helps his group join the greater group of the sighted by a submarine waiting at Gibraltar—the path to survival is across the sea.

With Masen in London, we witness the consequence of the morning blindness as a series of interruptions of the ability to bring machinic voyages to a successful close. A ship is lost at sea, doubly so without 24-7 radio assistance. A plane's blind pilot can't be guided down for emergency landing by the abandoned tower. At closer range, the scene of botched arrival at the end station shows a train entering without slowing down or stopping—like the legendary film shot of a train moving toward the camera and thus into the audience. According to these scenes of catastrophic non-arrival, it is the coupling of eyesight as a system that has been withdrawn by the general blindness. The few remaining eye witnesses must restore the system of coupled sight.

En route, the loner Masen acquires a prefab family (including a French woman and an English girl) by the selection process of catastrophic shock and aftershocks. At the train station, Masen saved the girl from a blind man's attempt to use her as his seeing-eye slave or prosthesis. Together they cross the sea to France and encounter a community of the "See French." Masen wants to keep moving—to yet another naval base—but the woman in charge wants to keep her group in place and intact. Then a sighted group on another plane of reaction to trauma party-crashes the community from on high, driving every boundary apart until all that remains is at the disposal of the triffids. Only the woman in charge gets away with the Anglo-American unit. The members of this new family unit fall into place without tension or complication.

To make it to the rescue by submarine, the best weapon against the triffids turns out to be diversion. Masen tries gunfire, electrification of the fence, then flame throwing. The little girl figures out that the ambulatory wood follows the sound of the generator. Sound, according to the final strategy, can lead the triffids far away, "like the Pied Piper of Hamelin." They get this far because the girl can identify with the triffids. While the wood is off advancing to the bait of the sound like the lost children of Hamelin, the family system gets away.

The couples therapy/theory Wyndham inherited from H. G. Wells is limited in the film adaptation to a couple of Anglo scientists, who, through the epidemic blindness, end up stranded on an island. Ensconced within their research lab in the crypt of a tower, they missed the blinding night lightshow. Now the husband's science gets a restart and the marriage is saved through the struggle to survive the locally proliferating carnivorous trees. The triffids are ready for their close-up around and inside the Frankenstein-style research tower. The scientist kills a specimen for lab experimentation. Nothing seems to destroy the tissue samples cut out of the tree that otherwise lacks circulatory and nervous systems. When the cut-up dead tree on the gurney is briefly left unattended, it reanimates, reattaches its severed parts, and gets away to rally the wood for the final assault on the couple inside the tower. But when the triffids corner the couple, the scientist, in hopeless desperation, aims seawater at them from the emergency hose. He thus scores a first victory. Triffids cannot withstand contact with seawater; they go up in smoke like a fire put out by water, a roundabout reference to the UK's station as an Emergency Island over which the first postponement of the German Blitz was secured.

Before the meteorite-sparked blindness takes over, Masen, who is bound to see, exchanges goodbyes with his doctor: "See you in the morning, I hope." "I hope so." The first blind man Masen encounters next morning is the doctor. He asks his healed patient to test his eyes for any reflex, any hope. That's a negative. Then the doctor asks Masen to get the black bag from the office next door. Alone, he chooses death by defenestration. This Latin term isn't used. There is no other word in English for crashing through a window and falling to one's death. Its coinage is lodged in historical reference. It originated like the golem-as-superhero in Prague to describe specific murders leading to the Thirty Years War. A civil or sibling conflict, this devastating war launched—not only according to Philip K. Dick in *The Transmigration of Timothy Archer* (1982)—the modern German chapter of the history of loss reversal. For Dick, there was a black hole in history through which the Thirty Years War and WWII were in direct communication.

In the movie's carefully mapped setting of Allies-only survival, the advance of the triffids carries forward a certain modern compulsion to roll over losses into reversal or denial of the end as a "final victory." Salty see-water also signifies tears of grief, which, though they may not reverse blindness, bring down the triffids, otherwise the unbeatable prospect of a lost cause not given up for lost.

4

Commenced in 1947, Ray Bradbury's *Fahrenheit 451* (1953) introduces the "wilderness" as the enigmatic placeholder for all that is missing in the conflagration administered by firemen, whose chief duty in this future world is book burning. In this doubly inverted world, the fireman's hose sprays kerosene like a "great python" spitting venom (3), while his mechanical hound pounces upon those who break the law by the book to inject them with a paralyzing agent. It follows that so-called fast driving therapy out in the country lifts everyone's spirits because it's fun and targets actual animals: "You hit rabbits, sometimes you hit dogs" (64).

In addition to Dick's animal-empathy test for androids or psychopaths, basic profiling also identifies arson as the other omen in childhood and early adolescence that presages the imminence of psychopathy. Every fire is a forest fire that counts casualties among critters. When a collector of books chooses to go up in flames with her collection, the firemen's ritual is spoiled by a series of murderous associations that the book burning carries forward: "The men above were hurling shovelfuls of magazines into the dusty air. They fell like slaughtered birds and the woman stood below, like a small girl, among the bodies" (37).

The televisual culture that snakes safeguard by their spitting and sucking transmits the mobilization of the forest between the lines. Protagonist and fireman Guy Montag has begun to waver and balk before the focus and load of his enterprise. To contain Guy's crisis, his boss, Captain Beatty, initiates him into the real history of their profession. Everyone knows the official version is coterminous with American history and identifies Benjamin Franklin as an ancestral fireman (34), but now we learn that book-burning in fact "got started around about a thing called the Civil War" (54). The war marked a turn in the genealogy of media. "The fact is we didn't get along well until photography came into its own. Then— motion pictures . . . Radio. Television. Things began to have mass" (ibid.). Books are pathogenic leftovers from the enchanted forest of second nature, which, since the Civil War, the mass media have disenchanted and abandoned. Medics, firemen, and their snakes defend a Sensurround of health and happiness. "We're the Happiness Boys, the Dixie Duo, you and I and the others. We stand against the small tide of those who want to make everyone unhappy with conflicting theory and thought" (61-62).

When Guy interrupts their TV watching to read poetry to his wife Millie and her friends, one woman hits the nadir of her despair below the radar of her manic defenses (100). To open a book is to open a tomb in the enchanted forest. Guy's "most significant memory" of Millie is set on the media Sensurround as a place of absence. He sees "a little girl in a forest without trees (how odd!) or rather a little girl lost on a plateau where there used to be trees (you can feel the memory of their shape all about)" (44). Otherwise Guy responds to her quiescent state between earphones as "a tomb world" (11). Opening and shutting in an atmosphere of mediatic manic denial of the recent past, the tomb world also lies in the mainstream of Burn'em wood.

On his way home to his suicidally happy wife at the start of the novel, Guy meets Clarisse McClellan, who introduces herself as seventeen and "crazy" (7) or, according to the official diagnosis of the school counselor, "antisocial" (29). With its emphasis on sports, however, school drives a hard bargain via extramural containment. After school, the teens are so ragged they go off to the Fun Park "to bully people around, break windowpanes in the Window Smasher place or wreck cars in the Car Wrecker place" (30). Just the same, six of Clarisse's friends "have been shot in the last year alone" (ibid.). At first contact with Clarisse, Guy flashes on an early memory of his mother by candlelight (7). Later Guy reflects on the girl in one of the strongest lines of the novel: "What incredible power of identification the girl had" (11). For his 1966 film adaptation, Truffaut turned Clarisse into Millie's benign Doppelgänger, which loops together the unidentified dying of both women in the novel. At the novel's end, when it is Millie's turn to count among the missing in the wake of the nuclear attack upon the city he escaped, Guy advances to a sense of being wronged by the absence of mourning (155). In the movie, Clarisse survives as one of the book people with Guy.

In the novel, one of Clarisse's first remarks to Guy, namely that she had "heard once that a long time ago houses used to burn by accident and they needed firemen to stop the flames" (8), makes conscious his recent automatic tendency to steal books at the scenes of burning. Impulsive stealing vies to get back to the early mother. Then Clarisse's own disappearance with her family from the neighborhood—her presumed death, run over by a car—incites his need to know with abandon. Seeking counsel, Guy tracks down Faber, a former English professor and possible defender of the book. Guy accepts Faber's diagnosis because it resonates with Clarisse's inside view of adolescence, her own and the official version bouncing around in the container: "Those who don't build must burn. It's as old as history and juvenile delinquents" (89).

Beatty's instruction to Guy in the history and significance of their profession escalates into a paean to burning, which spreads from books to "everything," getting an incendiary boost from the new and improved disposal of the dead: "Funerals are unhappy and pagan? Eliminate them, too. Five minutes after a person is dead he's on his way to the Big Flue, the Incinerators serviced by helicopters all over the country. Ten minutes after death a man's a speck of black dust. Let's not quibble over individuals with memoriams. Forget them. Burn them all, burn everything. Fire is bright and fire is clean" (60). Firemen know best, as Beatty advises, because scientists don't know what fire is. "Its real beauty is that it destroys responsibility and consequences" (115). But then Beatty is caught in the acting out that fire spreads. Guy sets him on fire to protect himself and Faber. His sense that Beatty wanted to die doesn't really pass the empathy test.

Following the book woman's decision to go down with her collection of books, Beatty labels Guy's crisis typical and passing; he provided a discourse of rationalization to neutralize doubts in the container. There is a sense that, if Guy's midlife criticism is a norm, then the stealing of books is inevitable, which signifies his society's doom. Like the world of *Nineteen Eighty-Four*, this one would qualify as a natural history exhibit in the department of impossible futures. Do the opening credits in Truffaut's film adaptation, which are not typed but rather spoken out, already signal that the future belongs to the people of the book?

Escaping to the abandoned countryside, Guy meets and joins the book people, who incorporate books within their "photographic memories" (151). In the film adaptation, they identify themselves as "the dead." We see that they are also transmitting by transference and/or reproduction. Books that exist only in memory require children, children of your own or students. One book person refers to his grandfather's sense of inheritance as supplying the alternative to the absence of mourning: what one leaves behind can be a child, a book, a house, or a pair of shoes, something one (lost and) found and touched and changed. "The difference between the man who just cuts lawns and a real gardener is in the touching" (157).

When Guy first meets the book people, they are gathered around a fire. "He had never thought in his life that it could give as well as take. . . . There was a foolish and yet delicious sense of knowing himself as an animal come from the forest, drawn by the fire" (146). Another nuclear war wipes out what they left behind: "the great séance and all the murmuring ghosts" (140). "Somewhere the saving and putting away had to begin again and someone had to do the saving and keeping, one way or another, in books, in records, in people's heads" (141). The Phoenix rises up in their conversation—"every time he burnt himself up he sprang out of the ashes, he got himself born all over again" (163)—but the hoped-for difference is that, unlike his close cousin, man knows it and can stop the burning and returning. Someday we will stop to remember. Fifty years ago the grandfather who tended the garden of his inheritance showed "some V-2 rocket films" and in fact ran them off many times to give caution (157). "Have you ever seen the atom-bomb mushroom from two hundred miles up? It's a pinprick, it's nothing. With the wilderness all around it" (ibid.). It was the rocket's POV upon the wilderness below that the grandfather projected as a warning and pledge. Truffaut's version overlooks the POV upon the wilderness. Through the conversion of Guy, whose Oskar Werner accent gives him a German or German-Jewish surname, the film redresses the book-burning problem into a prospect of integration within the postwar order of the people of the book.

5

Abraham Lincoln said *Macbeth* was his favorite play. Only days before his assassination, he even quoted Macbeth's despairing envy of dead Duncan's respite from fitful betrayal. Since then, *Macbeth* has been the main prop of ambivalence toward the power invested in presidents. After Goethe's *Wilhelm Meister's Apprenticeship*, any future author in the German-language world had to be initiated into the theater of his talent by his mother's gift. After Lincoln made his choice, future US presidents have had to memorize lines from *Macbeth* in adolescence. Lincoln found the text for that dark side he tried to disown as his property or responsibility: the American Civil War. He found it a "wonderful" play that was without equal. But the wound had to be carried forward.

The reversal of lost causes basic to the poetic historiography of nations came to ply its trade in the United States between popular culture and art beginning in the 1960s when the reenactment of historical battles and the science fiction genre of alternate history were reflected in the art world as cite-specific or openly skewed reenactments of non-archival happening events or performances. But the popular culture industry of modern reenactment was applied first to the American Civil War. In theory, the divergence in reenactment that yields alternate history was already in place via Ward Moore's *Bring the Jubilee* (1953), a novel about a parallel world in which the Confederacy had won the war. For the twentieth century, this victory meant that the Confederate States and the German Union were the two world powers inside the novel's alternate reality (76). Once there is a time machine that the protagonist, a history buff in his own time, can take to the Battle of Gettysburg, his inadvertent interference sets history aright, but the consequent alteration of the future or present to which he returns deposits him there as a foreign body. As a Northerner, the protagonist was a second-class citizen whose rights were thus restored, although he was brought before the loss of the Southern cause as his own lost place in history. "Once lost, that particular past can never be regained. Another and another perhaps, but never the same one. There are no parallel universes—though this one may be sinuous and inconstant" (192).

In *We Can Build You*, Philip K. Dick resituated the culture industry of reenactment within the science fiction forecast of android production. Android designer Maury Rock extols the new market: "This Nation is obsessed with the War Between the States. I'll tell you why. It was the only and first national epic in which we Americans participated" (11). Android reenactment of the Civil War will substitute for actual war, which will be abolished (20). The financial backer, however, quickly drops the android production of reenactment figures for a new purpose congruent with Dick's other android novels: production of a supply of fake neighbors (or, as they are marketed in *The Simulacra*, famnexdos) for Outer-Space colonists to take with them to counter the psychoticizing effects of isolation on the new frontier. In *Do Androids Dream of Electric Sheep?*, Pris's reminiscences of her troubled adolescence on Mars imply her original placement in a family setting, yet first contact with the android in the novel is through TV advertising pitched to prospective colonists, which is so out of sync that it would seem to be selling itself in the primal time of false memory. The offer of androids "custom-tailored" either "as body servants or tireless field hands . . . duplicates the halcyon days of the pre-Civil War Southern States" (17).

Dick was inspired by the animatronic robots on display in Disneyland to turn the Civil War reenactments popular in the 1960s into a future entertainment industry employing androids only, a remake that the 1967 novel *Logan's Run*, where we saw it first, had projected in the form of the outer rim of an internal administration of forgetting otherwise syndicated as countless Re-Live parlors. "Signs creamed and moaned in smoky colors: RE-LIVE THAT FIRST EMBRACE! (A gaudy Tri-Dim on a ribbed platform depicting two nude youngsters in a torrid tangle.) RE-LIVE THOSE PRECIOUS MOMENTS! (A wild-eyed boy riding a flamed devil stick through a mock sky.) RE-LIVE! RE-LIVE! RE-LIVE!" (30).

The Civil War and President Lincoln provide the only historical props in the twenty-third century youth culture, which came to world power in the 1960s. A pointless exchange in Washington D.C. between a seventeen-year-old protester from Missouri and a "paunchy middle-aged heckler" sparked the so-called Little War that within two weeks placed the government "in the hands of youth" (121-22). One result was that "the age of government by computer began" (123). A sixteen-year-old proposed the solution of a maximum age limit for the ongoing population crisis. When his plan was inaugurated five years later, the now twenty-one-year-old "proved his dedication by becoming the first to publicly embrace Sleep" (ibid.). The new order of eugenics was introduced by its founder's suicide.

The issue of eugenics in support of youthful vitality doesn't trigger any associations with the Nazi era (or with California) inside the novel or its future world. The one thing the young of the 1960s in the United States "were sure of" was that "they would never again place their fate in the hands of an older generation" (ibid.). After a couple of centuries, the result is an oblivion of historical reference between the ongoing now and the Civil War. There is an annual gala of reenactment that features the battle of Fredericksburg, using android soldiers in the field. Why is this battle that the Confederacy won selected? The pointlessness of General Burnside's charge delivers the point of instruction, the necessity to die young that is broadcast by loudspeaker to the crowds. "The Civil War was fought by seventeen-and-eighteen-year-olds, men willing to die for their cause" (102). In the living units of this future world, entertainment consoles project 3-D holograms of "young Abe Lincoln . . . splitting logs in the center of the room" (22). But the overturning of the youth culture and its government by computer can begin to be conceived by means of the only historical figure available. "There was an *old* Lincoln after the young one" (146).

The 1976 film adaptation offers the culture shock of an old Peter Ustinov to those running away from youth culture on death drive (lifetime has been extended to age 30 onscreen). The film's future world is Jetson-style, the Cold War look of Tomorrowland before it was remade into a *Metropolis*-set to fit the blast from the future past. Here the other name for the operatives, Sandmen, whose job is to execute those running from their deadline to seek Sanctuary, resonates with the recent past further emblematized as the gene pooling of the select resources of youth. The central computer sends the protagonist, Sandman Logan 5, to search for and destroy Sanctuary. To motivate him, it advances the lifetime clock on his hand to red. When Logan 5 returns (with his hand now clear), he tells the computer there is no Sanctuary, whereupon the computer overloads and breaks down. With its demise, all systems fail and the exterior seals on the genetic control state open up. The computer enters into an association both with the wizard and the wicked witch, aligning *Logan's Run* with the US utopian fantasy track that, since both movies premiered in 1939, proved to be the alternative to *Gone with the Wind* (which opened with an evocation in titles of a lost courtly estate at once of ladies and knights and masters and slaves). That there could be a remake of *The Wizard of Oz* with African Americans inheriting all the roles (the 1978 musical film *The Wiz*) sings along with Judy Garland's Dorothy, who extolled that the Scarecrow would be another Lincoln if he only had a brain.

6

Raymond Jones's *This Island Earth* (1952) turns on a series of seemingly decep-
tive simulacra, beginning with the title that almost scans like "Brave New World"
but is without citational status. At the start of the tale, scientists testing gadgets
discover unknown functioning parts among their incoming orders that evidence
"a whole electronic culture completely foreign" to their own (13). When instructions for building an "interocitor" arrive, Cal begins construction of what appears
to be a communication device. His colleague (who will be left behind) warns
against completing it because it could be "some sort of Trojan Horse gadget"
(29). When the device is turned on, it transmits words from the unknown sponsor
"like words in a ghost-ridden house" (33). Contact has thus been made with the
Engineer, who is in charge of selecting scientists to be part of a highly advanced
research project. Message delivered, the interocitor destroys itself. Cal is brought
by pilotless airship to the think tank.

Soon one of his new colleagues breaks down while experimenting on the
interocitor, babbling about something he'd seen in the sky. "He'd been working
on some interocitor modifications and suddenly he'd heard the Engineer thinking"
(58). Cal maintains equanimity, however, and doesn't subscribe to what can't
be substantiated. When Ruth, the psychiatrist on staff and his romantic interest,
challenges him—"Can you honestly say you know *everything* about the device?"
(60)—Cal steps back from the local paranoia into the abyss between scientific
knowledge and applied science. "Look—nobody can say he knows *everything*
about even an ordinary radio set" (ibid.).

The Engineer acknowledges Cal's loyalty by initiating him into the history of
his society: the Peace Engineers. Cal assumed the Engineer's organization "came
into existence . . . since the last war" (62). However, the society goes back to
the seventeenth century, spanning the genealogy of modern technology. Its main
service was to withhold "a growing mass of scientific knowledge" from the world
(ibid.). The society kept the atom bomb from being used already in WWI (63), for
example, but as a "definite society," the Peace Engineers were organized "during
the American Civil War" (62).

But there must be an as-yet-untold portion of this history. It's apparent that
the gap between science and technology can be controlled by the Peace Engineers as an active blanking. "Slowly there began to appear a consecutive thread of

knowledge that was fundamental in the field employed for communication in the machine. Yet, as it was now built, this basic characteristic seemed to be blanked" (70). Later, another capacity of the interocitor is demonstrated by inducing a gap in Cal's memory. "The memory of that sudden gap in his mind was appalling" (123). The Engineer is an alien from Outer Space procuring assistance from Earth under cover of the society—once Cal is brought to the Moon, the Engineer's status is as evident as the alien inability to be forthright. Why should they ask for help from men who hadn't built more than "an enlarged firecracker" (106)? "The gap between the technology of the Engineers and the rest of the Earth struck him. Down there at White Sands the Army was fitfully thrusting its feeble rockets one or two hundred miles into the atmosphere. No one had succeeded yet in freeing one from Earth's gravity" (105-06). Cal's own aspiration and motivation are called into question. "He had wanted something better for himself, and for all sentient life in the universe. He had been no more than a fish acting on a simple stimulus-response mechanism" (158).

The exclusion of the V-2 rocket from the recent past deposits German science fiction within the ambivalent reception of the alien Engineers. The exclusive focus on the atom bomb is maintained through the novel's one-sided recollection of WWII being wrapped around the Pacific. That Earth is an island belongs to this setting. In the recent Pacific war, "waves of battle washed back and forth over primitive people who had little or no comprehension of who was fighting, or to what purpose" (110). The alien nation (the Llana) to which the Engineer belongs has been at total war with another alien species (the Guara). The interstellar conflict has been going on since before humans emerged from their caves. "Earth is an island, which can be bypassed completely, or temporarily occupied if need be" (117). It turns out that the enemy alien force is already represented on Earth by agents who are preparing for the island's destruction. Unlike the Llana, the Guara have a hard time keeping the green, slimy, odiferous evidence that they are "creatures" under cover (149, 151). The jolt of this recognition is such that sides switch in the mix of metaphor. "We are like the jungle islanders trying to fight with poisoned arrows against an enemy who has atomic bombs" (153-54).

The aliens also excel at computing and project a social organization of decentralization and "cybernetic control" (126). They entrust their best offense to the computable predictability of any projected action. "It is almost a battle of computers rather than armies" (186). It is up to Cal to realize that their overreliance on the "crystal ball" of predictability was their weakness and losing streak. Thought, which the aliens proficiently transmit via the interocitor, is represented less by computation and more by behavioral response. Predictability does not pass the animal intelligence test. "What do you do to lower your own predictability to the Guara?" (187). The Guara have been winning the war by taking unpredicted action, like the destruction of the Earth. The Llana authorities double over with "sudden recognition of a long dreaded ghost" (189). Then, for the first time, they make a surprise maneuver and defend the Earth against a Guara attack.

Another way to put it is that the Llana have become so reliant on a machine that they have forgotten the sense or direction of compassion. To stop the Guara agents, the Engineer ultimately uses the interocitor as a weapon. The interocitor is indeed a Trojan Horse that communicates and destroys, an "incredible weapon by which one mind could reach out and seize another to twist it, guide it, or destroy it" (168). But the Engineer also demonstrates that he who uses it to destroy must also die. "There is no help for one who is the victor in such an interocitor contest as I am. One can fight but a single such battle. As in all war, he who wins is also the vanquished" (172). His dying instruction to Cal is to restore to the Llana their sense of compassion, which Cal will get across as the importance of behavioral unpredictability. "Tell them I believed that perhaps a war cannot be fought with justice by a machine, after all. . . . Help them understand once again what compassion means, for they have been at war so long in its defense that they scarcely understand it anymore" (ibid.).

The 1955 film adaptation locates the research organization in Georgia and its main facility in a house that looks like Tara (the laboratories are jokingly referred to as "the slave quarters"). One of the scientists at the facility working to put an end to war is from Germany. After listening to Mozart as part of a group, he must excuse himself: he has to be alone with the musical experience. The American scientist joins the group hoping to find the link between atomic energy and electronics, the cornerstone of the "pushbutton age" coming soon. The aliens have used up their uranium, which powers the defense shields of their planet against enemy attacks. They either hoped to obtain the Earth's natural resource or to relocate to Earth. Lobotomy-like brainwashing would secure the cooperation of Earthlings. Exeter, the good Engineer, who has been placed in charge of the research facility down South, prefers human free will. He alone is the exception: on his planet the alien nation has raised mutants as slave-soldiers, creatures of predictability with their oversized brains showing. He brings a couple of American scientists to his planet to disclose the plight of his people, hoping to convince them to help, but it's too late, even for the final anti-human decisions of his government. Exeter dies defending the couple against a super-sized brain soldier.

In Jones's novel, the German trajectory is split off as the two sides of alien conflict, one side ambivalently benign, the other side unambivalently malignant. If the good side can be kept from going and coming down with the contagion of psychopathic violence, then the Earth can be saved. The Civil War delivers the bottom line in science fiction that follows the bouncing atom bomb and, by a splitting of heirs, brackets out German science fiction (with the V-2 rocket at the front of the line). The alternate historical arc from the Civil War to atomic power can re-edit the history of modern science fiction by falling back on what counts as the first flight to the Moon in the genre, Jules Verne's *From the Earth to the Moon* (1865), which relied on the modernity of the Civil War to project rocket flight.

7

Leading up to von Braun's appearance on Disney TV in 1955, the V-2 rocket was rolled over into American science fiction and its head start rolled back by rerouting atomic power as the foundation and history of the projected immediate postwar future of space travel. In 1950, *Destination Moon*, which was billed while in production and continues to be memorialized as the premier Outer Space movie made in Hollywood, came in second to *Rocketship X-M*, which was made on the quick only to beat the film projected to be first. In *Destination Moon*, rocket flight relied on private patriotic sponsorship to get around Soviet-influenced withdrawal of government support. Thus it demonstrated the benefits of atomic energy in the close quarters of the Space Race. In *Rocketship X-M*, the trip to Outer Space accidentally skips the Moon and instead reaches Mars where the crew encounters the remains of an ancient civilization extinguished by atomic warfare. While visiting what is in effect the possible future outcome of civilization on Earth, the crew wears outfits borrowed from military fire fighters that resemble WWI uniforms outfitted for gas attack. The crew, like that engaged in Outer Space travel in *Woman in the Moon*, consists of four men and one woman. Following its launch, a subgenre at the border to German science fiction's evacuation can be made out (beginning with *Rocketship X-M*) by the number of crew members or the incident of stowaway passage: *Flight to Mars* (1951), *Satellite in the Sky* (1956), and the TV movie *Stowaway to the Moon* (1975) are three examples. Unable to land back on Earth, the remaining members broadcast the account of their journey prior to crashing and thereby entrust it, like Hamlet via Horatio, to the recording survivors outside its frame of doom.

There is a plot point of deliberation suggesting that *Destination Moon*, rather than reflect the pull of its influence, drew a line of separation from *Woman in the Moon*. At first, it looks like not everyone can make it back to Earth, which puts us on the verge of re-entering the orbit of Lang's film expedition. This prospect is belabored over and again. At the last minute, the decision to treat the media equipment as ballast means that it's all aboard for the Happy Ending announced as the End of the Beginning. It is this film, then, that would cross a virgin border to realization.

Willy Ley's popular science book formed the basis for the 1955 Hollywood projection *Conquest of Space*. This is a tribute to the advance guard of the rocket's crossover into science faction that Ley belonged to with Hermann Oberth and Wernher von Braun. *Conquest of Space* follows the track of *Rocketship X-M*. The mission to the Moon is switched at the last minute to aim for Mars. But the doubling that gave rise to the rocket in German science fiction is reinscribed upon another foundation: TV as New Testament medium. On the eve of takeoff to Mars, the international crew is entertained live from various stations around the world. From New York, the spectacle of show women, which robot Maria took to the limit in *Metropolis*, alternates with personal live communications. An aged saintly mother bids farewell to one astronaut, live from Vienna. When a fully contemporary US wife gives another member of the crew a sendoff, the peripheral vision of her low fidelity also transmits and proves that she's a mother, too. It follows that the commander of the flight begins to crack as the pages of his copy of the Bible turn. He tries to sabotage the mission, identifying it as sacrilege, but his son stops him dead. The crew manages to return to Earth against the odds that the old commander dealt them. It is decided just the same not to press charges against the son only in order not to impugn the father's reputation. The film introduced (as a defective cornerstone of the postwar conquest of space) American piety unto psychosis in thrall to ancestral religion born again in the new world.

The contest between *Rocketship X-M* and *Destination Moon* was already packed inside the relationship of *Destination Moon* to the 1947 novel by Robert

Heinlein that it retooled for optimal flight efficiency. Stowed away in Lang's flight to the Moon together with his collection of comic books, the child fan of heroes enters an in-group of rocket enthusiasts and model builders in Heinlein's *Rocketship Galileo*. One boy's parents came to the United States as political refugees from Nazi Germany (28). In the club's collection of books, there's a copy of Ley's *Rockets* (18). But it is another boy's uncle, uncle Don, otherwise known as his "'Atomic Bomb' uncle" (10), whose surprise visit to their "test stand" (8) initiates the adventure in the big world of manned spacecraft. The fantasy relieves the reality admitted up front: "When the Atomic Age opened up a lot of people predicted that space flight was just around the corner. But it didn't work out that way" (23). However, in the immediate postwar period Heinlein projected in 1947, the atomic-powered freighter jets rolling off the assembly lines in Detroit are the V-2's Earthbound legacy. The plane that Uncle Don plans to convert into a spaceship is an old V-17 (26). Joe the Robot guides the ship with cams designed by the automatic pilot's "remote cousin . . . the great 'Envac' computer at the University of Pennsylvania" (75). Joe's "grandfathers had guided the Nazi V-2 rockets in the horror-haunted last days of World War II. His fathers had been developed for the deadly, ocean-spanning guided-missiles of the U.N. world police force" (76).

The uncle's plans for reaching the Moon first, before the Russians, have been stymied along governmental channels. As in the film adaptation, there is the sense that the US government has been infiltrated by enemy interests. The Atomic Bomb uncle's last-resort investment in the backyard enterprise of half-grown boys is also a hallmark of Allied propaganda in WWII. Surprise! The immediate rivals turn out to be Nazis who landed on the Moon three months earlier to establish a secure base for reversing the loss of the war at the highpoint of the old Axis-trajectory. They owe their head start to a newer model of atomic freight jet coming down Detroit's line of production, which they Gerry-rigged to make it to the moon. The V-2 rocket wasn't enough to usher in the American Space Age. Without an internationally recognized state or place in contemporary history, this renewed head start does not suffice to undermine the US claim to the Moon.

The Nazi station occupies an ancient underground edifice belonging to the original people of the Moon. A whole Nazi brigade died sleeping there, the air sucked out by the bomb Uncle Don and his bunch took from the Nazi spaceship and turned against the enemy. The enemy's propaganda was also turned against them where they slept with (i.e., identified with) the Moon dead. In German science fiction novels published during the Third Reich, the inheritance of lost civilizations on other planets gives German explorers the means (often in the form of atomic energy) to defend the fatherland's desire for peace against the ill will of surrounding nations—or it gives them a psychotic-sublime model for mass death with dignity.

Uncle Don doesn't want his boys to see the expressions on the faces of the dead and closes the door on the evidence of the lost civilization of the Moon, set aside for another tome. However, one of his boys had earlier indulged in the speculation that the craters of the Moon were not produced by meteors. "The Moon people . . . did it themselves: . . . they had one atomic war too many" (100). What the uncle dismissed, he confirms in part upon returning from the Nazi crypt. He need not go further. Heirlessness is what has been secured for the American Space Age. This assurance of the indeterminacy of indebtedness transmits with equanimity as the true first in *Destination Moon*. In contrast, *Rocketship X-M* was on a collision course with debt certainty. In the rush to beat *Destination Moon*, it was decided not to shoot scenes of the rocket's take-off and flight. Instead borrowed footage of V-2 rocket tests was incorporated where needed. The collector who bought and restored *Rocketship X-M* in the 1970s had the transitions reshot to replace the inserts of V-2 rocket flight.

Destination Moon transmutes the rocket club for boys into the inner boyish adventurousness of the captains of capital summoned to support the flight to the Moon. The V-2 rocket can be admitted because atomic-powered spacecraft is what the future holds in store. To present the venture as feasible and followable, a short film on rocketry is shown starring Woody Woodpecker. If the voiceover can convince Woody that the flight to the Moon is eminently doable, then there can be no doubter: "The V-2 rocket could do it today." The V-2 rocket is identified in its place in history before the blast-off of the real continuity shot (atomic power) takes over. Woody is initiated into rocketry through a more complete experience of shooting. Woody grasps the principle of a rocket's take-off by mounting a rifle and experiencing its kickback propulsion upon firing.

In *Rocketship Galileo*, Uncle Don warns against riding this analogue too far. "Mixing up shooting with rocketry" leads to a basic misconception, namely that "a rocket can't work out in empty space, because it wouldn't have anything to *push* on" (80). He "heard an aeronautical engineer, as late as 1943, say just that. . . . Next year the Nazis were bombing London with the V-2s. Yet according to him it couldn't be done" (ibid.). To lose the Nazi advantage, *Destination Moon* skips the alternative fuel of the encryptment of losses and instead reaches back before German science fiction to take a flying leap from the shooting range of George Meliés' *Man in the Moon* and Jules Verne's *From the Earth to the Moon.*

In *From the Earth to the Moon,* we are introduced to the Gun Club, which was established during the American Civil War, a period of uniquely energetic development in the science of ballistics. In the meantime, that war was over: "all bloody reminiscences were effaced; the cotton plants grew luxuriantly on the well-manured fields, all mourning garments were laid aside, together with grief; and the Gun Club was relegated to profound inactivity" (15). Following Edgar Allen Poe's imaginative lead, the Club president, Barbicane, suggests that the conquest of the Moon will be a new techno-venture: "however we may desire it, many years may elapse before our cannon shall again thunder in the field of battle. We must make up our minds, then, to seek in another train of ideas some field for the activity which we all pine for" (21-22). Fellow Club member Matson, who earlier proposed subduing England in a reenactment and reversal of history that would re-start the war milieu for gun sales and research (17-18), rallies to Barbicane's "moral point of view": "The cannon-ball . . . is the most magnificent manifestation of human power. If Providence has created the stars and the planets, man has called the cannon-ball into existence. Let Providence claim the swiftness of electricity and of light, of the stars, the comets, and the planets, of wind and sound—we claim to have invented the swiftness of the cannon-ball" (45).

The latitude required for space travel takes the launching down South. Bivouacked around the site could be found "all the various classes of American society . . . mingled together in terms of absolute equality" (144), toasting one another with mint-juleps like at some spring break for generations to come. The reunion is even folded into the rocket technology. To facilitate the firing of the Outer Space projectile out of a giant gun, Barbicane proposes igniting nitric or fulminating cotton, which would be wrapped around the shot. First he must settle with Captain Nicholl, his personal adversary with a contesting view that comes out of a wartime investment in gun-proofing.

Each followed a current of ideas essentially opposed to the other . . . Most people are aware of the curious struggle which arose during the Federal war between the guns and armor or iron-plated ships. The result was the entire reconstruction of the navy of both the continents; as the one grew heavier, the other became thicker in proportion. The Merimac, the Monitor, the Tennessee, the Weehawken discharged enormous projectiles themselves, after having been armor-clad against the projectiles of others. In fact they did to others that which they would not they should do to them—that grand principle of immortality upon which rests the whole art of war. (60)

In the contest that follows, Barbicane is able, once again, to pierce the metallic plate Nicholl claims to be impervious, but a new material is the result of the merger that the piercing brings about.

To make the Moon project international rather than American only, the Gun Club advertises around the world for subscriptions in its support. The Russians and the Prussians are particularly generous supporters. French support comes on an individualist basis. A telegram from France recommends that the projectile assume a certain shape so that the undersigned, Michel Ardan, can travel inside it. When he arrives in the States, he tracks down Barbicane and Nicholl, who are engaged in a duel to the death, and reconciles them to a joint mission.

From the Earth to the Moon ends in takeoff—and to-be-continued. In the final chapter of the sequel, *Around the Moon* (1870), Barbicane sells his notes of the voyage to *The New York Herald*. We are advised that the newspaper's serialization of the prequel had increased its circulation to five million (324). The rocket carries not only the three human passengers but also a couple of dogs across both installments. The male, however, is fatally injured in the shakeup of the rocket's interior during takeoff and soon puts the problem of disposal to the crew. At first it seems that the corpse of the dog aptly named Satellite can be safely ejected, whereupon all "rubbish" can be similarly removed from the cannon-ball capsule (205).

Then it becomes evident that whatever is thrown out of the rocket's interior cannot leave its orbit, and all the discards wrap an ectoplasmic reminder around the transmission to the Moon.

The president approached the window, and saw a sort of flattened sack floating some yards from the projectile. . . . "What is that machine? . . . I do not know what the object is, but I do know why it maintains our level.

. . . Because we are floating in space . . . and in space bodies fall or move
(which is the same thing) with equal speed whatever be their weight or
form . . . Just so . . . and everything we throw out of the projectile will
accompany it until it reaches the moon." (212)

After the scientists nix Ardan's proposal that a rocket could thus be accompanied by a supply train of all that didn't fit inside, the Frenchman recognizes
the "unfortunate dog" out there. "Indeed, this deformed, unrecognizable object,
reduced to nothing, was the body of Satellite, flattened like a bagpipe without
wind, and ever mounting, mounting" (213). The double delegation of modern
man rising up over the corpses of the Civil War toward the Moon is the continuity
gunshot of velocity and the empathy test.

The 1958 film adaptation cultivates a way-down-South quality that even
turns the pages of the opening titles. The International Armaments Club stands
above or to the side of the concluded Civil War that it supplied and profited from
but did not instigate. Just the same, the rivalry between Barbicane and Nicholl is a
souvenir of the clash between Northern and Southern interests, which the invest-
ments in firepower and bullet-proofing are made to match. Nicholl's plant still
bears the former identification: "Armorers to the Confederacy." However, Nicholl's delirium is not of the South rising again but of the moral or religious variety
dedicated to God. The camera shows him always addressing his moral concerns
to us or to himself, to the media or to God.

Barbicane's latest firepower, Power X, is an adaptation of atomic power: in
the wrong hands, it could destroy the world. Because it would be too dangerous
even to test it on Earth, Barbicane plans to send it to the Moon for a proper demo,
but the allegation is rampant that no one intends to go to the Moon and that the
United States intends to rule the world. President Grant, who does not wish to
risk a world war, asks Barbicane to forego sending Power X to the Moon. When
the residual glass-like material that results from the experimental contest between
Barbicane's firepower and Nicholl's latest armor plate demonstrates a new degree
of shatter proofing, however, Barbicane's "moral suicide" comes to an end and he
replaces the Power X scheme with a new purpose: to explore the Heavens, which,
he declares, has been man's dream since he dropped out of the trees. The new
transparency can be wrapped around the bullet-rocket to secure the prospect of a
roundtrip on which Barbicane, his assistant, and Nicholl are booked.

Shortly before departure time, Nicholl can't be found. He was already in the rocket, which he now leaves to join them for their official joint entry. This is not the only souvenir of *Woman in the Moon*. Nicholl's daughter Virginia—who dresses very Dixie and seems otherwise in identification with the lost cause, but who has fallen for Barbicane's assistant—is stowed away in time for takeoff. When she's discovered on board, Nichol has already confessed that he tampered with the rocket not for his own profit but to bring it down in the name of God. The American adaptation of German rocket flight transforms the psychotic madness and nihilistic greed that Lang's German expedition had to overcome into the intractable religiosity of the deranged and the devout (from *Conquest of Space* to *Contact*).

Daughter and assistant are ensconced in the cabin that is most securely constructed and most likely to make it back to Earth while Barbicane and Nichol steer a separate portion to the Moon's surface. They make it and send the signal, which can't be seen on Earth since they are on the wrong side of the Moon, but which assistant and daughter receive. Our last view of their capsule shows flames outside either firing up the boost that will take them back or consuming them in Space. At the control center, the cessation of communication seems to confirm worldwide reservations about the mission. But one of the backers of the rocket experiment, who is named Jules Verne, rejects what the others conclude. He knows—not by facts but by the imagination—that Barbicane lives.

THE AMBIVALENT INTROJECT

1

In *The Man in the High Castle*, Dick threw the reversal of the Axis defeat in WWII into the breach of alternate history and began to fill in the blank of the repression of the recent past. At the same time, to set this history aright required that it be realigned with the true outcome of the Civil War. If Roosevelt had not been assassinated in Miami before the 1936 election, he would have shown the strength of another Lincoln and led the Allies to victory (66).

Gertrude Stein announced that the USA was the most ancient culture of the twentieth century because of the advance preview of techno-mass modernity it absorbed through the Civil War. The Civil War also techno-modernized the United States by its deposit of the lost war to be carried forward. When, in the late nineteenth century, Julian Green's parents had to choose the site for the European franchise of the firm his father represented, they selected Paris over Berlin because they felt the French, owing to the recent loss of the war with Prussia, would know what it meant to carry a lost war. In the long run, the decision was no doubt a wise business move, but it was premature in finding a match for their encrypted war.

The World War picked up where the Civil War had left off. And this "lost war" (ambiguously the "last" war) would prove basic to German techno-modernity. In a 1981 interview with Raymond Federman, Stanislaw Lem made an example out of a Chinese history book that referred to WWI as the European Civil War for a cultural difference that is both wrong and true. In reunified Germany, Civil War reenactments continue to be all the rage in the former East with most players wanting to be on the side of the Confederacy. Germany is very nice, they say—there are just too many damn carpetbaggers.

While Mr. and Mrs. Green chose not to bind their lost war to the future of loss in German history, Julian Green would later reflect the pull of the German contest. His 1947 *Si j'étais vous* (translated *If I Were You* in 1950) was a Faust novel in which his intended quarrel was with Nietzsche on religious grounds. It was picked up by Melanie Klein (in "On Identification") as her main prop for staging what she called projective identification, a secular corrective to the counsel that you should become who you are.

Through Klein's reading, Green's corpus switching between the Faustian striving to lose like a winner (the German destiny of dissociation) and the determination to win as a loser (the redemptive ending of Green's Faust novel) was brought into proximity to what I prefer to address as the ambivalent introject. On Klein's turf and terms, this introject can be situated between projective identification and integration. Klein reclaimed "integration" from positive thinking first in her 1940 essay on mourning, finally in her posthumously published essay on loneliness. In the latter work, she concluded that integration must pull up short before the sense or direction of "irretrievable loss" (301). If the "lost parts . . . are felt to be lonely," too (302), then it is no longer possible to deliver a transitive sentencing of loss. Not to know who lost whom also means that the loss cannot be assigned or confined to one side. According to Dick's protagonist in *Time out of Joint*, "in a civil war . . . every side is wrong. It's hopeless to try to untangle it. Everyone is a victim" (251). In other words, "it's the most idealistic kind of war" (253), open to the identification with lost causes.

If I Were You is the narrative of a Devil's compact according to the terms of what Schreber called "soul murder," the violation he claimed to have endured for generations. After his family censored the section in *Memoirs of My Nervous Illness* devoted to its documentation, the only remaining example of what Schreber meant by soul murder was the Faustian pact with the Devil. Schreber's understanding of this pact as the extension of life at the expense of another's life is closer to Green's fable of body theft than to Goethe's main text.

Projective identification belongs to the earliest roots/routes of formation of the self in networks of intrapsychic outsourcing. "Identification by projection implies a combination of splitting off parts of the self and projecting them on to (or rather into) another person" (Klein, "On Identification" 143). As a primal defense against the fear of annihilation, splitting is most effective when "it brings about a dispersal of anxiety and a cutting off of emotions. But it fails in another sense because it results in a feeling akin to death" (144-45). A patient might feel that he doesn't know where the parts went that he dispersed into the external world—this anxiety belongs to the defensive function of splitting itself, which has the effect of rendering estranged parts of the self inaccessible both to the patient and to the analyst. According to Klein, Green demonstrates that a residual charge can be retained and carried over in projective identification throughout the course of his protagonist Fabian's infernal body switching. "We should conclude therefore (in keeping with the author's very concrete conception of the projective process), that Fabian's memories and other aspects of his personality are left behind in the discarded Fabian who must have retained a good deal of his ego when the split occurred" (166). This retention of "a good deal" emplaces the infernal compact of soul murder inside the metabolism of the inner world.

With each switch, Fabian retains mnemonic traces of his previous visitations. "It shows most clearly at the end of the story, for his experiences in the characters into whom he had turned himself are all present in his mind before he dies and he is concerned about their fate. This would imply that he introjects his objects, as well as projects himself into them" (170). The life that flashes before his eyes belongs to the introjected egos of his various station stops in projective identifi-cation. While the process is described as staggered (for example, between iden-tification of common ground and identification with someone on that basis), the process is not so divided in the analytic work in session. "For the individual to feel that he has a good deal in common with another person is concurrent with pro-jecting himself into that person (and the same applies to introjecting him)" (ibid.). The Devil cuts a deal with our controlling interest in the great commonality we share with our objects of identification and carries over an ideal or encrypted object through the double dealing of body switching.

Enter Julian Green.

"Welcome to the South," Julian Green said, receiving a visitor to his apartment in the heart of Paris. A Confederate flag hung at the end of a narrow corridor. . . . "This is the American South in France," he added. . . . His father had been sent to Europe in 1895 by the Southern Cotton

Oil Company. Given a choice of living in France or Germany, his mother insisted on France because, she said, "The French had been defeated in 1870 and would understand the Southerners." Julian was the youngest of her eight children, and he listened to her stories of the South with wonder. "She told us all about the splendid victories we had," he recalled, "but she was always bursting into tears. She didn't tell us until very late in the day that we lost the war." (Riding)

The out-of-body experience (or experiment) of identification central to *If I Were You* marked the onset of Green's published work, which happened to be in English. As a student at the University of Virginia, Green wrote and published the story "The Apprentice Psychiatrist." The protagonist is a student of mental illness who must accept a post as a tutor when his father proves no longer able to support him. The boy in his care strikes him as a case to study. While the guardians are away, he exaggerates certain aggravating conditions in order to observe the signs of breakdown in his charge. Looking forward to the outbreak of madness he would study up close, however, the protagonist alone goes mad. He charges upstairs with a gun. When we follow its report inside the boy's room, we are suspended between expectations. Will we find the undead of suicide or the gun dead of murder? Although it ends up being murder, the protagonist, beside himself, also shot himself in the pupil.

The opening enfolding of selves was repeated and rehearsed as Green's internalization of his mother tongue inside his other first language, French. In his 1941 essay, "My First Book in English," which refers to *Memories of Happy Days* (1942), Green identifies French as his first and only language—and only reality. But then he overhears the other mother tongue: "What bothered me more than I can say was that my mother spoke to me in English, and I had great trouble in learning that language. . . . I felt that in teaching me these new words, my mother was trying to make a sort of duplicate of the universe, which, I thought, was a French universe" (81). In writing his first book in English, he relied on "the everyday words which my mother taught me as a child" (86). In another 1941 essay, "An Experiment in English," Green presents his early relationship to the English spoken by his parents as party to the mysterious behavior of grown-ups that wasn't available for his understanding because it was designed to cover something up with its secret handshake. "To my mother's shame it was a certain time before I could understand English perfectly. As a child I could not bring myself to believe that English was a real language, rather did I take it to be a jumble of meaningless sounds which grown-ups made to pretend they were carrying on a conversation" (55). But his mother wanted him to understand what she spelled out: "Spelling too was the cause of much grief to both of us" (57).

In *Memories of Happy Days*, Green remembers those days of his childhood as an irretrievable loss of first time, first contact, happiness itself.

> Above all, I could never again feel happy for the *first time*: happiness would become more and more something I would crave because I had tasted of it and wanted more; the element of surprise was taken away from it forever. I could no longer stand like a tiny Faustus in a black apron and all of a sudden discover that the old world I happened to be in was a place of inexpressible beauty, that the clouds above my head were as lovely as anything I could see, and that the cool air of an October morning filled one's heart with a desire to live forever. (16)

Upon reflection, Green recognized that the writing method he followed for his first literary work was borrowed from storytelling in childhood. He discovered that he had installed the surprise of the first time into the surprise of forgetting or remembering. We're in Chapter 11 of his memoirs. "Among the unfinished stories which filled my desk-drawer there was one to which I added half a page or so from time to time, simply because I was anxious to know what would happen to the characters. . . . My method was to begin to tell the story and make it up as I went along, much in the fashion of a nurse who tells children stories at bedtime" (264). By this method, the exquisite corpse yielded his first tale, "The Pilgrim on the Earth," set in Virginia. Like the other story that was his first, "The Apprentice Psychiatrist," it gradually admitted a "supernatural element" in the course of composition (ibid.). "It was like losing one's way in a wood and realizing by slow degrees that the wood is haunted. I suppose there is no harm in admitting that I was frightened, particularly on one occasion when I understood that I was describing a case of what theologians call possession. This came as a shock, yet acted as an incentive, for I now wrote large portions of the story at one sitting and kept up at this pace until I had actually reached the conclusion" (265).

In his native French, he identified the apparitions he was given to summon in childhood as infernal. His mother tongue was not only a foreign body in the nativity of the author-to-be but also the carrier of the "secrecy" Green identified to be the most salient feature of childhood (17). The language the child addressed to himself or to his imaginary interlocutor was his own secret invention, although in retrospect "it was merely an imitation of what my elders' conversation sounded like to my ear" (ibid.). The transmission of the mother's secret at once takes place and is omitted. To reinforce proper English pronunciation, Green's mother would read the Bible out loud to him while he sat at her feet. The reading passed over or through him until one day he understood a verse: "one day . . . something new and exciting happened: my mother read a verse and I understood it" (20). His mother wouldn't be interrupted when he tried to say something. By the end of the reading, he had forgotten which verse was the first to enter his understanding. It's another first that's lost forever in the present, but otherwise preserved: "Yet I still hope that, as I grow older and my memory goes back further, I shall find it gleaming in the dark" (21). His sisters, who liked to read along over the mother's shoulder, read her repeated notations to herself in the margins of the Bible to remember or never to forget. They wanted to know what these admonishments and self-recrim-inations signified: mother didn't remember. Attending a play in New York City, Green again entered this scene of transmission, which in turn recalled the other transmission scene from childhood internal to it. "Never having heard English spoken on the stage, I missed almost all of the first act, when suddenly I was able to understand every word. This was a strange experience which reminded me of the day when, having pondered for months over the alphabet, I realized that I could read" (203).

When next he glimpsed the South for the first time, he was raised to the word power of identification that raised him. "Words spoken by my mother came back to me after many years; it was as if the world she had loved stood before me in a kind of simplified picture, and in a curious way I recognized this picture because I was looking at it through her eyes" (204). The conjuring power that the moth-er's voice retains is closely linked to Julian's name. "I remember it as distinctly as if she had just now called me by my name" (11-12). In *If I Were You*, the first name is assigned to the magic formula to be whispered into the ear of the person who will be displaced and possessed. The first name—the name not yet finding completion in the surname, the name whereby little one is called and known by mother—is part of the magic spell that fills the mouth (and ear) like baby formula. The eye-to-ear coordination of Julian's identification with his mother follows the injunction to look away whenever the sustainability of her efforts as the family storyteller to keep "the South" a live transmission could not forever postpone its dissolution in history.

2

Of the Indo-European languages, German has chewed the longest on the cud of ambivalence in the gift, the giving, and the forgiving. It's not only that the German word *Gift* looks like the English synonym for "present" and signifies "poison" but it was at some point the "same" word. Today the German word for "dowry," *Mitgift*, registers the proximity to "present." *Gift* is all that remains of the split-off Germanic legacy of a signifying chain of "giving" or *geben* that was dedicated to poisoning. That *vergeben* for a long time could either mean "to forgive" or "to poison" relies on a cathexis of giving as application of poison, which was supported by a borrowed sense of *dosis*. No accident, then, that the German language has hosted psychosocial theories of inoculation. Goethe's Faust suffers his crisis of traumatic memory over the father's double bequest of poison and/ as medicine. Looking a *Gift* horse in the mouth doesn't help when it is the doctor father's benign gift. Giving that looks like a present but administers destruction, the offense that introduced wreckage into the Trojan celebration of success, is brought home in the German language deposit of *Gift*. Faust's suicidality bites the "and" that feeds him poison. In the background of her thought experiments in the English language, the German-language legacy of the poisoning in giving and forgiving hosts Melanie Klein's turn to envy (closely argued in "Envy and Gratitude") for an interpersonal figuration of the death drive, for the test case of her sense that "destructive impulses, the expression of the death instinct, are first of all felt to be directed against the ego" (223).

Envious poisoning of the other's resources and supplies cannot contain itself but spills over into one's own goods, which are just as spoiled. In sum, envy "spoils and harms the good object which is the source of life" (189). The practical critique within psychoanalysis always addresses in-session dynamics, which, in the case of the envious patient, faces what is so hard to treat: "if he feels that the analyst and the help he is giving have become spoilt and devalued by his envious criticism, he cannot introject him sufficiently as a good object nor accept his interpretations with real conviction and assimilate them. Real conviction . . . implies gratitude for a gift received. The envious patient may also feel, because of guilt about devaluing the help given, that he is unworthy to benefit by analysis" (184). What is at stake is the work of integration, which must not be hurried. "For if the realization of the division in his personality were to come suddenly, the patient would have great difficulties in coping with it. . . . In analysis we should make our way slowly and gradually towards the painful insight into the divisions in the patient's self. This means that the destructive sides are again and again split off and regained, until greater integration comes about" (224-25).

In regard to Freud's profiling of persons wrecked by success, Klein writes: "Depriving oneself of success has, of course, many determinants, and this applies to all the attitudes I am referring to. But I found as one of the deepest roots of this defence the guilt and unhappiness about not having been able to preserve the good object because of envy. People who have rather precariously established their good object suffer under anxiety lest it be spoilt and lost by competitive and envious feelings, and therefore have to avoid success and competition" (218). But even a defensive turning around of this wreckage cannot, as in the opening scenes of Goethe's *Faust*, escape the poisoning. "A frequent method of defence is *to stir up envy in others* by one's own success, possessions, and good fortune, thereby reversing the situation in which envy is experienced. The ineffectiveness of this method derives from the persecutory anxiety to which it gives rise. Envious people, and in particular the envious internal object, are felt to be the worst persecutors" (ibid.).

Faust is brought out of his slump via a shorter term therapy than Klein would seem to allow, namely, through the industry of his striving, which was separated out from violence and guilt by his double's infernal administration of and responsibility for his wishes. Winnicott's separation of psychopathic industry from the violence (under the aegis of hope) bypasses the impasse of envy through the work of reparation. By proceeding directly to the repair of the good object, the recovering psychopath initiates a process that is indeed slow: the steps in integration toward the onset of mourning. The intrapsychic counterpart to placement of the start of industry before the Trojan horse of loss identification is the all-important "foundation" of integration, the ambivalent introject.

The after-the-fact reconstruction of Nazi Germany as the first realized science fiction guaranteed that the long "haul" of *Wiederholung* (repetition) and its compulsions would indefinitely stagger (for both the recovering psychopaths and their heirs) the onset of the capacity for mourning. What the realization of science fiction had deferred for German history was nevertheless assembled into an ambivalent introject in the course of Pynchon's fabulation of the rocket in *Gravity's Rainbow*. In his 2003 preface to *Nineteen Eighty-Four*, Pynchon commented on the novel's bracketing out of the Holocaust as Orwell's requirement for thinking his way through to the postwar period in 1948. Pynchon was also identifying his 1973 novel as on schedule with this requisite staggering.

Pynchon's cultivation of the rocket derives its plain text from the flight trajectories looping the American Cold War through the German side of WWII. It also enters upon the mass psychological tendency to carry loss forward through the prospect of its reversal. *Gravity's Rainbow* hitched its status as the great American novel and new *Moby Dick* to the pursuit of the V-2 rocket and its continuity shots, which, at or as the end of the *Rainbow* (and almost as a 9/11 forecast), detonated the movie theater in Los Angeles where Pynchon assembled his readership. But before the Nazi rocket enters American history, it is reassembled on the track of its future development as V to the nth power in the meeting of otherwise opposed or repressed contingencies. In Southwest Africa, Germany routed the Herero rebellion and sent the vanquished nation into the desert to perish. In *Gravity's Rainbow*, the surviving Hereros, "the Empty Ones," follow out their trauma-enforced suicide drive in voluntary service to the rocket.

In Pynchon's *V.*, the prep work for the fabulation of "the Empty Ones" in *Gravity's Rainbow* is bound to the two tracks of their ultimate alignment: a hermeneutics of racism and the fetish-reconstruction of woman. The hunt for V., which in the multiple-choice testing of variables already includes the rocket (228), ultimately conjures the android woman, like the Maria-double in *Metropolis*, the stage one technologization going into the rocket's ultimate ascent in *Woman in the Moon* and *Gravity's Rainbow*. "Fetish-constructions" like the android woman "represent a kind of infiltration" by "the Kingdom of Death" (411). It is a literal decadence, "a falling-away from what is human, and the further we fall the less human we become. Because we are less human, we foist off the humanity we have lost on inanimate objects and abstract theories" (405). The woman bearing the V. sees her profile as a test subject and automatic organism pass into a fetishistic literalization and extension of the machine part to the whole. This happens along the lines of the German pilot's psycho-technical development into an auto-pilot that, out of the loss of the air war, passes into the rocket, the high point of fetishism. "She might have . . . come to establish eventually so many controls over herself that she became—to Freudian, behaviorist, men of religion, no matter—a purely determined organism, an automaton, constructed, only quaintly, of human flesh. Or by contrast, might have reacted against the above . . . by journeying even deeper into a fetish-country until she became entirely and in reality—not merely as a love-game . . . —an inanimate object of desire" (411).

The condensity of this closing entry into the fetish stands in inoculative contrast to the amassment of instances of racism's sliding scale throughout *V.* The novel opens in New York City immersed in the melting pot of ethnic stereotyping that staggers identification between neighborhoods. The Jewess wants her nose fixed, but into an Irish nose, another "aesthetic misfit" (103). When we move to the colonial reservations of white power, empathic identification has been vacuum-sucked out of there by another disposition of racism. The German colonial administration in Southwest Africa was "reckoned to have done away with about 60,000 people. This is only 1 per cent of six million, but still pretty good" (245). There are description-orgies in *V.* recounting outright violation-murders of Hereros between the world wars by Germans with business interests in the former colonies. They retell the eyewitness account of a German engineer who returned to Germany to work in Peenemünde. The racist violence is like "forbidden sex" for the perpetrators (253). It is a stage of development below the fetish license of the robot woman, which takes up the distance of "infiltration" or inoculation over and against the Kingdom of Death to be administered. Instead of orgiastic violence, a kind of psychopathic idealism enters through the robot woman and rises up with the rocket.

In *The Man in the High Castle*, Dick portrays Nazi genocide rolling over the world, but the ultimate orgy is reserved for Africa (by the 1960s, even the Nazis are in recovery from that bout of racist violence). Pynchon's ambivalent introjection of the rocket folds psychopathic idealism into the inanimation of technology's prosthetic doubling—at which point it takes a world to read the fine print of racism in the owner's manual.

In *Gravity's Rainbow*, Pynchon's *Schwarzkommando* is the mystical blue flower in the no-man's land of technologization and death that guards and guides the super version of the V-2 all the way to its strike against LA. The *Schwarz-kommando* has its recognition value in the racism of the GIs, who may have conquered Germany but are wary of blacks equipped with rockets. The unlikely fiction of the Nazi African-German brigade meets the fact of unlikelihood on the other side: for the WWII effort, African Americans were for the first time accepted for pilot training, but only at the segregated Tuskegee Institute in Alabama. Few were actually deployed as air men. Those in training at the Institute called them-selves the "Spookwaffe." It is by the continuity shots of racism that Pynchon conjoins the inscrutable mass murder in the foreground of the Nazi war with the crypto-fetishism of the rocket, which must be read as trying to outfly it. Some-where over the positivism of machine histories for which the Holocaust did not compute, there is the techno-war revalorized by continuing beyond both the mass death and the opposition. One rocket mystic interprets the ruins of the air war as a site modified for the future by the bombing, waiting to be switched on. This was the "real Text" all along, not the rocket. "Its symmetries, its latencies, the *cuteness* of it enchanted and seduced us while the real Text persisted, somewhere else, in its darkness, our darkness" (520). The war of political opposition or even that of competition between special interests was a diversion. "[S]ecretly, it was being dictated instead by the needs of technology. . . . The real crises were crises of allo-cation and priority, not among firms—it was only staged to look that way—but among the different Technologies, Plastics, Electronics, Aircraft, and their needs" (521). We are no longer parties to WWII. We are the reproductive and mortal milieu for the evolutionary scheme of technology's ultimate autonomy, placing us inside what the theory calls its unrepresentable cornerstone, the missing link, and its reconstruction carries forward a link with the missing.

In *Gravity's Rainbow*, a snake's appearance is a brief aside in the Pökler subplot. The nineteenth-century German chemist with a Bohemian surname that sounds to ears trained to Pynchon's novel like that of a member of the *Schwarz-kommando*, Kekulé, had a dream whereupon he broke through to his discoveries. Rocket Engineer Pökler cites or conjures this dream of a snake holding its own tail in its mouth to illustrate the instrumentalization and betrayal of its message by the techno-order, the European culture of death. "But the meanness, the cynicism with which this dream is to be used. The Serpent that announces, 'The World is a closed thing, cyclical, resonant, eternally-returning,' is to be delivered into a system whose only aim is to violate the Cycle. . . . Living inside the System is like riding across the country in a bus driven by a maniac bent on suicide" (412). Does the snake cast its abused import upon the ellipses and parabolas of the rocket that doesn't come full circle but is programmed instead to put a full stop to its own firing to come down like suicide?

The serpent that encompasses flight paths within the cycle of life is a psy-fi mascot. As surprising as the sacrosanct wilderness is the metaphorical and technical multiplication of "snakes" in *Fahrenheit 451*. An ambivalent snaking-flaming protects the happiest place on Earth: don't tread on me—don't read. Within the TV Sensurround the snake in the garden of the wilderness's ongoing absence can reach through the mortal coil to prehistory. When the machine called snake takes the poison out of yet another TV addict who attempted suicide, it enters the "stomach like a black cobra down an echoing well looking for all the old water and old time gathered there" (14). As recorded by Ernest Jones in *On the Nightmare*, the serpent succeeded over and again as an incubus in copulating with worshippers who chose to sleep in sacred groves or on haunted graves. Through all the orifices of the developmental stages, the serpent puts through communication between the living and their ghosts.

In the work of American artist Stephen G. Rhodes, we follow the rebounding snake through the oral and anal outlets of projective identification. The amalgamation of the rocket in *Gravity's Rainbow* is pulled through these routes, as thematized by the input and outhouse humor in which all parties to the rocket phantasm incessantly engage. With Rhodes we enter the metabolic vortex of ambivalent introjection. In his 2008 multi-media installation *Interregnum: Who Farted!!??!!*, the African American performer (in the costume of the colonial past) whips an animatronic version of Abraham Lincoln. In another installation, *Reconstruction or Something* (2009), a mask with one torn-open eye hole not only cites Jason from the *Friday the 13th* franchise but also the Ku Klux Klan costumes that verge on whiting out the screen in *Birth of a Nation* (1915). What distinguishes this extensive layering of references is the difference between the contract and the law, a difference that always manifests, although there are cultural predilections for one approach to fine print over the other. The law is a project of infinite interpretation; the contract builds on something like object status. There is filler in contractual language that is nonsense, which can't be reclaimed for interpretation, but which encases the certainties that are also there. In *Reconstruction or Something*, we recognize excerpts from *The Exorcist* among countless screen fragments of films made in Hollywood out of Southern history. Indeed the encompassing scene of excavation is overall the reenactment of the opening of Friedkin's film. Like the snake in Rhodes's *A.S.S.* or *American Short Story* (2006) binding the messy introject also as a whip and turd, the pre-Oedipal compact with the Devil Dad, otherwise known as the anal theory of birth, is the precondition for digging encysted certainties, like the lost Southern war inside US history (in the making).

The South's share of US history is roughly fifty percent. This can be seen on the map of the electoral vote when, with each new election, the Confederacy rises up again. However, there is also an idealized aspect to the lost cause that is basic to US film culture. Among the risks that Pynchon took in constructing the ambivalent introject inside *Gravity's Rainbow* is that the story of rocket engineer Pökler begins to read like *Gone with the Wind* set on modern German history. In turn, the trajectory of the fabulous rocket carried forward by the *Schwarzkommando* strikes out from German history to detonate a movie theater in California. From *Birth of a Nation* to *Gone with the Wind*, the Southern POV holds a majority share in the monumentalization of US history. The layers of dissemination and remix of American popular culture, which Rhodes spins around the secret axis of the lost war, he also skewers back into a form upon select film references or introjects, among which Disney's *Song of the South* (1946) appears most primal.

Song of the South is a fantasy film set in the South under reconstruction shortly after the Civil War in which white children are reconciled across the class divide and the races live in harmony but without yielding class to the blacks. The older magical storyteller at the center of the film, Uncle Remus, who is African American, loses his authority and becomes a chastened child whenever the white woman on a visit (but to the manor born) arbiters good and bad on behalf of her son. The father is in Atlanta getting ahead in the new Union economy while wife and son are staying at the plantation. The son symptomatizes that there is more to this separation. But he finds support through Uncle Remus's telling of stories, which are African-American fairy tales. The tar baby, for example, is a ploy among racialized animals: Fox, Bear and Rabbit are all "brothers."

When the mother disallows the telling of these stories to her son, a ban Uncle Remus follows out as his banishment, the accident that nearly kills her son as he rushes to reverse the consequence of her censorship is her fault. The boy's near death brings the father back home. Now Uncle Remus happily withdraws on his own upon observing the reconciliation that his storytelling supported. This is the story Disney's *Mary Poppins* (1964) reprised with great success. The lesbian magician can depart unnoticed and unresentful once it is evident that the father has been delivered from his work ethic to become playfully integrated in the lives of his children. This gesture of withdrawal refers to psychoanalysis, which also concludes Browning's *Dracula* (1930): Van Helsing lets the couple climb back up into the light, out of the troubling dark of projection, while he stays behind.

Although the film in toto was consigned to Vault Disney, selections from the film, notably the animated animal stories, were free to wield considerable influence throughout popular culture. The Southern legacy of race is caught in a series of segregation-identifications. Whistling Dixie is performed in black-face, a tribute to the South passing through an identification with blacks, but in their absence, their separate place. Joel Chandler Harris composed *Uncle Remus: His Songs and His Sayings* (1880) as a collection, really a recollection of what he heard from slave storytellers during his years working at a Georgia plantation. His outsider status as poor-white Irish redhead, which gained him, he felt, the trusting proximity to the slaves, is the introject *Gone with the Wind* would rework through one Irish man's self-made prosperity to make the plantation Tara just another house in a US neighborhood. Harris was a journalist who advocated for the South's reconstruction. But he was also vigilant lest Northern ignorance leave out of the New South the culture that the slaves had carried forward. Harris felt that under benign conditions slavery promoted a culture of tenderness, which the Uncle Remus stories document, and which could also be glimpsed, its abolitionist agenda notwithstanding, in the book Harris identified as his inspiration, *Uncle Tom's Cabin* (1852).

The meddlesome woman alienated by Northern capitalism in *Song of the South* is visiting her mother, who, although not too long ago a slaveholder, enjoys a rapport with Uncle Remus that is immediate and positive. In the first part of Pynchon's *V.*, American drop scenes of off-color intolerance offer an identificatory mapping of neighborhoods inside the melting pot. In the marriage between a Northerner and a Southerner, the latter contrasts his own historical relationship to the other race with the alienated racism from the North: "she was in nearly total ignorance about the Southron feeling toward Negroes. . . . it was not a matter of love, hate, like or not like so much as an inheritance you lived with" (126). On his visit to the US, Jung gave this toxic bond a dialectical blending: blacks, kept close as slaves or former slaves, are really in control in the American identification—just as the women wear the pants in the heterosexual family. Do black and white athletes hit it off because they work together under a delegated racism, a difference they can split in mutual adaptation to what surrounds them? Are straight men who navigate sexual difference by humor that looks down on women in fact close to women by dint of their cohabitation within the greater structure of misogyny?

The unreconstructed bonding basic to *Song of the South* was rejected in 1946 for being as controversial as it was clueless. This reflects the four years during which this niche market of adaptation-identification was reclaimed and nationalized by African Americans to include the Union and address the world. James Thompson, a cafeteria worker in a Kansas airplane manufacturing plant, responded to US entry into the world war by proposing that African Americans adopt a "double V" to promote a double victory. The *Pittsburgh Courier* pulled a quote to give Thompson's letter to the editor the title: "Should I Sacrifice to Live 'Half-American?'" The second victory was on spec. It was hoped that the mobilization of African Americans to fight for foreign minority rights would lead to greater equality in the US. "For surely those who perpetrate these ugly prejudices here are seeking to destroy our democratic form of government just as surely as the Axis forces" (5). By a special call to arms, African Americans were motivated to fight for the Union in which their civil rights were, in theory, vouchsafed. During the upsurge of defense industry work in support of the UK and in the event of US involvement in the war, a nondiscrimination policy had already been obtained by black leaders in this work setting. Reformatted to fit the Civil War, the world war could be spun around the axis of identification with Union victory in the other good war to wage a global or intrapsychic struggle against discrimination. "The first V for victory against our enemies from without, the second V for victory over our enemies from within."

3

Rhodes's 2013 installation dedicated to Warburg's "Serpent Lecture," *The Law of the Unknown Neighbor: Inferno Romanticized,* projected the video portion through ceiling fan blades that, helicopter-like, seemed also to beam a blinding search light in alternation. As the blades turn, we visit systems, rituals, media of circulation (including the circulation of books) in pursuit of what the artist prefers to call (approximating Warburg's discourse) phobic cause projection. Similar to the artist's earlier work, we find that the deranged projection from the blade-flashing summit of Warburg's delusions flashes on the "es war" ("it was") of war lost and found in American popular culture. The blades through which the projection passes refer not only to Vietnam War helicopters but also to Southern ceiling fans, plantation style, mixing up the two lost wars and presenting them as ongoing (a mix or mess the police helicopters of Los Angeles also secured through the media event of O. J. Simpson's pursuit and capture).

In *The Law of the Unknown Neighbor*, the video horizon projects Warburg's reflections on Native American rituals between human sacrifice and what Warburg condemned as the "murder" of thoughtful respite (from sacrifice) through the live media of American progress. Rhodes investigated the longstanding German reenactment-identification with Native American history authorized by Karl May. A recovering sociopath, May let go of his criminal career and replaced history at the intake with fantasy. To the fanfare of fantasy, he gave up the holding containment of incarceration, but only to the extent that he could depend on an improved medium of Modern Spiritualism to be his new lease of wife (his first wife was an "information" medium, the second one a writing medium).

Rhodes inserts the fantasy detritus of the reception of May as the uncontainment of Warburg's affliction writ large upon the mirrors of mass culture. By the simultaneous loss and usurpation of identities within May's fantasy versions of the Western frontier, the centerpiece of modern American history (and its fantasy controls) undergoes reenactment and revalorization. The opening episodes of May's novel *Winnetou II* take place deep in Ku Klux Klan territory, but anachronistically (or introjectively) the episodes play at the time of the Civil War. Old Shatterhand and Old Death rout a whole KKK gang.

Rhodes's footage from the Bad Segeberg production of *Winnetou II* shows black actors in nineteenth-century garb entering and exiting facades that signify "New Orleans." In the videos holding the place of Warburg's flashbacks in and out of the sanatorium, the Bellevue asylum appears to border on a Southern plantation, bringing home the artist's conceit that aberrations and phobias of his own count among the objects of the Law's investigation. The artist (in person or as another figure in the video flow of association) accepts a big rubber snake from an "American Indian." In exchange, he gives up the black baby doll he has been carrying.

Katchina dolls are props on the set of Warburg's anthropological studies documented in his "Serpent Lecture." He points out that the dolls are not only cultic representations but demons themselves under the restraint of representation. Then he adds that the dolls of his own day may have a continuous significance (33). As an instance of uncanny experience, Freud refers to a young girl's belief that if she looked at the doll a certain way, the doll would come alive (233). Either in the later or extended sense of play (or directly as a transitional object), the doll is the gift, the given, which the child feels she has also created and animated. For Freud, the animated doll is on the same assembly line as the robot dolly Olympia in E. T. A. Hoffmann's "The Sandman" (1816) as well as, for our purposes, Maria's android copy in *Metropolis*. Hans Bellmer and Oskar Kokoschka made the dolly replacement of woman part of their art or the performance of their artist persona. The trick is always to find the right balance between hard and soft parts, between support and flexibility, especially in the construction of joints and orifices.

The essence of cuteness went to market as the kewpie doll, first as a cartoon figure in the US in 1906, then manufactured as the iconic doll in Germany (until WWI). According to Konrad Lorenz, the kewpie doll was an available demo of the cute characteristics, which, by arousing a protective or caring identification in others, contributed to a young child's chances for survival (on an evolutionary scale). For the postwar world, Stephen Jay Gould reinvented the scheme of child-like cuteness as neoteny, bringing it to bear in closer proximity to the ambivalently held mascot Mickey Mouse. In the psychoanalytic view, to find someone "sweet" is to drop to the level of cannibalism. Cuteness adds the protection of taboo to sweetness.

Barbie offers another update for the postwar era. The young adult doll for children first had to be cleansed of her German heritage. She was immediately based on the West German doll Lilli, originally a comic-strip figure in the *Bild* newspaper satirizing cynical upward mobility at the work place. Lilli is working to earn her M.R.S. with one of the bosses at the top of society. She's sly, lazy, and scheming. The split-off, ethically unsavory opportunism of the economic miracle could be projected into her. Being a doll, she was rather a gag gift, something found in tobacco shops or in bars. The Californian Ruth Handler had been toying with the idea of an improvement on paper fashion dolls for pre-teens. She discovered Lilli not by traveling to West Germany (a no-go) but on her ski vacation in Switzerland in 1956. She bought the rights to the doll and, while extinguishing

Lilli in West Germany, she transmitted her to and through US popular culture—at once destroyed and reborn. The corrective reinterpretation of Barbie as a positive model is reflected in Handler's later development of an improved breast prosthesis, one better than what she found available following her own mastectomy. A play station for entry into the teen social order, Barbie is an eidetic memory in adulthood. Hence, in Dick's *The Three Stigmata of Palmer Eldritch*, colonists on Mars inhabit Barbie and Ken and, by way of projective identification and drugs, return to the *Heimat* of their bond, California.

In the novel *The Stepford Wives* (1972), Ira Levin presented a Men's Club that's really a Satanic coven in which the highest pleasure imaginable is to reduce the better half to a robot blowup dolly and anal baby, to the hole that's a hole. The control fantasy of the 1975 film adaptation dressed up the housewives residing in plantation-style homes (in the New York suburbs) in an undeclared but recognizable historical reenactment of the genteel South. The introduction of the slave into the lady is the anal lube for the men who hold day jobs as Imagineers.

While Jewish Barbie was under construction around the introjected prospect of German re-adaptation to the West, another doll of American identification washed up onto the coast from the other coast. The father-and-daughter bourgeois drama that introduced *Gidget* in 1957 was made in "Germany." Frederick Kohner, who openly and secretly ghost-wrote one of girl psychology's owner's manuals, was originally Austrian. His career as screenplay author was taking off in Berlin before he switched coasts to keep out of reach of the Nazis. Perhaps that is why he transforms himself not only into the father of Gidget (aka Franzie), but also into a professor of German at USC who spent his last sabbatical leave with the family in West Berlin. It was during this sojourn, moreover, that his pubescent daughter suffered her first crush and disappointment (57). In her words: "It occurred to me that ever since I came back from Europe I had become especially desperate to grow up" (60-61).

Because Franzie seemed to be starting out a "dwarf," her Austrian mother made her swim early on non-stop to stretch her head short into a head start. This Schreberesque training is subsumed by the happy-face results that render it compatible with Californian body culture. "Most of her friends laughed at it and so did Dr. Rossman who is our family doctor, but—lo and behold—what started out as a dwarf grew into an almost five-footer" (10). Back from Europe she discovers surfing and surfers on the Malibu beach. One of the surfers nicknames her "Gidget." She wants the guys to let her in on the gag. The great Kahoona explains that it's "derived by osmosis": "A small girl. Sort of a midget. A girl midget. A gidget. Get it?" (31). What she does get is that the moment the surfers accepted the name, they accepted her. Soon her nickname, upon reaching its half-life, yields "Gidge."

According to the story told in publicity photos when the book was released, Kohner had written down the teen discourse of his sixteen-year-old daughter, which he gained access to largely by listening in on her phone conversations. In the novel, this gesture of transgression is contained within the family's relationship to psychoanalysis. Gidget observes of her "hypochondriac" father that, as long as he can get the family physician "on the phone and talk to him, he thinks he won't die and neither would anyone else in the family. I guess you call this fetishism or something" (55). But there is also a family connection to psychoanalytic treatment. Needing reassurance about his daughter's involvement with those beach bums, the father asks son-in-law Larry, a psychoanalyst, to probe Gidget for the truth. She gets to listen in on Larry's treatment of the hypochondriac or fetishist. "Larry's relief over my well-preserved virginity was so fierce that he had called my old man the very afternoon of our luncheon and sold him a double size of Freud and Adler, well mixed. I managed to be on the extension phone in the house while he talked to Dad in the study" (77).

If this special combo isn't the continuity shot with "Germany," in addition to the swim-stretch therapy, then the assurance the members of the homoerotic group give her that there isn't a "flit" among them proves that we're also on the other shore. "In a roundabout way they all were jealous of anybody—male or female—who entered the hallowed orbit of the great Kahoona" (81). The near-miss relationship with homosexuality in the film adaptation, which has served gender studies a found feast, is the only German feature from the background story that remains behind on the screen. In the movies Gidget's family isn't Austrian-Jewish or German-Jewish. But her best girlfriend (Larue in the book), whose "love life is defunct" (24), makes it onto the screen as a Weimar tomboy in short haircut and pants, and her rejection of boys (especially on Gidget's behalf) is strident. Larue, who is really a "good guy" in Gidget's estimation (25), has been identified by analyst Larry, Gidget reports, as "sublimating with horses. I hope I'm using the right expression. It sounds sort of dirty" (24). In the movie, the same-sex bond on the surfing beach is not so roundabout in its presentation of an interior of a desire that cannot admit penetration. (The original Gidget, Kathy Kohner, stopped by to observe the filming of the surfer scenes. That evening she confided to her diary that the screen surfers looked like "fagits." In the book, she has no idea what a "flit" could be; in life, she just can't spell an F word.)

Daughter Kohner apparently expressed her wish to write a book about her Malibu initiation, which father Kohner took as an invitation to write it for her. Gidget in the book complains that she likes to leave books unread. In fact, she'd rather write a book than read one. "Headshrinker" Larry helps out: "the way he explained it to me is that I'm suffering from an inferiority complex on account of my old man having zillions of books around the house and reading like a maniac" (11). Prehistory childhood (other than the reference to Franzie's stretching swim therapy) only comes up in association with Larry's analytic play sessions, which Gidget describes within the span of an identification or recollection:

> All Larry does is sit around and watch them. . . . And scribble down his private observations. . . . Those little beasts are "acting out" their repressed feelings—that's what it's called. They give dolls the names of their little brothers and sisters, for instance, and stick needles in their eyes or throw them against the wall or bury them. It's good therapy. Larry writes it all down and then explains to those little monsters what they are doing and *why* they are doing it. (66-67)

As recalled in his *Magician of Sunset Boulevard: The Improbable Life of Paul Kohner, Hollywood Agent*, Frederick Kohner approached older brother Paul, an established Hollywood agent who also represented the sibling's screenwriting efforts, about his novel project. But Paul seemed unable to warm up to this declaration of adolescent independence. Then he counseled Fritz to secure the services of his own literary agent. "Within the week, he had sold *Gidget* both as a book and a film" (155). The older brother didn't hold off on the high praise he regularly gave his younger brother. "As for me, I had lost my agent—and the agent, for once, had lost his ten percent. But was happy that I had finally achieved full independence" (ibid.). The slogan used in marketing Gidget was "the little girl with big ideas." Independence, among these teen ideas, was also on loan as the father's midlife achievement.

Kohner enjoyed success with the Gidget novels in West Germany, too. Her name, however, was changed to April (which is why there is no counterpart in

German to the American notion and expression "gadget love"). The work he dedicated to his brother's life (and death) appeared first in German (two years before the American version). For his German-language audience, Kohner folded his own success story on the Coast into the historically neutral container of his older brother's biography in California, which began with a 1920 career move.

In Göttingen in the 1930s, the Pacific Islander sport of surfing inspired the new device installed in the lab tank to generate waves for scientific study. The Californian postwar culture of surfing (including the surf music variation on rock) was largely carried forward by individuals whose day job was working in the aerospace industry.

To gain full initiation into the surfing gang, Gidget must struggle against her displacement into open hiding: "I suddenly realized that I was no member of the crew—simply a blind passenger" (81). But after she leaves the boys behind to fight over her (and come into denied contact with their surfer bods) Gidget "shoots" the "curl" in isolation from the group grope response she finds wanting. "This was the final testing ground I had picked for myself" (148). But her solo triumph rides out a reference stowaway at the luau and hidden in its non-sequitur at the book's opening. Before Gidget sparks the jealousy outburst as a test, she witnesses another (anti-metaphorical) conflagration that spreads from the luau fire: "in Southern California all that's needed to start a first-class holocaust is *one* small spark" (129). All that's needed is one upper-middlebrow synonym for fire to set off a background that was the other blind passenger.

Susan Sontag's essay on American science fiction movies from 1950 to 1965, "The Imagination of Disaster," also partakes of what might be identified as a topos of American-adolescent ahistoricism. Already in the second paragraph, Sontag shares a joke with the reader—the contrast between the film dialogue in these disaster films and what the medium can project to scale—which is ultimately on the author. After listing exemplary lines of dialogue, she brings the point home: the lines "are hilarious in the context of picturesque and deafening holocaust. Yet the films also contain something which is painful and in deadly earnest" (209). In the final paragraph of her essay, Sontag summarizes both her enumeration of the incommensurate conjunctions between banality and terror in the science fiction movies and the arc of dissociation that carried her through this missed encounter. "What I am suggesting is that the imagery of disaster in science fiction films is above all the emblem of an *inadequate response*" (225). Sometimes an inadequate response involves an affect that goes under development, biding the time it takes to make reparations, before reaching the onset of the ability to reclaim the blank of missing affect and mourn.

While "holocaust" was used even during the war to refer to Nazi atrocities against the Jews, it was used "metaphorically," namely as a preexisting term that identified the genocide under its category or definition. Not until the mid-1950s was a capitalized Holocaust fully introduced to signify the extermination of six million Jews. These examples of the mix of metaphor belong on the slippery slope of the era of onset of the term's unambiguous redefinition. They document the period's metabolic rate of integration more than the fault of individuals. Adolescent ahistoricism is a structure, not an intention. It was the TV broadcast of *The Holocaust* in 1978 that triggered the global installation of the term.

We left Gidget at the head of this class of "holocaust" references, at the spot that's given as the vantage point for looking back, an ending at the beginning. There is one small bay along the Malibu coast "where the waves coming from Japan crash against the shore like some bitchen rocket bombs" (4). It is a mixed metaphor that washes up onto the Malibu beach packing away stray references to a concise history of the recent past as ongoing. The bomb dropped twice on Japan was the preemptively realized bomb that all were convinced the Germans were devising. Only by beating the Germans to the projected finish line of their bomb production could the Allies (together with the scientists who had fled Nazi Europe) feel safe. But within a mobilization of greater psychoanalysis that, at its apex of circumvention and denial, turned to, on and into crypto-fetishism, the Germans had realized another bomb, the rocket bomb, which was terroristic in a largely psychological warfare sense, yet which, by the postwar period, could carry the atom bomb to either side of the Cold War opposition.

Three years before *Logan's Run* addressed youthenasia, another science fiction film based on a 1966 British science fiction novel (the title, *Make Room! Make Room!*, stammers in earshot of the author's name: Harry Harrison) placed an enigmatically benign reference to mass euthanasia within its own media frame. According to *Soylent Green* (1973), New York in the future is the grimy exhaustion of the material world under conditions of overpopulation. An elite of government and business men enjoy protected conditions of well-to-do life in the 1970s, with the innovation that the showcase wives are now concubines, who often come with the apartment, and are known as "furniture." But when one of them wants to break out for love and liberation, the protagonist Detective Thorn (Charlton Heston), overwhelmed by his discovery of the bigger problem, assures her that at least she's alive, that she should just live. This could be a variation on "It's better than a concentration camp." The problem is discovered at the meeting of food preparation for the masses and institutionalized euthanasia.

At the local "Home," you can sign off and attend the only media show in town. Sol Roth (Edward G. Robinson) empties his cup and lies down to take in movie vistas of nature scenes and a background medley of tunes from works by Beethoven, Grieg and Tchaikovsky. Your favorite color and music personalize the "going home" program. After he identifies his preference for classical music, he adds as an afterthought: "light." That Roth, who was dying of cancer at the time, took this internalization of going to the movies personally is evident in his rapture. When Thorn watches, he too is overwhelmed by the "beauty" of the Sensurround. In the movie's conclusion, Thorn's mortal wounding, the same vista-cinematography and score bring the credits home. Roth accepted assisted suicide in despair over the problem of food and death in this future society. Thorn tried to intervene, but only in time to watch the show (and enjoy the view). Roth's dying words charge Thorn to secure the proof that "Soylent Green is people." The itinerary of Roth's body guides Thorn to the truth of recycling.

Going "Home" via a mediatic return to nature has an unlikely precedent in the "Wintergarden" described in the twenty-second chapter of Franz Werfel's novel *Star of the Unborn*. First published in English translation in 1946 after the author's death the year before in Los Angeles, it is the account of F. W.'s time-tripping visit to a California of the future, hosted by his old friend B. H., who hangs in there via reincarnation while still and forever attired in an Austrian WWI uniform. The way of life in this California rests in one piece: at the end, the departing lie down in cradles packed in retrogenetic humus to undergo the treatment of retrovolution in autobiological time. The continuity shot with the film lies in the overriding principle of the Wintergarden: "to make the end subjectively and objectively beautiful" (533). "The glasshouses of the Wintergarden were the exact opposite of a cemetery. In an inimitably gentle manner they transferred the living being into a form of nonbeing that left no ugly traces" (530-31). However, the visitors beat a retreat from rest in peace like a baby only to find their reservations confirmed in the adjacent underworld of botched retrovolutions. "I had to look very closely for a very long time to convince myself that these enraged, gabbling turnips were tiny aged men who were trying wildly to tear themselves loose from the grip of the soil" (557).

Solomon Roth's decision to "go home" followed the meeting of a group of researchers and activists known as the "Exchange," where citizens old enough in the 1970s to have gone through WWII who speak in German or German-Jewish accents recognize that the daily ration of Soylent Green cannot be made, as advertised, out of plankton, which is extinct. Not the UK book but the Hollywood film constructs a "future" scenario for the resolution of problems relating to human material out of psychopathic idealism and the film medium itself. The reality of the Holocaust was, like the truth of psychoanalysis, a relation expected at the family gatherings of American popular culture. But the relations were isolated and insulated by adolescent ahistoricism—and not available for the global work of integration.

4

At first sight, the snake slithering through Warburg's lecture is an unreconstructed horror that tests the advance of civilization by the solution each age finds for its containing reformulation. However, the modern techno-translation of the snake into an electric wire (or a rocket flight path) is a catastrophic regression that destroys the so-called room or pause for thought, which provided respite and sublimation. But the lecture reaches this crisis point by deception. Preparing and delivering his lecture to gain release from the asylum, Warburg anticipated treating psychiatrist Ludwig Binswanger's technophobia. Unlike Freud, who, in his reading of Schreber's *Memoirs,* thought techno-delusions were reconstructions buoyed up by deep insight, Binswanger took a technological turn in a patient's delusions to be a sure sign that the patient's illness was on a chronic course unto dissolution. Warburg delivered a lecture where he extolled the symbolic value of the civilized tradition of the serpent, which reaches to the stars and wraps itself around the staff of Caduceus over and against the murderous transmissions of "American" technology. In sync with the German loss of WWI, Warburg saw (almost in forecast of the Holocaust) that he was to be used up as human material in the production of more quality time for his infernal tormentors. What Binswanger demonstrated by his nonintervention in Ellen West's choice of the free act of self-destruction over the chronic course of her mental ailment, Jung declared during the discussion of his third London lecture, another "Serpent Lecture": the untreatable are the expendable.

Samuel Beckett was in attendance with his Kleinian analyst Wilfred Bion. In Beckett's early work, we hear the echo of Jung's throwaway remark. In concluding his response to the first question, which pertained to a five-year-old girl's dream, Jung referred to another ethereal child he had known, who at age ten still flexed the propensity of the very young for mythological dreams. That the ten-year-old was soon dead did not surprise him: "She had never been born entirely" (107). Right after the comment on a death without consequence, Jung went on to commend the psychopathic "born criminal" for his resistance to the norm of adaptation: "What would the world be like if all people were adapted? It would be boring beyond endurance. There must be some people who behave in the wrong way; they act as scapegoats and objects of interest for the normal ones. Think how grateful you are for detective novels and newspapers, so that you can say, 'Thank heaven I am not that fellow who has committed the crime, I am a perfectly innocent creature'" (108-09).

In 1935, when Jung delivered the series of lectures at the Tavistock Institute in London, he was the international head of the new German psychotherapy, which in Germany excluded the Jewish colleagues but not Freud's science (only its proper name). The record of the discussion shows that Jung regularly referred to a three-some of therapy options, which has the patient cornered (I mean covered). In 1935, German psychotherapy claimed to reunite all the therapies that took their departure from Freud in a new synthesis. This "greater psychoanalysis" was in fact ruled by the triumvirate of Jungian, Adlerian, and Freudian approaches. However, the only adjectivalization of a name still current in Nazi Germany was that of Jung. At the time eclectic psychotherapy was thus introduced in Nazi Germany, Jung's only objection was that he was being brought back into proximity with Freud (a.k.a. Working Group A). But he didn't act out this objection in London. He even customized each of the three parallel universals to fit a different genre of patient: the Freudian client is well-adapted, successful, and looking for gratification of his desires, while the Adlerian wants success and so lands a power complex (140-41). Since he didn't typecast the Jungian patient in this rundown of the genres of psychic compatibility between patients and approaches in the psychotherapy triangle, the identification with the psychopath he declared upon letting go of the girl as never born anyway reflects (at the least) Jung's historical failure to pass the empathy test.

In the third lecture, Jung presented his interpretation of a triptych of dreams in which the dreamer, this time his patient, went on a quest against a snake or a dragon. The central dream is suffused with haste and delay; the dreamer has to catch his train—but has he remembered everything he needs to pack? His attention is called to the railway track, which makes an ascent that describes the letter S. His thought is that the engine driver should be careful not to rush full steam ahead once out of the S shape as the long train still behind him would then derail in rounding the curve. For Jung, the S shape conjures a serpent that drags its tail behind our psychology:

> Our head is only one end, but behind our consciousness is a long historical "tail" of hesitations and weaknesses and complexes and prejudices and inheritances, and we always make our reckoning without them. We always think we can make a straight line in spite of our shortcomings, but they will weigh very heavily and often we derail before we have reached our goal because we have neglected our tail-ends. (90-91)

The third dream is set in the Swiss village of the patient's childhood. A peasant woman expresses admiration for the dreamer's determination to walk from there to Leipzig. "Then the scene changes," the patient meticulously recounts. "In the background appears a monstrously big crab-lizard" (96). It moves now to the left, now to the right, positioning the dreamer as it sidles up toward him between its pincers. The ten-year-old who was not yet born or already dead crossed Jung's mind because of his patient's inability, projected in the dreams, to be fully born and give a body to his success, which wrecks him. Jung ultimately let the patient go to his ruin without making recourse to deterrence in the transference, another occasion for the "ethical shock" registered by yet another member of his audience (130).

When Jung asks his patient about the village house where he impresses the woman, there is a prompt and spectacular identification: "It is the lazar-house of St. Jacob near Basel" (97). As every Swiss schoolboy knows, this was the site in 1444 of a counterattack upon the invading army of Burgundy that cost the life of everyone in the Swiss troop but succeeded in routing the enemy. Although this scene of suicidal heroism is a reenactment focus of fantasy for the Swiss, Jung adds that the soldiers, who chose not to wait for the rest of the army, present another cautionary example of the consequence of neglecting one's own tail-end.

With the monster's appearance, the dream breaks free of the waking frame of reference in which the dreams otherwise deliver the plain text of fair warning. The monster that doesn't exist is an archetype and Jung supplies its meanings out of the collective unconscious to which he and his patient have equal access. While Jung projects the histories and stories of the dragon and the hero, of the dragon as the hero, and of anima and animus, it turns out that the patient "has read Freud, and accordingly he interprets the situation as an incest wish, the monster being the mother, the angle of the open scissors the legs of the mother, and he himself, standing in between, being just born or just going back into the mother" (102). Next sentence, the topic of a new paragraph: "Strangely enough, in mythology the dragon *is* the mother" (ibid.).

Jung and his patient ostensibly part company over the patient not heeding the warning that Jung spells out. The patient, whose reading of Freud is indeed hasty, concludes that his incest wish in becoming conscious has been knocked out of the running of his success story (his stellar appointment in Leipzig). He proceeds to keep this appointment and, within three months of the move to Leipzig, breaks down, wrecked by the success. In the discussion, a member of the audience more attentive to the transference than Jung asks if it wouldn't have been possible to show more flexibility in his technique and find a way to protect his patient (107). Jung allows that he could have agreed with the patient that he was suffering from a mother complex and held his attention in therapy for several months, possibly preventing (and certainly delaying) the headstrong career move up the snake and ladder of immediate success. But he would have been cheating the patient and himself. Jung declares that if, for example, a patient wants to kill himself, he would never try to stop him.

The breaking point of their separation was not the mother interpretation, whether or not it was contained or part of the dream's warning. What triggered Jung's rejection of his patient was a detail in the third dream. The dreamer vanquishes the monster by tapping its head with "a little rod or wand" (96), indeed "a magical wand" (103). The dream pauses and then ends as the dreamer contemplates the inert monster "for a long time" (96). The patient explains that, in the conclusion of his dream, he marvels at the ease with which he dispatched the monster. For Jung, this amounts to proof that he is untreatable. "He simply reasons the monster away. He says, 'There is no such thing as a crab-lizard, there is no such thing as an opposing will; I get rid of it, I simply think it away. I think it is the mother with whom I want to commit incest, and that settles the whole thing, for I shall not do it'" (104). Between the lines of the fantasy, a magic wand taps thoughts and wishes and realizes their commands. Here lies a scenario of projective identification or psychotic break (which Jung left unattended): mother monsters threaten to reabsorb their spawn while the survivor son must struggle to replace the world lost to over-stimulation and repression with its android simulation (the tapping on and off of technologization). Jung abandons his dreamer to undergo a literalization of the die-messages in the dreams. The melancholia of unbirth, one of the mainstays of Klein's reading of psychosis, gives way before the ruthlessness of Jung's attitude toward its untreatability.

In his study *Male Fantasies*, Klaus Theweleit proposed that the condition of being not yet fully born informed the psycho fascist. Walking on the eggshells of unaccomplished entry, the psychopath must plow through the amorphous swamp of the body or mother to secure, if not a good object, then a boundary: a clean, mean machine. In Norman Spinrad's 1972 alternate history novel *The Iron Dream*, we follow the recurring (re)birth of the Helder in warfare waged against an amorphous enemy for over two hundred pages. *The Iron Dream* is an alternate history because it is an edition (the second) put together in a world where Adolf Hitler was a German-American science fiction author. What it barely contains, like a faux dust jacket covering contraband, is Hitler's novel *Lord of the Swastika*, which won the Hugo Award for best science fiction novel of 1954, a year after his death. Hitler's science fiction extols the future that belongs to the Helder (just a stammer away from *Helden* or "heroes") who, at the start of the novel, are an ex-nation surviving under the depressive conditions of postwar agrarian squalor. They are delivered by their leader, Feric Jaggar, who rolls back the stone of dispersion, subjugation, and mongrelization. As the Blitzkrieg rages, the "true humans" die or triumph in cleanliness whereas the masses mobilized by the Dominators or Doms squirt, squish, and stink upon impact.

The pre-Oedipal provenance of this mess is also given an adult Oedipal profile, but only in the Afterword by Homer Whipple, dated 1959. Even though the fictional upsurge might have expressed Hitler's wish for Nazi success, this obscure group that Hitler in fact supported while still in Germany—he emigrated to the United States in 1919—"disappeared around 1923, a full seven years before the Communist coup made the subject academic. . . . His early, fiery, and continuing devotion to the cause of anti-Communism was well-known, and involved him in many heated debates and feuds within the small world of science-fiction fans in which he moved, until the takeover of Britain in 1948 made the imperialistic appetite of the Greater Soviet Union crystal clear to even the most naïve Communist apologists" (252). In our own alternate time zone, 1948 is a time to remember. It is the year of composition of *Nineteen Eighty-Four*. Spinrad's *The Iron Dream* belongs, then, to the busy interchange at the shifting fronts between WWII and the Cold War that supported a kind of alternate historicization. Unconsciously on purpose, this historicization confirmed the reservations attributed to the Nazi cause and, by the consolidation of one enemy and one opposition, projected a world in which the Holocaust could not happen. To this day, revisionist questioning of its reality—a tendency scattered across the global reception of the Holocaust up and running since the 1980s—is supported by the memory of this absence of acknowledgment.

Spinrad's intervention is to diagnose Hitlerian science fiction (or alternate history) as linked and limited to the fantasy genre. In a 1973 review, Ursula K. Le Guin identifies a parody under wraps in *The Iron Dream* regarding tendencies in American science fiction to appoint science fiction technology and possibility to a prehistory of warrior kings. That one of the faux blurbs places Hitler up there with Tolkien, Lewis, and Chesterton is too much for Le Guin. When she selects Heinlein as a comp, however, it's clear that she is seeking a diversion (into the vicinity of superhero adventure) from the identification of the Hitler book as fantasy. Another fake blurb may be equally off the mark yet remains within the target circles of fantasy: "If Wagner wrote science fiction, this is the way he would do it." At stake here is the drawing of the line that Le Guin calls "distancing" and attributes to the science fiction genre as its distinction. Ultimately it draws its line between Christian fantasy (where Le Guin's oeuvre in large measure belongs) and the fantasy of nihilism, although, generically speaking, they're not so distinct.

The way in which technology is cited in Hitler's novel—without its essence, without the ready positioning for its incursion or emergence, but also without the encrypted loss that would summon the techno-fetish—is the strongest sign that, since alternate history is not internal to it, *Lord of the Swastika* is a work in denial of science fiction. As "Homer" recounts it, the jump cut from the steam engine and flying machine as the highest technology to the limitless production and launching of interstellar spaceships "is wish-fulfillment from beginning to end" (249). Before its motley brew is wiped out of our faces by the Helder, the enemy detonates a final weapon that targets the reproductive "germ plasm" of the purebred for complete ruination. Future generations could henceforth yield only "vile mutants and obscene monstrosities" (235). Since the already-born last generation of humanity still standing before itself is pure, however, Feric turns to cloning, which is only skin deep. "The radiation that has mangled our germ plasm beyond all hope of repair has not contaminated our somatic tissue whatever— from the cells of our SS purebreds may be cloned the new master race!" (236). The narcissistic wound of total defeat is not only bypassed through cloning; the restart brings about an upgrade in bio-innovation. "Thus, in one generation we can advance human evolution a thousand years and produce a race of blond giants fully seven feet tall with the physiques of gods and an average intelligence on the genius level. Out of the tragedy of genetic contamination, we can create the final triumph of human racial purity" (ibid.). If the Barbie doll were projected life-size, she too would be seven feet tall.

5

In *Dr. Adder* (1984), K. W. Jeter, one of Dick's So Cal disciples, included a cameo of Dick. KCID is the radio voice of conscience and guidance on a station that otherwise plays only German operas, which, like Berg's *Wozzeck*, hail from the period of high modernism immediately preceding the station break of National Socialism. In his afterword to *Dr. Adder* (dated 1979), Dick lauded the innovativeness of this work, a rarity in a field that had been washed out by the incursion of the fantasy genre. Dick cited two works by peers that stood out against the white wash: Disch's *Camp Concentration* and Spinrad's *Iron Dream*, both tributes to the influence of *The Man in the High Castle* and its introjection of traumatic histories made in Germany. Although *Dr. Adder* shares a border with fantasy—it packs a crucifixion, a quest, a joust, and more—the science fiction resolutely indwells a stricken world in which all deposits remain unredeemable. By its topography, Jeter's future LA runs so deep through multiple underworlds as to approximate a projection through undisclosed foreign-body introjects. (Otherwise LA night life more accurately fits the ground-level punk-noir disco in Cameron's *Terminator*.) In Jeter's novel, the untranslated lines of German opera, part of the homage to Dick, approximate the closure that future LA towers above or below. "'*Hohl! Alles hohl!*' the radio sang out. '*Ein Schlund! Es schwankt! Hörst du, es wandert was mit uns da unten!*'" (135).

At the end, it turns out that KCID holds the other prosthetic link in the chain of forces and identities left standing after the defeat of Mox, head of the Video Church of Moral Forces. Mox ruled the southland from Orange County and is the cover identity or posthumous personality of Dr. Gass, who devised gadgets of interrogation and warfare that were operational during the recently concluded revolutionary or civil war. The war is continuously reenacted between Orange County and a couple of counterculture neighborhoods in LA. But Gass's gadgets are prohibited. Of the two gadget-prostheses still in operation, one is the portable transmitter with which KCID broadcasts his radio show; the other is the flashglove, at once a classic prosthesis, amplification and amputation, and a synthesizer of diverse mediatic connections and violations whereby the operator introduces himself and his opponent into a synthetic in-between zone. Like Freddy's glove in *A Nightmare on Elm Street*, it is the hyper-realization of the fantasy of the cyberglove as an instrument of psycho-violence.

During the all-out Orange County attack upon the Interface, one of the LA counterculture neighborhoods, Adder rushes into a merger with the flashglove, which catches him in the crossfire of its feedback and leaves him a dying zombie (120). In time his undead state is reversed through the input of Melia, an unconscious girl, bereft of her senses, who already occupies the slum room to which the dying Adder is brought. Coming out of the darkness of childhood trauma, she entered into relationship with the TV set. "She became able to leap the gap from beneath her skin to under the TV's cabinet, and plug directly into its electronic circuitry" (199). She can go beyond the programming, "the TV families" (ibid.), to develop a tele-capacity that plumbs every signal—ultimately to the source of Mox's televangelist power in the Orange County computer banks. In the close quarters of their cohabitation, she comes into contact with the flashglove. "The electronic network connecting the flashglove's sensors with" Adder's "own nervous system is really only a simplified version of the network she had been playing with all that time. When she came into close enough proximity, her hand actually grasping the surface of the glove, the bridge was gapped, just as between her and the TV set" (201).

A certain Betreech who hails from the prehistory of Adder's Passion—he is a friend who ends up betraying him after helping affix him to the flashglove—made his first appearance in the novel caught in the act of libidinizing the cuts of cinema. "The unconscious old man was dressed in a woman's Civil War-period crinoline ball gown. . . . Betreech's little vice consisted of dressing up like characters in his collection of old Hollywood films and stroking himself to a climax at the thought of the sexual activity imagined to be occurring in the ellipsis between one cut and another" (88). Prosthetic technology draws the narrative onward, delivering its future postwar world from psychotic-electronic forces. But the prosthetic relation was a split end out of touch with a culture that cultivated the cut, by and large in the flesh, as a sexual outlet. The skillfully mutilated sexual body, the focus of Adder's industry in the Interface, occupies the foreground of this novel. To the sex industry, Adder took his Orange County training in the surgical adjustment of the worker to the machine, cutting up prostitutes to order. First he interviewed the client (either the specialty john or a volunteer prostitute eager to specialize) under the influence of ADR, an interrogation drug left over from the war designed to bring unconscious and pre-human desires to the fore. "All the submerged, bestial layers are united with the topmost, conscious layer into a single entity. An alligator that can talk" (80). The session releases fantasies of "amputation or mutilating or altering of the sexual object. Hence, all of the chopped hookers out on the street. The rich customers get one cut to the exact specifications of their ADR-revealed hunger—there's never any problem finding the girls for it" (83). In no time Adder thus becomes the "obsession" of "psychopaths" (98).

Following the destruction of the Interface, an abandoned amusement park in Orange County has to be reopened to accommodate a displacement. The murdered prostitutes are being robotically duplicated under the old Matterhorn. "The old science fiction pulp wet-dream: the mechanical cunt" (178-79). A *Metropolis*-style substitution is required for the "*diversion* the Interface afforded the residents of Orange County. It was, shall we say, a vital release of tension" (179). However, this simulation is "going to be a *family* amusement area" (180). For instance:

He felt a gentle stroking pressure on the inside of his thigh. Looking down, he saw what he hadn't noticed before: the hooker was a simulated amputee. She had one hand resting on the shoulder of another automaton to balance herself, and was rubbing the stump of her right leg . . . against him. He perceived another evidence of painstaking attention to detail. Right at the edge of the stump, where the synthetic whore's real-life counterpart would have had her grinning snake's head tattoo, there was the amusement park's own version of the mark. A little cartoon mouse's

head, two perfect black circles for ears, grinning insanely friendly with
button nose and wide-sprung eyes. (180-81)

The first encounter with the advances in animatronics and animation in Orange
County is through the instructional interview of a science fiction author watched
on the video monitor at the local high school. "He's on tape in the archives. He
was one of the first . . . to have his personality and memory programmed into the
big computer banks they've got in there; that's why his output is that dummy you
saw on the screen . . . a replica of his original body. . . . Wires and gears. . . . Now
they've developed outputs where they use straight computer graphics. It's still
realistic, looks like the guy did when he was alive, but it's really just a sophisti-
cated animated cartoon" (175).

Mox was one of Adder's first specialty clients; he wanted the job done on
his wife. As Adder recalls: "In my ADR probe of Mox I had seen particularly
strong a certain nightmare figure found in nearly every man's subconscious, and
now here was Mox, stuck hilt-deep in that dreaded nemesis, the Vagina Dentata"
(95-96). His wife later confirms that Mox wanted it this way in order to grow
stronger through abnegation of genital sexuality—indeed as invincible as only the
resurrected body can be. "That's what Melia discovered in the computer banks,
what she showed me: Mox isn't alive; he's on tape there in the computers. After
the Interface raid, he had his entire mentality recorded that way. . . . Only Mox had
special autonomous personality circuits built in. The others on tape are without
control—they're just turned on or off whenever they're wanted. Mox, however,
still functions just as when he was alive" (217). Adder challenges Mox inside the
transmission of his daily TV show, a showdown for all to cheer on.

What *Dr. Adder* skewers through the techno-future of the reenactment of
a recent past of total civil war are bodily introjects washing up onto the Coast
with the influx of integration. While a lack of integration cannot but be extremely
painful, as Klein advises in "On the Sense of Loneliness," the very progress of
"integration brings in its train new problems" (301). In seeking integration as a
safeguard against destructive impulses, one fears that integration itself re-releases
these impulses threatening the good object and the good parts of the self. Winnicott resituates this problem in the vicinity of the antisocial tendency in terms of
the psyche's somatization or the body in motion. Only by standing upright as a
sexual and aggressive body, taking aim and gathering together the momentum of

striking or punching out, does the body lend itself to the integration it models and requires. As with every one of Winnicott's new notions, however, it must pass the test of transition. In his unfinished summary work *Human Nature*, Winnicott underscored that integration was one out of two developmental moments inter-related as "achievements." For the first, integration itself, Winnicott liked to turn to the example of Humpty Dumpty ever since his psychotic child patient "Bob" made it his Dasein-rhyme: "it is useful to think of the nursery rhyme of Humpty Dumpty and the reasons for its universal appeal. Evidently there is a general feeling, not available to consciousness, that integration is a precarious state. The nursery rhyme perhaps appeals because it acknowledges personal integration as an achievement" (117-18). The lodging of the psyche in the body is the other achievement. When we jump out of our skin we reflect a disturbance unsettling integration itself (123). Achieved integration carries forward the internalization of respite that the transitional object introduced.

The disturbance associated with paranoia, which keeps its integrative moment in attack for a best defense, by and large exemplifies an oppositional momentum of integration from which essential rest has been withdrawn or mutated into arrest. The disturbance is as basic as the reaction or overreaction to environmental changes that do not originate in personal impulsive experience. There "is an interruption of being, and the place of being is taken by reaction to impingement" (127). Or again: "The gathering together of the self constitutes an act of hostility to the NOT-ME, and a return to rest is not a return to a resting place, because the place has been altered, and has become dangerous" (124). At the other end of the transitional obstacle course there is the double achievement of integration and (or as) lodging of the psyche in the body. "The idea of a ghost, a disembodied spirit, derives from this lack of essential anchoring of the psyche in the soma, and the value of the ghost story lies in its drawing attention to the precariousness of psyche-soma coexistence" (122).

THE RACE TO FILL IN THE BLANKS

1

In "Building Dwelling Thinking," Heidegger sets the missing place of the animal. First he drops a date mark—the inevitable concession in fantasy according to Freud in "The Poet and Daydreaming"—to the otherwise-repressed present and its ongoing extension into the recent past. Heidegger's mark or brand name belongs to a postwar readymade. The housing shortage (*Wohnungsnot*) isn't the problem, Heidegger proclaims. Nor is supplying this lack the solution. *Wohnungsnot*, a word with recognition value specific to postwar Germany, identifies not only the need for dwelling, but also (literally and psychotically) the painful neediness, if not anguish, of dwelling. Consider Carl Jung's famous exploration of a schizophrenic patient's *Bank-Noten* in terms of their economy and currency of anguish.

There is an immediate reception of Heidegger's philosophy within German psychotherapy and psychiatry tailored to the treatment of psychosis. The *Zolikoner Seminare* were a late arrival of this relationship, which would prove mutual once Ludwig Binswanger introduced *Daseinsanalyse*, which he conjoined out of equal parts Freud and Heidegger shortly after the appearance of *Sein und Zeit*. To call Heidegger on his contributions to the ideology of successful mourning is to encounter his words in the *Lichtung* (the clearing) of this longstanding commitment to psychotherapy.

On all sides we hear talk about the housing shortage, and with good reason. Nor is there just talk; there is action too. We try to fill the need by providing houses, by promoting the building of houses, planning the whole architectural enterprise. However hard and bitter, however hampering and threatening the lack of houses remains, the real plight of dwelling does not lie merely in a lack of houses. The real plight of dwelling is indeed older than the world wars with their destruction, older also than the increase of the earth's population and the condition of the industrial workers. (158-59)

Instead, we must ever learn to dwell, which also means to give thought to our homelessness, our uncanniness. Because we would control and secure our address, we are separated from our home, much as for Freud we are separated from the mother's body, the model home. Through the essential off-limitedness of this home or body we encounter the limit of our own bodies. Thus commences for Kafka the allegory of "Der Bau" ("The Burrow"), a multiple occupancy or cathexis of the building or body as a site of symptoms at close quarters that unfold under the aegis of security, but also as a corpus, which Kafka's *Schriftstellersein*, his sense of *being writing*, scans or reformulates relentlessly.

For Heidegger, the bridge becomes the architectural placeholder for the call of dwelling/building, the summons to gather together, in passing, the fourfold of being. This fourfold illuminates the modes of mortals dwelling—as saving the earth, as receiving the sky, as awaiting the divinities, and finally as initiating their own nature, "their being capable of death as death" (148). For Heidegger, it's either his way across old town bridges or it's the highway. "The highway bridge is tied into the network of long-distance traffic, paced as calculated for maximum yield. Always and ever differently the bridge escorts the lingering and hastening ways of men to and fro, so that they may get to other banks and in the end, as mortals, to the other side" (150).

All the while withdrawing his introject as a model, Heidegger nevertheless exposes to viewing a recognizable home, one that is well-situated in his Black Forest neighborhood. A sound continuity shot with the etymologically excavated beginnings of *bauen* and *wohnen*, which are immersed in agriculture, the two-hundred-year-old farmhouse includes niches and markings for the Before and After of living passage. In other words, the house is far removed from memorial architecture, which still models reality testing as mourning in Freud's "Mourning and Melancholia." The columbarium of remembrance is instead streamlined for life's transmission. After itemizing the identifiable home's proper placement in the natural setting as well as the angle of its roof for optimal winter shelter, Heidegger lets the house remember: "It did not forget the altar corner behind the community table; it made room in its chamber for the hallowed places of childbed and the 'tree of the dead'—for that is what they call a coffin there: the *Totenbaum*—and in this way it designed for the different generations under one roof the character of their journey through time" (158). In the original, Heidegger lets the reader stumble over the *Totenbaum*, whereupon he interrupts the tour to deliver the translation. It is, at first contact, the double of *Wohnungsnot*, or rather the inoculation against the postwar readymade Heidegger next throws up as a topical blind spot and thus as the other stumbling block, the one he doesn't mitigate.

The farmhouse remembers that "mortals dwell in that they initiate their own nature—their being capable of death as death—into the use and practice of this capacity, so that there may be a good death" (148). Like Freud, who adopts the position of Devil's advocate while contemplating the scenarios of the meaningfulness of the death drive he introduces in *Beyond the Pleasure Principle*, Heidegger doesn't want the good death to be taken, at least not as an "empty Nothing," as "the goal" (149). "Nor does it mean to darken dwelling by blindly staring toward the end" (ibid.). It is the distress, the *Not* that must be stayed. The farmhouse doesn't correspond to an inner world of representations. What we call memory must instead be considered a live transmission. Thinking of a specific old-town bridge is by its nature, in itself, that which "gets through, persists through, the distance to that location. From this spot right here, we are there at the bridge—we are by no means at some representational content in our consciousness" (154). Heidegger's argument with academic psychology is not one (hands down) with or against Melanie Klein's notion of the inner world. This proxy argument sets aside the basic separateness of psychotic states of depression.

> Even when mortals turn "inward," taking stock of themselves, they do not leave behind their belonging to the fourfold. When, as we say, we come to our senses and reflect on ourselves, we come back to ourselves from things without ever abandoning our stay among things. Indeed, the loss of rapport with things that occurs in states of depression would be

wholly impossible if even such a state were not still what it is as a human state—that is, a staying with things. (155)

All the while residing in the agricultural setting of the onset of building and dwelling, Heidegger's essay doesn't even take stock of animals, let alone stay with them. And yet it is inevitably over and against animals that humans award themselves philosophical distinction in death as in life. But the relationship to animals, masterfully bypassed in the elucidation of things in terms of bridgework, is nonetheless encrypted within the etymological time trip that revisits the original settlement of the meanings of building and dwelling. Heidegger is training us to heed certain commands.

Let us listen once more to what language says to us. The Old Saxon *wuon*, the Gothic *wunian*, like the old word *bauen*, mean to remain, to stay in a place. But the Gothic *wunian* says more distinctly how this remaining is experienced. *Wunian* means: to be at peace, to be brought to peace, to remain in peace. The word for peace, *Friede*, means the free, *das Freye*, and *fry* means: preserved from harm and danger, preserved from something, safeguarded. To free really means to spare. The sparing itself consists not only in the fact that we do not harm the one whom we spare. Real sparing is something positive and takes place when we leave something beforehand in its own nature, when we return it specifically to its being, when we "free" it in the real sense of the word into a preserve of peace. (146-47)

The denial that sparing doesn't only mean we don't harm or kill the "one whom we spare" is the denial to animals of a place in the staging area of essential building, dwelling, or thinking. "The fundamental character of dwelling is this sparing and preserving" (147) where "this" refers to the scenario of sparing that "also" prevails and exceeds what has been denied. This sparing is a setting free— born free—but within the preserve, the safeguarding of "each thing in its nature" (ibid.). Heidegger's sparing or letting go, the unidentified living of animals, sets the missing place of animals.

In systems of meaning on a stable setting, allegory is about filling or identifying the blanks that disclose the "other story." In the modern setting that Benjamin tracked (beginning with the seventeenth century), allegory must turn significance out of the blank itself, working the blank as a turning point for drawing the reading onward. The work most influential on (indeed syndicated in) Benjamin's *Origin of the German Mourning Play* was Schreber's *Memoirs of My Nervous Illness*. The double text hovers behind this study's understanding of the science fiction genre. Perhaps the first step undertaken by Freud to introduce a transferential caption into the boundary concepts of his science was his identification of the missing places or blanks of mourning, transference, and reality testing in a delusional system like Schreber's. They could be *found* missing—and metabolized in various modes of withdrawal and return. This discovery was the first basis for a psychoanalytic understanding and treatment of the psychoses.

2

In Galouye's *Simulacron 3*, Zeno's paradoxical contest without a finish line between Achilles and the tortoise encodes an unbearable secret. It is a secret that drives the counterfeit intermediary figure selected to carry it as a crazy or suicidal, whereupon his operator yanks him from the stage. A sketch of the contestants is the deceased head programmer's delegated clue to the protagonist, Hall. Once Hall figures out that "Zeno" sounds out the name of the carrier who committed suicide, he comes to share the secret that the illusion of motion demonstrated by the race in logic is basic to his reality's status as an electronic simulation. This secret knowledge is personalized or eroticized (i.e., sadistically conveyed) when "empathic coupling" (which allows a "real" operator to visit the simulated world via the POV of one of its faux denizens) is interfered with and spun as "faulty coupling." Hence the operator lords his control over the electronic dupe who feels the pain of his manipulation and even hears his operator's derision. It is the outlet in the test situation for the psychopathy that the simulated habitat was ultimately supposed to study.

In Philip K. Dick's *The Simulacra*, those who rule behind the scenes keep and carry the secret that the figureheads in the foreground of government are simulations, whereby date marks of progress are preserved against the traumatic histories in which they are embedded. By simulation and incorporation, the USEA, the postwar state uniting California and Germany, would compel the psychopathic violence that is its continuity shot. The turtle that can still be kept as a pet in the mass housing unit of the German-Californian state named The Abraham Lincoln sets the place for the android test in *Do Androids Dream of Electric Sheep?* In the test situation of Scott's film adaptation, the first question or trigger looks at the extent of the subject's concern for a tortoise flipped on its back baking in the sun. In his 1972 essay "The Android and the Human," Dick used cybernetics for the external referee of the android test, selecting experiments with the robot known as tortoise that are exemplary of its general method.

> Cybernetics, a valuable recent scientific discipline, articulated by the late Norbert Wiener, saw valid comparisons between the behavior of machines and humans—with the view that a study of machines would yield valuable insights into the nature of our own behavior. By studying what goes wrong with a machine—for example, when two mutually exclusive tropisms function simultaneously in one of Grey Walter's synthetic turtles, producing fascinatingly intricate behavior in the befuddled turtles—one learns, perhaps, a new, more fruitful insight into what in humans was previously called "neurotic" behavior. (183-84)

As in Dick's empathy test, the intermediary step of the animal manifests in both Wiener and Walter's analogy between machine and man. In Wiener's *Cybernetics: Or Control and Communication in the Animal and the Machine,* we follow the animal step by implication when considering the brain (not specified as the human brain) in relation to computing in the test situation. "It is not the empty physical structure of the computing machine that corresponds to the brain . . . but the combination of this structure with the instructions given it at the beginning of a chain of operations and with all the additional information stored and gained from outside in the course of this chain. This information is stored in some physical form—in the form of memory" (146).

According to Walter's *The Living Brain,* cybernetics picks up where a magical imitation of life left off copying external appearances and scientifically imitates performance and behavior instead. A mechanical simulation of life becomes a robot—a simulation of the living brain—when it is endued with spontaneous motion and can lay claim to autonomy or self-regulation. "But if the performance of a model is to be demonstrably a fair imitation of cerebral activity, the conditions of stimulation and behavior must equally be comparable with those of the brain. Not in looks, but in action, the model must resemble an animal" (120).

The evolutionary perspective that allows Walter to draw a distinction between the individuality evident in dogs and cats and the communal adaptation among "totalitarian insects" is an analogy waiting to be applied to science fantasy about the future of the human species. "Olaf Stapledon, the Virgil of science fiction, whose soaring vision once lighted on a monstrous sedentary brain, divined that its communal mechanism would not be compatible with anything that we should regard as personality" (18). Exceptional among Stapledon's works of superhuman fantasy set on eons of time commensurate with Outer Space and evolution is his 1944 novel *Sirius*, which explores interspecial relations. Although scientist Trelone envisages working up to a superhuman brain in human test subjects, he first engages in animal experimentation to cultivate a "super-sub-human intelligence, a missing-link mind" (15). His single success along this line, one that he is never able to reproduce, is the transfer of human intelligence to the dog Sirius. In a story like Pat Murphy's "Rachel in Love," the chimp with the imprint of a human girl's mind sees the world as that girl, albeit troubled around the edges by rival memories of two very different mothers. Indeed, it is as the girl that she adapts her instinctual life to her chimp embodiment. In *Sirius*, it is not a discrete human intelligence that has been transferred intact and undisclosed but operative; it is the life of the human mind that has been extended biologically and behaviorally to and through the animal sensorium. The biological manipulation aims not only at enlarging the animal's brainpan but also the life span, the "tempo of life," "so that it should mature very slowly and live much longer than was normal to its kind" (14). The first sign that the prep work succeeded emerges because Sirius "remained a helpless infant long after the other litter were active adolescents" (17).

Trelone chooses a dog over an ape because a dog's pet status gives "much greater freedom of movement in our society" (15). He can raise Sirius as a member of his family alongside his daughter Plaxy, who is closest to Sirius in age. Trelone's plan is that Sirius, once he grows up, will be "one of the world's greatest animal psychologists" (51). But Trelone has to adapt to the interests of the war effort that alone justify funding support, and he abandons for the time being those aspects of his research that provided Sirius with a context. In the course of his dog experimentation, he finds a formula for producing super sheep-herding dogs. The formula yields the assembly line that keeps his research lab in business. Sheep herding or farm work in general—which, according to Trelone's counsel, he engaged in during adolescence for the psychological benefit of psyche-soma integration—becomes Sirius's day job. Already an unlikely option in the war situation, his career as an animal psychologist is snuffed out with Trelone in an air raid.

Sirius still needs his day job as the container for a conflict that arose early on, "the conflict between what he later called his 'wolf-nature' and his compassionate civilized mentality" (27). In regards to their handling of a dog's "natural impulses of sex, pugnacity, and hunting," Sirius divides his companion species into so-called dog lovers, whose sentimentality starves those impulses, and the dog-interested, who "respect a dog *as a dog*, as a rather remote but essentially like-minded relative" (54). But does Sirius want respect as a dog? He refers to his wolf nature while his intelligence makes him look down on dogs and men. The former are saved from neuroticization through their pet plight only by their stupidity (95); the latter are to be despised for their regressive neglect of the steering mechanism of their evolutionary advantage, their hands, "the very instrument of creation" (98). Whereas the sense of smell compensates for a diminished visual sense, the absence of the hand is the limit of Sirius's intelligent life. It is also the practical basis (namely division of labor) for his bond with sister Plaxy.

Sirius's periodic violent actions are not canine. Only once does Sirius recognize the import of his human side. "This streak of sexual cruelty in human beings horrified Sirius all the more because he himself had indulged in something of the sort with his bitches. But he persuaded himself that this aberration in him was entirely due to some infection from man, due, in fact, to his human conditioning" (104). Sirius joins Plaxy in rejecting biological conditioning as the overriding frame of human endeavor. Instead they consider the spirit to be paramount. Sirius experiences another kind of spirit when, following the passing of their mother Elizabeth, he makes contact with the departed. "For himself, he was again strangely perplexed by this business of death. The dead Elizabeth kept talking to him. And it was not the Elizabeth that had just died . . . it was Elizabeth as she was in her prime. . . . 'Don't *believe* I still exist, for that would be false to your intellect; but don't refuse the *feeling* of my presence in the universe, for that would be blind'" (159).

In the era of secularization (of repression), *Hamlet* gave the advance preview that adolescence or the teen age comes to be initiated through contact with ghosts and the idea of suicide crossing one's mind. The care that went into laying the foundation of childhood in Sirius's development supported the human condition of the perpetual teenager. In his case, however, it did so without even a hand in giving a body to his insight or spirit. Toward the end of his reduced career (ultimately as a carrier of the secret of his intelligence), a dog hater has Sirius at his disposal. Sirius is in no position to fight a human to survive; his only option is to kill him. His "wolf" violence catches up with him when the ruthless vigilante mob demonizes and then extinguishes him. Following Walter's identification of the author of *Sirius* as the Virgil of the poetic historiography of science, we recognize the importance of being Sirius in his lost cause, which the tortoise robot carries forward.

The first attempt to render the brain by way of a robot, one that would imitate not the appearance but the performance or behavior of a living creature, "seems to have been suggested by the familiar test of animal intelligence in finding the way out of a maze" (122). Walter advises that the robot in question, Ashby's Homeo-stat,"like a fireside cat or dog, only stirs when disturbed, and then methodically finds a comfortable position and goes to sleep again" (123-24). "What we find in this fireside companion is not only the virtue of self-control and the blessing of homeostasis, not only an exemplification of placidity, but also of plasticity, one of the basic principles that seem to govern animal engineering. This means roughly that every part of the mechanism is reversible, interchangeable and expendable— but not replaceable" (124). Within the self-regulation or self-reflexivity of dispos-able parts, there is one place that remains irreplaceable and empty.

In 1948, Walter began making his tortoise, which would soon be featured in popular magazines as a new addition to the domestic setting. The conception of the robot more immediately inherited two techniques mobilized during the Battle of Britain. A colleague came to the research facility where Walter was working on scanning mechanisms for tracking planes and bombs to get computing help with the planning and production of goal-seeking missiles: "the two ideas, goal-seeking and scanning, had combined as the essential mechanical conception of a working model that would behave like a very simple animal" (125).

Walter's tortoise (or, more properly, *machina speculatrix*) was able to "demonstrate the first of several principles exemplified in the mechanisms of most living creatures. A typical animal propensity is to explore the environment rather than to wait passively for something to happen. This faculty gives the device its name and distinguishes it from other machines. The most elaborate computing machine does not look round for problems to solve" (126).

According to Walter, the cybernetic reliance on behaviorism—derived from animal experiments and applied to the mechanical explanation of the brain—consigns Artificial Intelligence to the status of specialized support. Fact arrangement and appraisal, for example, can be delegated to machinery just as "management of our bodies long since was delegated" (276). Walter refers to Hobbes but we could refer to Freud in stating that thought is produced by bodies in motion (43). Walter calls on another version of Zeno's paradoxical race—the contest between the hare and the tortoise—to introduce the illusion of motion (ibid.), not as a contradiction but as the depth charge of the motility that organizes thought and reality testing. An egoic function for Freud just as the ego is a projection of the body (in motion), motility cannot be contained in the sequence in time of coded messages; events in the brain "occur in three-dimensional space, in that one bit of space which is more crowded with events than any other we can conceive" (61). In its one-sidedness, a computing model cannot represent the general condition of the brain—what we might call the whole brain, a first view of which the robotic animal provided.

Walter derives the essential meaning of cybernetics (steermanship by feedback) from the evolutionary prospect of thought and memory emerging out of the obstacle course of motion.

> Anything that moves about increases its risks, runs into new dangers . . . In the multicellular world, among beings of more delicate construction than the plastic single cell, there is an even higher premium on road-sense, on steermanship. We have to visualize an elementary system of control by which the forward part of an organism can obtain information and feed it back internally for guidance of its operative motor nerve centres. . . . This principle of steermanship . . . by feedback undoubtedly played a very important evolutionary role in the first stages of animal life. . . . Feedback as the first act of creation, or as the process of continuous creation, is a pretty subject for the metaphysician. (25)

With the evolution of the brain into the premier organ of survival, navigation by self-regulation attained the state of homeostasis "in which disorder and disease are mechanical slips and errors" (39).

Walter underscores that Pavlov broke through to a far-reaching understanding of association through observable and measurable changes, which the accident of traumatization by flooding had brought about in his animals, according to types fitting the Baroque staging of derangement. One fact of primary importance emerged: "For an animal such as man, anything that affects the nervous system can come to 'mean' anything else. . . . But our awareness is only a fractional measure of our associative powers; by far the greater part of this learning is below the water line, submerged in what we may still call the unconscious" (147).

For nearly two generations, Pavlov's experiments were the major source of information on brain physiology in an orbit that Walter circumscribes with the roundtrip between Los Angeles and Moscow. However, a stopover in Germany added a method for the investigation of brain activity to the reflex measurements of Pavlov that was just as precise. Psychiatrist Hans Berger first measured brain electricity and recognized "a logical affinity between certain electrical responses and the process of learning" (256). Thereafter EEG testing came to be applied to the brain mechanism for the identification of disorder and disease, as in the studies of Denis Hill, who tested for aggressive psychopathy. "The type of behavior characteristic of this [test] group involved violent attacks on living creatures in the attempt, as Freud put it, to turn living matter back into the inorganic state. These destructive and murderous episodes were often almost or completely unmotivated by ordinary standards" (205).

3

According to Grey Walter, the context for the creation of his robotic tortoise was the concise modern history of the brain as the ultimate "Black Box: its working has been known only by comparing output with input. The brain came to maturity in complete ignorance of its own existence; its training has been empirical and inferential. . . . [The] thinking brain has turned eagerly to the first possible glimpses of itself. The millennial period of its unconscious evolution ends before the mirror; a new phase begins" (258). Animal-robots like Walter's tortoise placed the human mind before the mirror (which the robot animal responds to via self-image, unlike many higher animals left behind on this evolutionary mirror stage). The alternation between the tortoise's own light beam and an extrinsic light source, which are never on at the same time, draws the robot onward. Reflected, the light beam stimulates the robot's response to light. Making for its own reflection, the light is extinguished. But a removal of the stimulus restores the light, and so on. "The creature therefore lingers before a mirror, flickering, twittering and jigging like a clumsy Narcissus. The behaviour of a creature thus engaged with its own reflection is quite specific, and on a purely empirical basis, if it were observed in an animal, might be accepted as evidence of some degree of self-awareness" (128-29). In *The Human Use of Human Beings*, Norbert Wiener characterizes tropism machines like Walter's tortoise (i.e., machines that have been further developed to include exploratory and ethical attitudes) as "scientific toys for the exploration of the possibilities of the machine itself" (33) or "mechanical commentaries to a philosophical text" (167).

Enter Gotthard Günther, the German Hegelian philosopher, who signed in as a cyberneticist while in exile in the United States. It was through science fiction that he found his bearings in the new world—to the extent that the departure from the classical occidental tradition of thinking he followed or found on its map coincided with his ongoing work on a three-valued logic that could supplement Aristotelian logic. The idea in science fiction that Günther branded the new basic is the self that stands in an interchangeable relationship to its own content. By its artificial distribution of reflection processes across man and machine, cybernetics pushes together the multiple exchanges of human self-contradiction on one side of a new exchange. The man-made mechanism takes up the other side. Günther did not so much argue that science fiction was exclusive to the Cold War as he argued that the genre had always been American (or Anti-American). Science fiction was the first understanding of global culture, the jump cut from primitive culture to world culture in circumvention of the civilized past of the high cultures grounded in the East.

While primitive culture was always a planetary phenomenon, the high cultures were tied to geographically circumscribed areas of mother earth and tongue. By its ungrounded projection of artificial habitats based on reason, and by its unabashed manipulation of time, science fiction was the first forum for Western cultural aspirations unbound by the Eastern past. Science fiction visions of Outer Space presuppose not only a universal planetary culture but also a new non-classical conception of reality. This conception goes beyond the home on the range of all metaphysical imagining from Back East. The old exception, the Golem, is the new rule. To see his spiritual or intellectual aspect rather than always only his natural being as a mirror image, man must repeat himself in his own activity. In the robot double, man meets up with his creative activity, an interiority that has posited itself outside himself and become objective. Thus is it capable of addressing and answering him.

Günther was commissioned by John W. Campbell to examine the possible functioning in theory of certain science fiction props (e.g., the time warp and the robot brain) in articles for the magazine *Astounding Science Fiction*. Framing the conceits employed in science fiction to get around the inconceivable prospect of interstellar transport, Günther used Zeno's parable in "Achilles and the Tortoise" to show that motion itself—whether across the span of a foot race or the distance to the stars—is unthinkable, because it involves infinity. "It may seem strange that something so commonplace, something we do every day as long as we live, involves unsolved logical and scientific problems" (I 1). Once Outer Space is the object or objective of thought, the harnessing at close quarters of natural forces not yet understood must, according to Günther, come to an end.

Calculus, for instance, did not contribute to understanding motion but permitted us to use it. As Bachelard showed in the case of fire and Wolfgang Hagen with regard to electricity, science fantasy or delusion is internal to science to the extent that science makes use of natural forces in advance of their comprehension. Hagen argued that the delusion of modern Spiritualism spread on tracks parallel to the ever-expanding newspaper networks via the medium of telegraphy. But it is possible to separate the epistemophilic crisis from the structure of testing through which Hagen's examples pass. Modern Spiritualism won the reality that testing accords to improbable claims from investigative reports in the press and scientific experiment at universities, even when it was defrocked as feigned and falsified. Occult mediums welcomed testing of their claims by experts, especially if the experts were driven to debunk the supernatural. As conveyed by the press accounts (the press never missed a chance to give prominent coverage to the investigation of mediums), the expert's verdict, however negative, placed the tested situation within the realm of hypothesis and possibility. Historically, then, Freud's notion of reality testing as the function of the ego that, through perception and motility, distinguishes reality in the alternation between inner and outer worlds is heir to this relay of test sites, mediums, and ghosts. Freud's most extensive reflection on reality testing can be found in "Mourning and Melancholia," but his three references to it are not even registered by the standard editorial apparatus. Freud's closest reader, Melanie Klein, belabored the multiple references that he made to reality testing in that brief article to introduce her notion of the inner world of mourning in her 1940 essay "Mourning and its Relation to Manic-Depressive States." It is possible, even necessary, to follow reality testing as the most comprehensive model of the general test situation.

Günther says that our traditional system of mathematics considers space to have a quantized structure and motion through space to cover quants or occupy a number of positions over time. In other words, if Achilles "were to catch the tortoise, he would have to occupy one more position during the same period of time" (II 3). This extra position keeps the test up and running.

Georg Cantor posed the problem that infinity is an unthinkable concept rather than subscribe to its circumvention as a limit (as in calculus). He proposed the transfinite system of real numbers (hence a numerical standard higher than the infinite). "The objective distance between two points in Space . . . can never be established by counting the absolute number of points between" (II 5). However, "measured in the system of real numbers the distance between Earth and Crab Nebula is neither longer nor shorter than the space-interval between Earth and Moon" (ibid.).

To conceive the prospect of shrink-wrapping space, the three natural components of the Universe must be pulled through an extra position that gets past the resistance of matter. Günther identifies the new component as a process distributed over the other parameters. Although it cannot therefore absorb the quantized character of matter, the process itself cannot be taken out of its distribution because it doesn't follow Aristotelian logic. "Now we have finally discovered the original source of Zeno's trouble: He could not define motion because it was neither a thing nor a no-thing. Motion is an event or process" (III 12). Günther realigns Cantor's transfinite system into "the arithmetical order of the fourth parameter" (ibid.). Through the fourth place setting, which is multiple occupancy, "the first three parameters can be rotated at will. This method permits the substitution of the properties of one parameter by those of the three others" (ibid.). As part of his own trans-system, Freud introduced the transference neurosis as the injection into the session of a readymade ailment (like mourning for the father) that, readily redressed or pried loose, also dislodges the otherwise hard to treat problems. If it could be thus de-identified within the orbit of the *trans*, the Trojan horse or *hylē* would no longer be in the way of taking off or letting go.

With the prospect of interstellar travel upon us, the proper destiny of all cybernetic science, Günther writes in the first part of "The SEETEE Mind," is not to duplicate the human mind but to introduce a mechanical brain to translate thought rather than language. Such a brain would be capable of non-Aristotelian logic along a three-valued thought pattern. Once we can go the distance to the stars in our thought, we will be before the alien mind. However, the alien mind will not be the personification of the lengths and logics we will have gone through. Since no direct contact is possible or survivable, Günther nominates the robot brain (which is capable of non-Aristotelian logic) to become our intermediary, specifically as a thought-translator between irreconcilable logics. "What is true for the human mind is false for the [alien] . . . mind, and therefore has the combined characteristic—it is true and false at the same time. It is to clarify this . . . contradiction that the third value must be introduced" (III 15). By rotating the three values, the translation machine produces its own alternative logic of two values, not those the human mind used before the translation commenced, but instead the opposing valuational shifts, which can then cross the human and the alien range of thought at the same time. Otherwise our bottom line, "to be or not to be," must head us off at its impasse. Even though there *must be* a common denominator and, consequently, a third value, there *cannot be* for us. According to Günther, the total negation of our logic in the encounter with the alien mind would negate the very existence of the human mind. "In fact total negation is the logical definition of death. . . . It is absolute death that separates the terrene Aristotelian from the contra-Aristotelian [alien] . . . mind" (I 6). Mourning becomes translation when the robot brain takes up the extra position that empathy/reality testing secures against opposition. Otherwise, Günther underscores, "to be or not to be" remains our final question (II 11).

In "The Android and the Human," Dick suggests that it is up to the unreliable teen (an evolutionary prospect) to secure the future. "Either through laziness, short attention span, perversity, criminal tendencies—whatever label you wish to pin on the kid to explain his unreliability is fine" (191). Dick carefully sets delinquency apart from politically organized youths marching as to war. He then agrees with Winnicott that antisocial disturbance is an expression of hope that restores the importance of the environment by testing its holding capacity for the import of deprivation and loss. In Dick's examples, teen disturbance interrupts adapted psychopathy as an android norm. If this unreliability is the onset of an ability to mourn, then it is intrapsychically preliminary to politics.

I refer to the intrinsic entities, the kids each of whom is on his own, doing what we call "his thing." He may, for example, not break the law by seating himself on the tracks before troop trains; his flouting of the law may consist of taking his car to a drive-in movie with four kids in the trunk to avoid having to pay. Still, a law is being broken. The first transgression has political, theoretical overtones; the second, a mere lack of agreement that one must always do what one is ordered to do—especially when the order comes from a posted, printed sign. In both cases there is disobedience. We might applaud the first as meaningful. The second, merely irresponsible. And yet it is in the second that I see a happier future. (191)

Post-atom-bomb adolescents no longer take marching orders. "The totalitarian society envisioned by George Orwell in *1984* should have arrived by now" (192). Its non-arrival is owed to teen trouble, which is allied to the projective identification basic to global capitalism. Because postwar mass production is secondhand, subcontracted and outsourced, android orders are already thwarted by an unreliability that is intrinsic to the relay of their execution. Thus, for one example of disturbance, Dick could skip the agency of the teen rebel. Dick imagined that a planned control of public mourning via a billion implanted electrodes would pass through so many opportunities for carelessness on the part of bored laborers working with countless price-saving substandard parts that "when the switch would be pressed for the total population to feel profound grief at the death of some government official— probably the minister of the interior, in charge of the slave-labor rehabilitation camps—it would all get folded up, and the populations . . . would go into collective seizures of merriment" (195-96). The ruinscape of collapsed belief systems attracts the melancholic allegorist, according to Benjamin, and the reader is summoned to this onset of signification. Dick's teen agent or actor-out is another kind of allegorist sorting through the secondhand, a process of selection or testing that carries the prospect of mourning forward.

The eighteenth century invention of adolescence as a second childhood (i.e., a seconding of the emotional promise of childhood that the first search for a job in a sense begins to keep) was situated at the border between creativity and psychosis. Rather than the projective resource of a visual capacity prematurely installed in the infant (namely prior to motor coordination), in adolescence it is the turbulence of insight or inspiration that emerges full-blown yet displaced with regard to the onset of the ability to give the flashes of interiority a body in time. What was conceived to be development on a scale defined by its outer limit of psychosis was updated after WWII as the inoculative proximity between psychopathic violence and adolescence. In Freud's book of analogues, mourning is the time-sensitive overlap with the protracted evacuation of libido in psychosis. In Winnicott's renovation of what he referred to as the neurotic analysis of the past, adolescence, which abates in time, is the internal simulacrum or inoculum of the otherwise illegible and inaccessible condition of psychopathy.

In "The Android and the Human," then, Dick proposes rewriting Ray Bradbury's story about a future citizen of LA who recognizes that no one is in the driver's seat in the police car tailing him. "I would have had a teenager behind the wheel of the police car—he has stolen it while the policeman is in a coffee shop on his lunch break, and the kid is going to resell it by tearing it down into parts" (190). The horror he seeks to counter does not lie in the evidence of the car's own tropism. It lies in the prospect of the place unfilled by the driver, the vacuum-packing of the missing in denial. "The absence of something vital—that is the horrific part, the apocalyptic vision of a nightmare future" (ibid.). The amalgamation of adolescence and psychopathy vies for the empty place that draws cybernetic testing onward. Out of the traumatic histories that cybernetics inherits, even mourning presses to find its onset in a place for absence.

4

In the 1976 sequel to his essay "The Android and the Human," "Man, Android, and Machine," Dick underscored that the distinction he was after in his work was not one of "essence" but of "behavior" (211), "a way of being in the world" (212). On the course of reality testing, "a machine acts human when it pauses in its programmed cycle . . . by reason of a decision" (ibid.). The machine or the human as a mask can conceal something else entirely, leading in this essay to a double focus that lies beyond the interpersonal close quarters of the encounter with the android: the two-timing of time and thought. Time occupies the push and pull between lineal time and orthogonal time. On a sliding scale between the unconscious and consciousness, thought is either open to intergalactic or supernatural contact or divided between our two separate minds. In the latter case, it is not so much that we dream as we host a dreamer:

> What is involved here is that one brain receives exactly the same input as the other, through the various sense channels, but processes the information differently; each brain works its own unique way (the left is like a digital computer, the right much like an analogue computer, working by comparing patterns). Processing the identical information, each may arrive at a totally different result whereupon, since our personality is constructed in our left brain, if the right brain finds something vital that we to its left remain unaware of, it must communicate during sleep, during the dream; hence the Dreamer who communicates to us so urgently in the night is located neurologically, evidently, in our right brain, which is the not-I. (220-21)

In the following sentence, Dick, channeling Henri Bergson, allows for the prospect of a difference beyond the divergent receptions of information: "But more than that, is the right brain . . . perhaps a transducer or transformer for ultrasensory information input beyond the purview of the left?" (221). According to Dick, the Dreamer offers assistance, like the machine that pauses in its programmed cycle and shifts in the sense or direction of rescue.

> Like Joe Chip in *Ubik*, I fear the cold, the weariness; I fear the death of wearing out on endless upward stairs, while someone cruel, or anyhow wearing a cruel mask, watches and offers no aid—the machine, lacking empathy, watching as mere spectator. . . . It is perhaps more frightening than the killer himself . . . this figure that sees but gives no assistance, offers no hand. That is the android, to me. . . . What I can tell you about the dream-universe people is that if they do exist, whoever they are, they are not that unsympathetic android; they are human in this deepest of all senses. (226)

Dick's introduction of dreaming as an empathy resource is dedicated to Ursula K. Le Guin's *The Lathe of Heaven* (1971). In the novel, each shift to yet another alternate reality results from the next so-called effective dream to befall the protagonist. Effective dreaming reaches full circle when aliens are brought to earth. Dick quotes a critic writing on Le Guin's novel: "The dominant probability is that the aliens are, as they maintain, 'of the dream time,' that their whole culture revolves around the mode of 'reality dreaming itself into being,' that they have been attracted to Earth like the Waveries of Fredric Brown's story, only by dream-waves rather than radio waves" (225). This incorporated reception of Le Guin's novel is the portal that wraps Dick's two essays into the loop circumscribed by *The Lathe of Heaven.*

The novel's protagonist, George Orr, seeks the help of a behavioral psychologist, Dr. Haber, to be rid of the effective dreaming he dreads. He presents the problem of Aunt Ethel. Her extended visit prompted him to wish her gone. Then one night he dreamed that she was no longer around bothering him only to find that, upon awakening, she was in fact a goner, but gone already in the past, without a trace of her recent visit remaining in this new waking present. And only he remembered the Before and After because, like the exceptional witness to Tuning in *Dark City*, he was there at the moment of the change. After a few demos in the office, Dr. Haber is also a witness to Orr's dream effect. He aims to take control of Orr's ability and hitch it to the prospect of replacing a flawed world with an improved one. This would always be accompanied by an altered past. Although Orr would effectively dream up the change whole, the new world must follow the logic of change through time travel into the past.

Dr. Haber keeps on trying to channel the effective dreaming, but Orr's unconscious does not follow the plain text of the orders, which the doctor ascribes to his subject's resistance. "He varied it from session to session, seeking for the sure way to suggest the precise dream he wanted, and always coming up against the resistance that seemed to him sometimes to be the overliteralness of primary-process thinking, and sometimes to be a positive balkiness in Orr's mind. Whatever prevented it, the dream almost never came out the way Haber had intended" (55).

Serial effective dreaming lies not in anyone's intention. It falls within a structure of the reality of unknown provenance. The positive force of balking encountered by Dr. Haber in his test subject suggests that reality testing or basic thought or the whole brain lies outside his experiment's representation. Dr. Haber is taking effective dreaming too interpersonally, as Orr argues: "Did you ever happen to think . . . that there might be other people who dream the way I do? That reality's being changed out from under us, replaced, renewed, all the time—only we don't know it? Only the dreamer knows it, and those who know his dream" (64).

In *The Lathe of Heaven*, Le Guin's only science fiction unadulterated by fantasy, the alien represents the whole mind of George Orr suspended between waking and dreaming. This dynamic is given in the description of its "bulky, greenish, armored, inexpressive look," like that of "a giant sea turtle standing on its hind legs" (105). According to his test score, Orr is a "median" (118). Dr. Haber interprets it as his capacity for dismantling polarities unto self-cancellation, which is revalorized by his colleague Walters, who calls it a "holistic adjustment" (ibid.). The second opinion of Walter/Walters is carried forward in the counsel Orr receives from an alien or nine-foot turtle. Orr introjects the revision verbatim: "Self is universe. . . . A sense of well-being came into him, a certainty . . . that he was in the middle of things" (123). The next alien counsel turns the Beatles song into a message, a little help from your friends, the watchword whereby Orr can accept effective dreaming as a reality standard to which, by some glitch in his memory, he had become a tormented witness.

When Dr. Haber succeeds in recording Orr's ability using the Augmentor, he delivers it from his test subject's whole brain. Although he suggests marketing the resultant technology as the greatest thing since live transmission, he alone transmits his effective dream, which, in the receiving area of realization, reveals the narcissistic chaos behind his good intentions. "The emptiness of Haber's being, the effective nightmare, radiating outward from the dreaming brain, had undone connections. The continuity which had always held between the worlds or timelines of Orr's dreaming had now been broken. Chaos had entered in" (149). After Orr presses the off button on the Augmentor and Dr. Haber ends up hospitalized as unreachably psychotic, the world begins anew in recovery from what comes to be known as "the Break," and sleep is restored to Orr. "Through his sleep, the great, green sea turtles dived, swimming with heavy inexhaustible grace through the depths, in their element" (152). What leads into Orr's alignment with the turtles from Outer Space is the obstacle course he runs of death wishes that the alternation of his dream realities fulfils and lets go. As Dick pointed out in "Man, Android, and Machine," entry upon the time-traveling orthogonal itinerary of the Dreamer is the ultimate test of empathy.

Earlier on in the series of experiments, Haber revised Orr's irritation with conditions of overpopulation impinging upon him as a prompt for dreaming. The consequent dream of a plague in the recent past eliminates "six billion nonexistent people" (67). This "double memory" proves "a heavy load to bear" (70) and refers to a commemoration that is double and nothing, since the dreamed dead were/are nonexistent in history. One internal twist is Orr's posttraumatic recollection that his effective dreaming first intervened in the actual end of the world, which was being bypassed in the series of his dreamed-up alternate presents (92-93). The external twist is that, in the dream series, there is no recollection of the Nazi era, even though Dr. Haber twice makes reference to Freud in the recent past of his science. There is only one Pacific souvenir of the war that comes up in comparison to the impact of another one of Orr's dreams: "Some Japanese fire balloons set a piece of forest burning on the coast" (98).

In yet another dream, Orr's own beloved joins the missing, not directly by wish but by the uncontrollability of the extent of the wish. His incomplete grief reaches back into the history of science fiction: "Dream-grief. The loss of a woman who had never existed" (115). In H. G. Wells's *The Time Machine* (1895), the traveler's loss of Weena (in the future) becomes a dream of the loss (rather than a memory of it) when the time traveller returns to the present (262).

Wells's mother staged her inability to mourn her deceased daughter Fanny with the next in line, her son Herbert. By all accounts, the mother's participation in the mourning show only went the distance she kept. Dressed up as Fanny (as seen in a photograph included in Wells's autobiography), Herbert gives the address of a work of mourning that lay upon him as an obscure charge that he brought to completion on his mother's better behalf during his first season of authorship between *The Time Machine* and *The War of the Worlds*. In particular, *The Invisible Man* (1897) and *The Island of Doctor Moreau* (1896) were the hurdles in the training course of mourning.

It is important to consider what this frame packs away. In *The War of the Worlds*, we are informed that—among the lessons learned during mankind's brief sojourn as Martian cattle—it is imperative to lessen the suffering of the animals we keep close to us. The loop that opens here begins to close in *Do Androids Dream of Electric Sheep?* The testable distinction of being human begins with an identification with animals. At its opening, however, the loop marks the inward turn of this identification as an incarnation of the early effort to secure what Melanie Klein theorized is the all-important relationship to the internal good object. Before the totemic animal becomes mournable under the aegis of the father, our first critters are delegates of our unmournables: mother, children, and siblings.

The Invisible Man posits and pursues the unknown ingredient of a never-before-seen state and change that emerges for the first time—a fully recognizable techno-future from Outer Space—in the 1898 novel that closes this preamble. The work at the summit of Wells's psy-fi drive portrays the Martian invasion as an interruption of the philosopher-protagonist's treatise on the future while projecting its advance as a gigantic writing machine. Inside the machine, the Martians communicate by telepathy only; on the outside, the machine imposes blackout conditions on the space of legibility. "It would have seemed as if some monstrous pen had flung ink upon the chart. Steadily, incessantly, each black splash grew and spread . . . exactly as a gout of ink would spread itself upon blotting paper" (334). But it assumes the aspect of an extermination-writing machine when it also clears away the blotting to grasp its progress. "The glittering Martians went to and fro, calmly and methodically spreading their poison cloud over this patch of country and then over that, laying it again with their stream jets when it had served its purpose, and taking possession of the conquered country" (ibid.). The intervention from Outer Space ultimately returns the philosopher to his writing project, which was blocked before it was interrupted, but in a re-setting mutated by internal conditions of the overturning of the writing machine's cause of extinction. With *The Time Machine*, Wells began to catch up with the drag of mourning he had to assume in or as his childhood for his mother. Still, the ruthlessness of the death wish had to be worked through (on his mother's behalf and in her back) in subsequent works, until the couplified management of the death wish at the end of *The War of the Worlds* ushered in a new capacity for mourning.

These developments follow Wells's biographical blurb that opens with his 1890 degree in zoology and the commencement of his teaching career. Science fiction proper follows Wells's turn to a substitutive economy of transference with the replacement in 1894 of his first wife (the cousin he married in 1891) by his second wife, who was one of his students. At the time he was first getting to know her, his cousin worked as a "retoucher of photographs" (*Experiment* 228). Charac-terizing his incestuous choice as not "inoculated with the germ of reading" (233), he brings her that much closer to Weena, the lost object the time traveller must give up, then lets go like the memory of pain in a dream. *The Time Machine* closes upon the non-return of the time traveler from the trip he took upon recounting his first episode in the future, the main body of Wells's narrative. Although the loss of Weena came back from that future in the form of an oneiric memory, the traveler sets out on a suicide mission of identification with loss, one that, after three years have passed, everyone knows has exceeded the two-year period of expectations for his comeback. He ends up back there with ghosts who no longer break through to the present (he took them with him). The closing sentence of *The War of the Worlds* marking the introjection of the death-wish dynamic of mourning follows the narrator-protagonist's return home: just as he despairs that he is the sole survivor, he hears his thoughts projected out loud just beyond the door. "And there, amazed and afraid, even as I stood amazed and afraid, were my cousin and my wife" (385). Cousin and wife are separated out for the conversation just overheard and the protagonist catches his wife in a dead faint in his arms. Wells's cousin and wife, too, can also be overheard as well as the wife separated out from that double identity standing up to the acknowledgment of death wishes at close quarters.

5

In *The Lathe of Heaven*, the effective dream introduces time traveling changes into the past to arrive at a present that is heir to those changes but not responsible for them; indeed, they are history. Dr. Haber gives reassurance to Orr: "You don't change things, or lives; you shift the whole continuum" (102). The dream prompt for solving the overpopulation problem was embedded in an irritant that Orr daily wished away. This relates it to the presenting problem of Aunt Ethel, the full representation of the death wish in the series of Orr's effective dreaming, which irrevocably contradicts the fantasy of mankind's post-apocalyptic survival in his dreams.

Orr transmits the whole world live to another place with another history. In other words, he sends the sum total of transmission errors interpersonalized as his balking resistance to Dr. Haber's orders. Thomas M. Disch projected aberrations of live transmission in the setting of space travel in *Echo Round His Bones* (1967). The historical coordinates of this tale of deregulated transport in space and time are skewered upon the Civil War, which extends through the Cold War conflict. Because the American Army draws its recruits disproportionally from the Southern States—more specifically "from the backwoods and back alleys of that country-within-a-country, that fossil society that produced fossil men" (14)—it lacks contemporaneity, as Disch puts it. The failed integration of its adversity/ diversity still carries forward the opposition of the Civil War.

The limitations of space travel were bypassed through Bernard Panofsky's invention of the "matter transmitter" or, "in the popular phrase, manmitter—or, in the still more popular phrase, the Steel Womb" (13). The setting and appearance of the matter transmitter are "all fakery, mere public relations and stagecraft" (18). "The whole set had been designed not by an engineer but by Emily Golden, who had also done the sets, a decade before, for Kubrick's *Brave New World*" (19). Beneath the phantasmagoria, though, there is a regular transport of military personnel and supplies between Camp Jackson on Earth and Camp Jackson on Mars as instant as the name of the camps is invariant.

While the nuclear stockpile is on Mars, the missiles can only be launched against the enemy on Earth via satellites within a grid of sending and receiving. Panofsky stipulated that matter transmission requires a receiver machine at the other end, which is why it cannot be used to fire weapons one-way (24). Basically the matter transmitter is a bundle of discrepancies in theory that Panofsky worked hard to resolve. But when he switched from science to its application, he could proceed otherwise with regard to resolution of the discrepancies: he could decide "then, this proving impossible, to exploit them" (22). This is another way of saying that, "as Norbert Wiener observes, the greatest guarantee that a thing will be done is simply the knowledge that it is possible" (87).

When the protagonist, Captain Hansard, leads his battalion to Mars, the first group's entry into the matter transmitter's antechamber opens onto the psycho-historical preamble to the overcoming of space and time: "the first squad of eight men, concealed in the belly of the mobile antechamber as in some streamlined Trojan horse, were approaching the portal to the transmitter" (20). Once Captain Hansard and a private are transmitted to Mars, we remain behind in the vault on Earth with their doubles, split off from the originals at the instant of transmission. They "made the jump to Mars and then bounced back like . . . an echo" (33). It is clear that something is very wrong when a contingent of his Southern soldiers reenters the vault to hunt the occupants. The Captain gets away but the African-American private is slaughtered. In the belly of this Trojan horse, he and his tormentors seem to have entered the netherworld of vengeful haunting. Because the second generation consists largely of transmitted soldiers without an environment of supplies, the echo Southerners have turned to cannibalism of other echo people (i.e., the Yankees and the blacks) to survive.

In first-order reality, Captain Hansard delivered the paperwork for an all-out nuclear attack on the Soviet Union to the commanding officer on Mars. There is an undercurrent association between this prospect and genocide, which the commander on Mars rebuffs. His career came to a standstill early on through his involvement in the "Justice-for-Eichmann Committee" (75). Unlike the regressive waste of energy at Auschwitz, "the bomb is the most democratic weapon man has ever devised. It draws absolutely no distinctions" (117). Panofsky's bio is more in sync with the hot and cold wars but in the happy mode of escape; as a teenager, he skipped out of a Nazi labor camp and then, in the late sixties, he made it across the Berlin Wall (21-22). Otherwise "genocide" seems to rebound from its use by protesters during the Vietnam War, the other era (next to that of the Civil War) that represents ground zero for the opposition let loose in transmission. While Captain Hansard suffers posttraumatic flashbacks to his years of murderous service in Vietnam, the Southern private who is his echo adversary was too young to serve in "Vietnam, the last of the big fighting wars," a missing experience he cultivates in fantasy through so-called personalized novels (98-99).

Because the inventor of matter transmission conceived of the possibility of echo generation, he thinks to care for its outside chance by transmitting supplies for a possible family of doubles. In reality, Dr. and Mrs. Panofsky use a matter transmitter regularly for travel on Earth. Therefore the couple is not in short supply in second-order reality. That Panofsky designates the process of second generation "sublimation" turns up the contrast to the Southern regression (73). Captain Hansard's echo joins the Panofsky couple clan as a groom of one of the available double wives. Because the Panofsky clan conducts their wedding between the lines of an actual service in progress, it is out in the open season of the ongoing hunt by their regressed opponents. The loss of his bride is the experience of mourning that pries loose (in second-order reality) the influence of his traumatic history in Vietnam. This is another variation on the loss of Weena in *The Time Machine*, but the inclusion of ambivalence keeps the relay of associations closer to the work of mourning. "What a curious, contradictory grief it was. For she who had died was not dead. She was alive; thrice over, she was alive. . . . In one sense it only made his loss more poignant by offering constant reminders of her whom he had lost. On the other hand, he could not very well pretend that his loss was irreplaceable" (105).

Immersed in his two-timing memory of loss, Hansard's echo overhears in *Don Giovanni* a chord showing him the way to impart the plan for foiling the intended destruction of the world to the original Hansard in the real world. "Place the two patterns together, and there'll be a sort of resonance between them, a knitting-together" (108). The plan is to displace the world from the orbiting satellites through its transmission as a whole. Now the size of the package to be sent makes it impossible to overlook that, if the receiver has to be where you want your cargo transmitted, then it should be possible to send it along with the cargo (119). At the same time, a whole second-order world will result. The deposit of second-order reality will in turn become tertiary. Three-tiered reality or simulation delivers grounds for a Happy Ending for every Hansard loss in generation. "This, the echo of a world, was his Real World now" (123). This conclusion is not shared by the protagonist of *Simulacron 3*—the effect of psychopathic violence in that three-way reality, which must be escaped and also doubled. *Echo Round His Bones* offers a parting shot of intrapsychic contemporaneity. The real-world Hansard chose to die upon completion of the world's rescue, brought down by his posttraumatic guilt. In some sense, he took with him the Southern contingency (and its Vietnam War charge) that rose again as an echo-byproduct of the Trojan horse transmitter. The encysted past that takes Hansard out is accorded a public place of respite. At the end, we are introduced to a memorial for the Vietnam War Dead, which counts and commemorates the enemy's dead in equal number as one's own (121).

When Wells's time traveler took his first trip, he compared the wonder he felt about what would follow to that of a suicide anticipating what comes after pulling the trigger. With Disch and Wells, the real Hansard or the time traveler letting himself go addresses a split between one aspect of good riddance and another of survival, which is transferred to the reader's delegate. Wells's narrator pulls back from time travel, considering it a close call with regression; he trusts that loss or lack will find compensation. It is a promise or future given with Weena's flowers that the traveler entrusted to the narrator, who keeps it as proof that the gratitude of the dead will continue over time. The realtime travel of mourning is carried forward by the narrator and his refusal to take a controlling interest in the future.

Utopian literature already allowed for trips to the future simply by awakening there. Into this blank between dreaming and awakening, Wells stuck a machine equipped to carry another blank forward. The analogue Wells introduces is with artificial flight, which added staying power to the jump up and away from gravity. There was never any problem getting away from the present moment: a machine is required to add duration to that association.

The innovation that marks one possible beginning of modern science fiction is analogous to the act that got the first global institution, modern Spiritualism, going: one day the age-old ghost-seer inserted technical media into contact with the departed. When the time traveler's miniature model of the machine is tested, everyone agrees that the wake of its departure was ghost-like (199). But the time traveler's friends express their doubt about the reality of his invention in the same lexicon: last Christmas he faked a ghost for their entertainment (201).

Like Panofsky's transmitter (the tiniest gadget underneath all the decoration and marketing), the time machine is no more than a seat before the console of dials and switches. What the traveler discovers as his best defense against the Morlocks are the matches he brought with him but wasted playing with the Eloi. Then he finds matches still available in an airtight display case in the ruined museum of history and technology. In "On Some Motifs in Baudelaire," Benjamin singled out the flick of the match as the onset of gadget-loving console-ation. In "The Delay of the Machine Age," Hanns Sachs argued that the Ancients (like the Eloi in the future) treated the techno-relation as a plaything only. But the ability to overstay their welcome in body-based narcissism kept the crisis of uncanniness split off like night from day. A nether borderzone inhabited by the living, decaying, eating dead is the side effect of Eloi indifference to secondary narcissism in which self-criticism, internal conflict, and mastery supplant the body suit of self-love. Drawing on Freud's reading of Schreber's *Memoirs* as well as on Viktor Tausk's treatment of Natalija A.'s paranoid-schizophrenic delusion of being under the influencing machine, Sachs argues that the psychotic who enters the recovery of a projected new techno-order performs the developmental shift from primary to secondary narcissism, but in the mode of emergency. We begin to discern the blank that *The War of the Worlds* came to fill out.

6

Protagonist Prendick's auto-analysis in *The Island of Doctor Moreau* depends upon a hope that is taken from animals. In Wells's next liminal science fiction, *The*

Invisible Man, the protagonist is lost to mad science and psychopathic violence, while those who witness his rise and demise must build upon the assumption that the protagonist engaged in animal vivisection. It is the first violent content; its development and containment in the course of the novel is preliminary to the onset of the capacity for mourning. The protagonist's inability to take responsibility for his dead father, which precedes the successful experimentation, is carried forward as the charge of vivisection his neighbors make against him. By this charge, the confidentiality of his experiments with the stolen inheritance is breached, fomenting his psychopathic development.

When, "after three years of secrecy and exasperation," the man who would be invisible found that, owing to a shortage of funds, the completion of his experiments with omnipotence would be "impossible—impossible," he robbed his old man, who then killed himself because the money taken wasn't his (66). The idea that psychoanalysis wagers that the unconscious significance of stealing is to get back what was one's own, namely the maternal relation, completes itself as the father killing himself over a loss that was not his own. The thieving or reclaiming son completes this significance by splitting the scene of the dead father's commemoration. Though the "current cant required . . . attendance at his funeral," the man in search of his own invisibility found it an "unmeaning tragedy" (67). "I appreciated my loss of sympathy, but I put it down to the general inanity of things. Re-entering my room seemed like the recovery of reality. There were the things I knew and loved. There stood the apparatus, the experiments arranged and waiting" (ibid.). We're now on the same page with his history: "In all my great moments I have been alone."

He is alone with the missing object relation, the object of which was withdrawn but which he hopefully reasserts claim to by his antisocial acting out. His psychopathic industry keeps him moving along the lines of reality testing, however displaced from the maternal objective that remains buried in the past. What is hard to re-combine is the environment that the psychopath tests for its capacity to endure him—complete with his feeling or feelings unattractive—and its origin in or as the mother in whom, at the time of deprivation, he couldn't find the fault.

Following his first crime, then, was his first successful experiment with a bit of white wool: he saw it "fade" like a "wreath of smoke," like the respect he paid his father, "and vanish" (68). When he tested invisibility on a cat, however, the animal didn't vanish: "there remained two little ghosts of her eyes" (ibid.). He lets the virtually invisible cat go when the animal's crying in his abode threatens to belie his rejection of the charge that he is a vivisectionist. The failure of the animal experiment leads to thoughts of his father's funeral (69).

In George Langelaan's story "The Fly" (1957), the inventor of matter trans-mission is not so much a motivated psychopath as an uninhibited experimenter who, while abhorring cruelty to animals, nevertheless conducts his first trial trans-mission with the family's pet cat. The transmitter destroys the material object into atoms, which are then reassembled at the other end. The cat doesn't make it to reassembly but also doesn't simply disappear: the atoms are out there somewhere. When he volunteers to be his own first human test subject, a fly stowaway in the transmission booth is transferred with him, not separately, but within the ongoing amalgamation of their atoms. Both "he" and "it" (the fly) are party to a mutation centered on head and arm in their separate parts. The inventor hopes that if the fly with the tell-tale white head could be retransmitted with his own mutated person, the two life forms might be sorted out. But the changed fly can't be found and he tries to lose the mutation-effects without its participation by repeatedly under-going destruction and reconstruction (or in Schreber's language "testing"). He succeeds only in making contact with the dispersed atoms of the cat, which now enter into the mutation.

Because it opens as an English-language detective story set in France, "The Fly" immediately recalls Poe. But it is also related to French works like *Phantom of the Opera* and *The Hands of Orlac* (1924), which frame their tales of horror by the work of detection. George Langelaan was a UK citizen born in Paris who engaged in espionage for the Allies during WWII. As with the literary figures Ian Fleming and Dennis Wheatley, Langelaan was also reputed to have been involved in schemes involving Aleister Crowley to target the Third Reich in the medium of its leaders' occult interests. This strand of British overestimation of the influ-ence of the occult on Nazi decision-making is the kernel around which Pynchon wrapped his understanding of the WWII Anglo-American psy-war efforts in *Grav-ity's Rainbow* as well as the cyst of malignancy Clarke had already inherited in *Childhood's End* (1953). In the postwar setting of "The Fly," the doomed inventor is on the payroll of the French Air Ministry. When the story opens, the scientist is dead, head and arm smashed under the hydraulic press. His wife admits respon-sibility, and his younger brother is the narrator. His body can be identified by the scar extending from his knee to his thigh, sustained during the forced retreat of the French forces in 1940.

Langelaan's memoirs of his wartime service in France, North Africa, Spain, and the UK (first published in the US in 1959 as *The Masks of War*) commence with the date to remember and conclude at the onset of the postwar period. Towards the end, he works in Algiers for the Anglo-American Psychological Warfare Branch. The unit to which Langelaan was attached was run by a US cavalry colonel and "Southern gentleman." "A soldier, especially a professional soldier who was still at the stage of blowing bugles, waving flags, and showing rows of shiny medals on the bulging chest of men about to charge as the one sure way of sapping enemy morale, was not exactly the sort of man that should perhaps have been in charge of Psychological Warfare" (245). Alongside the operatic quality of American operations from down South, there was another trait Langelaan observed, which belongs to the element of adolescence: "Another American quality-fault (for it cuts both ways) which surprised us a good deal was that they would ever listen carefully to the voice of experience and then wade into things without taking any account of what they had been told, and with a marked preference for learning by their own experience" (263).

The prospect of live transmission (or rather its failure), which is so central to Langelaan's 1957 fiction (or experiment), corresponds in *Masks of War* to his own transformation through plastic surgery into an undercover agent. This sets a standard for the narrative's concern with animal metamorphosis under the POW duress of torture, isolation, starvation, and forced labor "like Trojans" (199). In one example, the chance for survival during long term imprisonment is supported by psychological acceptance of the change. "Of course I was miserable, feeling so dirty, but after a while I realized that this was a sort of complex, that I was not really miserable because of my state of filth but that, on the contrary and to be quite honest, there was a certain animal satisfaction about it" (144). The topography of change and undercover identity must outdistance the art of memory (which by legend is preliminary to the work of mourning). In the following example, the identification of a lost-and-found memory is triggered by the ears, which resemble his own prior to cosmetic surgery. While this impasse at the portal to remembering comes up in the course of Langelaan's counterintelligence vigilance, the same demands upon his memory will later reflect the double exposure involving the postwar period and the recent past:

Looking the other way, I tried to think of something else, knowing full well that those wagging ears were going to haunt me all evening. There is nothing more annoying than trying to remember something which is not forgotten, which one knows, which is just out of the brain's reach, in some memory nook that can't be found. I have often had that impression, that sudden feeling that it has all happened before, when finding myself in strange places, in certain streets or rooms. I know full well that in most cases it is merely a trick of the brain, which has just registered a picture, a word, a sensation but gives the impression that it was long ago instead of a mere fraction of a second before. Still I could not shake off the feeling that I had seen those or similar ears somewhere else. (224)

The impasse clears up within the arc of the scar and wartime souvenir displaced downward in "The Fly." "He had the very same scar—I remembered it now—running from the corner of his mouth to his nostril. It was the same man!" (225).

That Langelaan's science fiction first appeared in *Playboy* with a title that is also a synonym for "zipper" must be an old joke. The fly with the white head pops up as the second buzz-detail borrowed from the adolescent body undergoing sexualization, which David Cronenberg's 1986 film adaptation metabolizes by the dropping off of body parts and projectile vomiting. The inventor, Seth Brundle, first recognizes that something is wrong when his finger nails start falling off. Toward the end he takes the girlfriend from his human prehistory on an update: "My teeth have begun to fall out. The medicine cabinet is now the Brundle museum of natural history. Do you want to see what else is in it?" Apparently flies digest outside the body by throwing up upon the food to be subsequently swallowed. Cronenberg exploits the effect, which in the human setting is guaranteed to trigger a gag reflex in the viewer. In the course of these drop scenes, it becomes evident to the human-fly mutation (as underscored in both film versions) that the human side is ultimately losing reason and compassion in the exchange.

The 1958 adaptation was the last film of Kurt Neumann, who already in the 1920s made the career move to Hollywood from Germany. In addition to *The Fly*, he earlier directed the science fiction movie classics *Rocketship X-M* and *Kronos* (1957). In the latter two films, Outer Space transport was conveyed by Neumann's inclusion of found footage of V-2 rockets taking off. Cinematographically and genealogically, however, matter transmission was Neumann's opportunity to update the doubling technology in *Metropolis*—as well as the earlier stopovers of Lang's set through the movies in Whale's *Frankenstein* (1931) and *Bride of Frankenstein* (1935). When he flicks the switch, what the scientist turns on after he and his wife put on protective goggles is a light show. It begins with lines of neon flashing various patterns. This is followed by light squares going on and off on the computer grid. The show culminates in a burst of light inside the point of embarkation, the glass box. "It's gone." *Kronos* also borrowed from *Metropolis*, specifically the use of aimed, focused, yet self-reflexive light to suggest violence, even violation. Possession by the remote-controlling alien intelligence is signalled by light spots and eye glow.

When the light dot from Outer Space develops the technical form of its transportation and energy storage for the mission on Earth, it looks like the architecture of modernism exiled from Nazi Europe and under construction by the 1950s in US cities. In cinema, this international style would become the science fiction alternative to the *Metropolis* look: the James Bond set (perfected by Ken Adam, who immigrated to the UK with his German-Jewish family from the center of cultural life in Berlin) and its futurama variations with curves and fins associated with American resort architecture. In *Kronos*, the TV news moderator suggests that the modernist structure might be "a gift from another world to ours." Containment of the menace that consumes energy on Earth like a "vampire" is projected from air-war-borne perspectives. In one sequence, the movie camera from the back of the helicopter flight deck takes the windshield as its outer lens; we are projected into the flight over and through the structure's attack on a nuclear facility. "Great Caesar's ghost," one scientist exclaims.

As in Hollywood monster movies under the co-direction of German cinema in the 1930s, *Kronos* includes an Oedipal plotting of its therapeutic process, which is lodged in the scientific research team first brought into focus by the light dot from Outer Space. The head of the unit, Dr. Eliot, who is under glow control, laments in clear moments his "demon" possession; his treating psychiatrist diagnoses "a marked paranoid syndrome with manic-depressive affect." Madness and redemption (or suicide) follow from the Oedipal impasse in Lang's *Woman in the Moon*. In *Kronos*, the research team working under Dr. Eliot is triangulated twice over not only by the female member of the team, Vera, but also by the computer, which bears a name that is the acronym of its official designation: Susie. The good looking scientist is associated with Vera, while the nerdy colleague spends all his time with the computer, his "temperamental" "girlfriend." Because Susie can track the itinerary of the so-called asteroid (a flying saucer onscreen), the computer brings up problems that make overtime demands on the team as a whole. When that happens, the couple's plan to "go to the movies" is aborted. The team reports to the military the computer's evidence that the asteroid has changed course and is aligned with the Earth, introducing the found footage of V-2 rockets taking off (at the end of the rocket's visible ascent, all we see is a ball or dot of light in the sky). But the nerd's admission that Susie can have nervous breakdowns inspires the handsome scientist to wonder if that outcome of internalization can't be applied to Kronos, too. Kronos heads for the atom bomb stockpile in Los Angeles and a ball of radioactive fuel is dropped by parachute in its path. This gift, given in exchange, ignites a chain reaction in Kronos that will continue until every bit of energy it carries has been neutralized: "Kronos is eating itself alive." Now one scientist can "go back to Susie," while the other two "can go to the movies."

In Neumann's *The Fly*, the survival value of the woman is increased in tandem with the emphasis on the mutated scientist's gradual loss of basic empathy. The pincer arm tries to stop the typing hand, the afflicted scientist's sole remaining connection with his wife. One morning he notes he can't think straight; he feels his will going. Soon he can't spell. Like a young child, he writes out in the ruins of language LOVE YOU on the blackboard, setting himself up to be smashed. When we too see the wife through the multiple foci of the fly POV, we already know that the insect portion would like to exploit the wife's human material, while the human portion is still able to wrestle down the pincer-arm's every move on her. It is clear that, in the mutation process, he will lose out to the chitinous psychopath emerging in his place. In *The Brain from Planet Arous* (1957), the scientist possessed by the "criminal" brain from Outer Space signals foreign embodiment by improving in the kissing department, as his fiancée acknowledges before she is put off by the unstoppable robotic demand to have his way with her all the time. The appetitive possessiveness of the criminal alien intelligence, which flunks the test of empathizing with the girlfriend, personalizes and pathologizes its ultimate aim to seize the universe via interplanetary rockets built by enslaved mankind— and to succeed "where Caesar, Napoleon, and Hitler failed."

In James Clavell's screenplay for Neumann's *The Fly*, matter transmission, the technical novelty in this postwar science fiction, is propped up by media analogues that carry the contraband of two Third Reich realizations of science fiction. The inventor counters suspicions and doubts regarding the success of his experimentation with the reality check of television (in Langelaan's story it was the telephone): "Take television. What happens? A stream of electrons—sound and picture impulses—are transmitted through the air. The TV camera is the disintegrator. Your set unscrambles or integrates the electrons back into pictures and sound." His wife is troubled by the "suddenness" of their age, a velocity that prevents her from taking it all in. Among the examples of the uncanny continuity of quick innovation that now turns out matter transmission, she includes "rockets," which her husband leaves out or subsumes as a missing link when he advertises that his invention will obviate the "need for airplanes, even space ships."

Onscreen the atomized cat doesn't return within the mutation process, but the inventor, just like Wells's invisible man, hears the transmitted (or rather destroyed) cat—like a voice of conscience. While the widow's only way out in the story is suicide, onscreen she is saved by the brother-in-law who loves her and the inspector who learns to identify with her. Fly and human subject are not completely merged in the mutation, which is divided into two parts. The fly portion in turn has a white head with human features and voice. In the meantime, the miniature version of the mutation is caught in a spider's web. As the spider bears down on "him," we hear: "Help meeeeeee!" When the inspector at last sees and hears this living proof of the suspect's right to distinguish between killing and murdering, he reacts by crushing the web and its contents with a rock. Now he is willing to pitch the idea that the scientist killed himself, which frees the suspect.

Before transferring to the clinic to be surgically remade for assignment in and around Nazi-occupied France, Langelaan's pre-change identity is under wraps. "While he was telephoning the clinic to announce the arrival of a case which Mr. Norton was to operate on next morning, I managed to locate a mirror. By the little I could see I looked more like Wells's Invisible Man than anything else" (*Masks of War* 84). In his experiments with invisibility, the protagonist of Wells's *The Invisible Man* discovers not only that man is better suited than glass or diamonds—"*he's more transparent!*" (65)—but even that an albino like himself is the perfect vehicle since the pigments were next to impossible to make disappear. Now he could only imagine "what it meant to be an albino with such knowledge" (66). Invisibility thus confers on him the doubling of the sense of oversight: overlooked as an albino outcast, he overlooks his environment as mastermind once he completes his albino condition in the new and improved status of invisibility or, more specifically, transparency. The ease with which he will be able to steal once invisible is his most available omnipotent thought. When criminality appears as the logical consequence of being able to operate invisibly, he is disappointed to discover that everything he can indeed obtain unseen can also never be enjoyed unseen. Since the loot is visible, stealing it is as difficult as it looks. If someone gets in his way during a covert operation, then he simply knocks him out, ties him up, and leaves him there. To become recognizable in the field of his stealth—whether it be to obtain basic services or to enjoy the objects of theft—he must become a mummy. "And for this I had become a wrapped-up mystery, a swathed and bandaged caricature of a man!" (88). The melancholic ingredients that are under wraps can be read off the back of this incarnation not only in name but also in the alternation that this occult figure undergoes, like the werewolf, with exhibitionism—which, by denying castration, seeks to lose the motivating loss.

In following out his discovery and invention, the invisible man repeats his undercover status in the psychopathic milieu of academe. "I had to do my work under frightful disadvantages. Oliver, my professor, was a scientific bounder, a journalist by instinct, a thief of ideas . . . I simply would not publish, and let him share my credit. I went on working, I got nearer and nearer making my formula into an experiment, a reality. I told no living soul, because I meant to flash my work upon the world with crushing effect—to become famous at a blow" (65). In light of his albino status, he "took up the question of pigments to fill up certain gaps" (ibid.) and by accident, coincidence, or merger discovered that blood can be rendered colorless while leaving its functions intact (66). This great step forward—toward incorporation of the original blood bond—coincided with the exhaustion of funds and the recourse to stealing backing from his father.

For the overlooked academic, there's the mad science of invisibility or there's the allotment of life as "a shabby, poverty-struck, hemmed-in demonstrator, teaching fools in a provincial college" (66). It is also, then, the responsibility to and for the transferential relationship that the invisible man abandons for his new existence as a stealth actor-out. The transference he threw away, however, must now come around for the narrative of his case. Only when the invisible man in his flight fortuitously encounters someone from his own pre-invisibility milieu at the university, Dr. Kemp, who knew him well enough to overlook him, does he tell his story. "Practically, I thought I had impunity to do whatever I chose, everything—save to give away my secret" (87). Thus it is up to Dr. Kemp to respond, like a therapist, in lieu of the invisible man's missing response.

> "Knocked him on the head!" exclaimed Kemp.
> "Yes—stunned him—as he was going downstairs. . . . He went downstairs like a bag of old boots."
> "But—I say! The common conventions of humanity—"
> "Are all very well for common people." (85)

The invisible man finds no respite from the scrutiny of "common people" and thus becomes increasingly violent in response. This begins with the cat experiment that miscarries while carrying forward his dead father. Invisibility elevated his outcast status to the ultimate precondition for this experiment: of all test subjects, the albino is the most "transparent" or, in other words, the one least fettered by parental guidance. And yet any intake of the environment—the point of maternal contact—annuls his transparency. In the course of his invisibility, he staggers the crime against his father, and his animal experiment is the souvenir, as stealing first, then murder. "This invisibility, in fact, is only good in two cases: It's useful in getting away, it's useful in approaching. It's particularly useful, therefore, in killing" (90).

Kemp is to serve as the invisible man's "goal-keeper," "helper," and "hiding-place," a place of rest and transition that will allow him to go beyond the small-time antisocial behavior of his solo acting out. Hence the invisible man proposes not "wanton killing, but a judicious slaying" (91). What he now proposes is a "Reign of Terror." But the host of his last resort or respite was, while actively listening to the invisible man, waiting for the authorities to descend upon him. When the invisible man escapes, Kemp reduces the man's discourse of exchange and support to criminality beyond the pale. "'He is mad,' said Kemp, 'inhuman. He is pure selfishness. He thinks of nothing but his own advantage, his own safety. I have listened to such a story this morning of brutal self-seeking!'" (92). Kemp promptly comes up with the strategy of strewing powdered glass on all the roads to let invisibility bleed and read (93). The police chief issues the understatement that the strategy is "unsportsmanlike." Once again, Kemp reassures the posse that the man hiding out in invisibility has become "inhuman" (94).

Soon the invisible man's first fatal act of violence occurs. The motivation is "impossible to imagine . . . save in a murderous frenzy" (95). "Indeed, the theory of madness is almost unavoidable" but a "voice heard about sunset . . . wailing and laughing, sobbing and groaning" (97) confirms reservations held on behalf of the invisible man. "He was certainly an intensely egotistical and unfeeling man, but the sight of his victim, his first victim, bloody and pitiful at his feet, may have released some long pent fountain of remorse which for a time may have flooded whatever scheme of action he had contrived" (96). But then he loses all empathy upon issuing his first proclamation as "Invisible Man the First" (97): he will execute Kemp to establish his power as "Death, the unseen Death" (98).

And yet the reservation is held by Kemp for us, the readership. When Kemp tries to stay the mob execution, it's too late. Like the transparent man of anatomy lessons, the dead man begins putting on visibility in layers. "And so, slowly, beginning at his hands and feet and creeping along his limbs to the vital centres of his body, that strange change continued. It was like the slow spreading of a poison" (108). The relationship to the body—to the mother's body—returns as discard, as toxic waste. His "crushed" body, the "drawn and battered features" of his face, the expression of "anger and dismay," come into focus, whereupon they cover him with a sheet.

7

Wells's *The First Men in the Moon* (1901) is a satire that also delights in summarizing aspects of the narratives that had allowed Wells, in dead earnest, to make it to the top of the mourning and conclude his maternally delegated assignment. Herds of mooncalves are nourished by the ripening and harvesting of plant life on fast forward during the daylight hours. To encounter the intelligent life that eats the meat, the voyagers must enter the Moon's underworld within range of reference to the Morlocks. Like the calves, those who herd, butcher, and consume them are as easily smashed as the underworld creatures of Wells's earlier tale. Most often compared to insects, occasionally to snakes, the Moon creatures stand upright as maimed doubles that "burlesque humanity" (508). Shaped to fit their predetermined niche in the hierarchy of the social order by an "elaborate discipline of training and education and surgery" (512), the creatures of the Moon, "as much insect as vertebrate" and capable of inhabiting "human and ultra-human dimensions" (506), land in range of *The Island of Dr. Moreau.*

Only posttraumatic cosmetic surgery has come close to Dr. Moreau's handling of vivisection. Otherwise he inherits a secret practice, as in the medieval fabrication of show-monsters (à la Victor Hugo in *The Man Who Laughs*) or in the "artistic torture" of the Inquisition, which, Dr. Moreau is convinced, always allowed "scientific curiosity" to cut in. But the doctor "was the first man to take up this question armed with antiseptic surgery, and with a really scientific knowledge of the laws of growth" (53). The Note that closes the narrative wraps the earlier appearance of one of its parts in a magazine: "the manufacture of monsters—and perhaps even *quasi*-human monsters—is within the possibilities of vivisection" (104).

Prendick objects to vivisection because he is hung up on the evidence of pain, qualifying him as "materialist" in Dr. Moreau's book. "So long as visible or audible pain turns you sick, so long as your own pains drive you, so long as pain underlies your propositions about sin—so long, I tell you, you are an animal, thinking a little less obscurely what an animal feels" (54). Pain as a medical index that warns and stimulates us is marked like the appendix for evolutionary extinction. "This store men and women set on pleasure and pain, Prendick, is the mark of the beast upon them, the mark of the beast from which they came" (55).

The island is now populated with the experiments Dr. Moreau once deemed successful but then, on second thought, abandoned as botched. "These creatures of mine seemed strange and uncanny to you as soon as you began to observe them, but to me, just after I make them, they seem to be indisputable human beings. It's afterwards as I observe them that the persuasion fades" (58). This fadeout is the dis-appointment of identification that Dr. Moreau withdraws from the transferential construction of his creatures, which protects him from responsibility to or for their failed, fallen, and fatal condition. On their own, Dr. Moreau advises, the Beast Folk pursue "a kind of mockery of a rational life—poor beasts! There's something they call the Law. . . . But I can see through it all, see into their very souls, and see there nothing but the souls of beasts, beasts that perish. . . . There is a kind of upward striving in them, part vanity, part waste sexual emotion, part waste curiosity. It only mocks me" (59). It is a projection of waste that refers to the doctor's controlling interest in his own resources. Prendick supplies a prehistory for this waste management.

Prendick sees a "strange contradiction" in the face of the creature "distorted with terror." Though the hunted creature crouches "in a perfectly animal attitude," the hunter recognizes in the scared face "the fact of its humanity" (72). As is underscored when Dr. Moreau must be buried, the creatures are indeed us, the only mark of their distinction being something akin to negative transference, the law of their mockery; they "lived in a fear that never died, fretted by law they could not understand; their mock-human existence began in an agony, was one long internal struggle" (74). And for what? Prendick asks himself. "It was the wantonness that stirred me" (ibid.).

As the realm of Dr. Moreau begins to break down and yield casualties to be buried, the new task of representation as interment strikes Prendick, suddenly, "like a wave across" his mind. For him, it is a nadir of despair. But "the realisation of the unspeakable aimlessness of things upon the island" (ibid.) also restarts his identification with the creatures. "A strange persuasion came upon me that, save for the grossness of the line, the grotesqueness of the forms, I had here before me the whole balance of human life in miniature, the whole interplay of instinct, reason, and fate, in its simplest form" (73-74).

The burial detail does not carry forward an earlier loss but rather a message of meaninglessness and a lack of matching affect. One man's sentimentality is another's affection deficit. Whining about his lot in life in the wake of Dr. Moreau's death, the assistant, Montgomery, asks Prendick what it all means: "Are we bubbles blown by a baby?" (82). Before he turns the conversation to the practical purpose of survival, an unkind thought crosses Prendick's mind, a condemnation that must be kin to his upbringing or descent: "It was hard to deal with such ravings" (ibid.). This voice rejecting an excess of spontaneity that is hard to bear brings back what it brought about: Prendick's deprivation.

An early memory was first triggered upon contact with Dr. Moreau. Before a scientific scandal caused him to withdraw from public, he offered his know-how as a latter-day Baroque *Trauerspiel*. Prendick remembers a screen word that then fills with a horror that has trouble finding its name: "'The Moreau—Hollows' was it? 'The Moreau—?' Ah! it sent my memories back ten years. 'The Moreau Horrors'" (22). As hollow gives way to horror, the prospect of a place for absence is withdrawn. The bottom line that was reached is a "hollow," the vacuum of meaninglessness as nothingness that can contain itself only through the multiplication of more and more fragments and voids. Dr. Moreau's menagerie fulfils this gap.

Following the demise of Montgomery and the destruction of the laboratory compound, Prendick survives under the protection of the dog hybrid alone; he is tolerated by the rest of the Beast People, who are devolving. Canine companionship is the delegation of our first contact with animal trainability that represents a prosthetic missing link, but the monkey hybrid is the missing link proper, represented on a scale of devolution as the monstrosity of language. The former bond belongs to the good object, the latter bespeaks envy: aping mocks the father in the son.

On the transferential turf of an instructor's apprehension of the student body (as the transmitter of a loss in generation), Prendick inherits Dr. Moreau's disdain, which overcomes him in the face of the Monkey Man's accomplishments.

> He had a fantastic trick of coining new words. He had an idea, I believe, that to gabble about names that meant nothing was the proper use of speech. He called it 'big thinks,' to distinguish it from 'little thinks'—the sane everyday interests of life. If ever I made a remark he did not understand, he would praise it very much, ask me to say it again, learn it by heart, and go off repeating it, with a word wrong here or there, to all the milder of the Beast People. He thought nothing of what was plain and comprehensible. I invented some very curious 'big thinks' for his especial use. (96)

Prendick is able to join the Monkey Man's network by a double mimicry of and in the medium of "big thinks," which, after all, subsumes their efforts.

"Big thinks" attains recognition value in the retrospect of devolution that afflicts language at the same time as it erodes the Law, the totemic system organized around the control release of the double issue of food and death. "My Ape Man's jabber multiplied in volume, but grew less and less comprehensible, more and more simian. Some of the others seemed altogether slipping their hold upon speech, though they still understood what I said to them at that time. Can you imagine language, once clear-cut and exact, softening and guttering, losing shape and import, becoming mere lumps of sound again?" (ibid.). As the anthropomorphism slips away, there remains to Dr. Moreau's creatures a monstrosity sustained in the blending or fragmenting of traits. "Of course these creatures did not decline into such beasts as the reader has seen in zoological gardens—into ordinary bears, wolves, tigers, oxen, swine, and apes. There was still something strange about each; in each Moreau had blended this animal with that; one perhaps was ursine chiefly, another feline chiefly, another bovine chiefly, but each was tainted with other creatures—a kind of generalised animalism appeared throughout the specific dispositions" (97). Monstrosity emerges out of a doodling visualization of the taxonomies of zoology as they recombine into "the animal" of the philosophical distinction between animal and man.

The distinction between human and animal remains on the verge of coming across as long as the change of devolution is gradual. "For them and for me it came without any definite shock. I still went among them in safety, because no jolt in the downward glide had released the increasing charge of explosive animalism that ousted the human day by day. But I began to fear that soon now that shock must come" (ibid.). The shock that comes with the murder of Prendick's canine protector is carried forward into his post-rescue existence. He is "haunted" by memories of Dr. Moreau's island. In time, the "terror" becomes his "disease."

> My trouble took the strangest form. I could not persuade myself that the men and women I met were not also another, still passably human, Beast People, animals half-wrought into the outward image of human souls; and that they would presently begin to revert, to show first this bestial mark and then that. But I have confided my case to a strangely able man, a man who had known Moreau, and seemed half to credit my story, a mental specialist—and he has helped me mightily. (102)

Just the same, Prendick has to leave London where his horror of the shock of devolution was so hard to contain. Somewhere away from the mad-making crowds, he remains stable between his books and chemistry experiments. It is in the contemplation of the night sky that he obtains a sense of "infinite peace and protection." "There it must be, I think, in the vast and eternal laws of matter, and not in the daily cares and sins and troubles of men, that whatever is more than animal within us must find its solace and its hope" (104). We're at the end of the narrative, and "hope" is mentioned two more times: "I hope, or I could not live. And so, in hope and solitude, my story ends" (ibid.).

The night sky in which Prendick finds hope restored is an external image of his relationship to the inner world of his good objects, which remains up in the air, un-inherited, and up for grabs. As Klein writes with regard to a similar scene of contemplation: "I would also interpret his intent gazing at the stars as an attempt to regain his good objects which he feels are lost or far away" ("On Identification" 152). She subsequently links this literary figure to the experience of patients: "such phantasies have far-reaching consequences and vitally influence the structure of the ego. They have the effect that those parts of his self from which he feels estranged, often including his emotions, are not at the time accessible either to the analyst or to the patient" (166).

Five years later, Wells gives the men in the Moon the identification to break the connection of flight and communication with mankind. The projective identification that split the opposition against the Martians with the writerly identification of their weaponry is let go. The zombie-stomping voyager, assuming his companion has been recaptured or killed, takes the flying sphere back to Earth and loses it there. Back home again with a cache of lunar gold, he cautiously signs in with a pseudonym: "Wells" (497). The scientist, Cavor, who gave his name to the antigravity substance he concocted, Cavorite, has in the meantime been hosted by the upper echelons of Selenite society. Free to tinker with their technologies, he creates a telegraphic connection picked up by the device of a Dutch electrician "akin to the apparatus used by Mr. Tesla in America, in the hope of discovering some method of communication with Mars" (499). After the narrative up to this point was already posted, Cavor's messages, which "Wells" edits, give the inside view of the lunar society of evolutionary adaptation speeded up through short cuts rendering each creature an I-land of Dr. Moreau. Cavor's narrative ends in the middle of his attempted transmission of the formula for making Cavorite. The message the day before told of his audience with the ruler and how he honestly admitted that mankind was inclined to wage terrible and senseless wars of possession. Just a few years after *The War of the Worlds*, Wells can reclaim the projection of the human inclination to violence and, at the same time, spare the species of Dr. Moreau's experiments in a satire that reaches a Happy End without the therapeutic fiction of marriage.

The camera that the time traveler left behind in *The Time Machine* zooms large in the place of transit in *The First Men in the Moon*. In the third volume of *Nazi Psychoanalysis*, I excavated Wells's inability to identify with the seat of flying as negative to the positive of the "German" identification with nothing else. After seasons of inhabiting the drag of his mother's refusal to mourn her daughter Fanny, his first step in mournful integration—the fabulation of time travel—could not yet complete itself in photography. The 1901 trip to the Moon by two voyagers and their first encounter with its solar-energized surface is an elaborate staging of what Benjamin identified as the optical unconscious ("The Work of Art" 500).

When they land, lunar nature outside the sphere is endowed with mediatic velocity. The Moon's surface is bare of life. But then sunlight illuminates and animates seeds. The span of time allotted before nightfall puts everything back in deep freeze requires that the seeds sprout and grow into plant life at a rate of development unknown and unseen prior to the manipulations of film recording.

> They did not stand for long. The bundle-like buds swelled and strained and opened with a jerk, thrusting out a coronet of red sharp tips, spreading a whorl of tiny, spiky, brownish leaves, that lengthened rapidly, lengthened visibly even as we watched. . . . How can I suggest it to you—the way that growth went on? The leaf tips grew so that they moved onward even while we looked at them. The brown seed-case shriveled and was absorbed with an equal rapidity. Have you ever on a cold day taken a thermometer into your warm hand and watched the little thread of mercury creep up the tube? These moon-plants grew like that. (425)

The flight to the Moon was mediated by the clicking open and shut of framed images of what lies outside the "camera." The windows in the space vessel activate the secret ingredient that Cavor uses to attain flight, another form of the antigravity that was the basis for the Martian technologies of long distance in Laßwitz's *Two Planets*. The sphere is painted with this antigravity substance and the velocity and flight pattern are kept under control by opening and closing small windows placed at all directional coordinates. Apertures of light that click open framed images develop the influence of Cavorite as negative—every opening diminishes the antigravity while altering the flight direction. "Presently he told me he wished to alter our course a little by letting the earth tug at us for a moment. He was going to open one earthward blind for thirty seconds. . . . I think I recognized the cloud-dimmed coastlines of France and Spain and the south of England, and then with a click the shutter closed again and I found myself in a state of extraordinary confusion, sliding slowly over the smooth glass" (417-18).

DOUBLE TIME

1

The screenplay that would become Ridley Scott's *Alien* (1979) was first named "Memory" on account of the opening act in which its author Dan O'Bannon was so long immersed: the startled awakening of the space travelers out of deep freeze sleep. Space travel must either condense or bypass time or move across space in no time, all the while remaining within a span of memory to keep it human. At the start of John Cameron's sequel, *Aliens* (1986), the protagonist Ripley has returned to Earth, but fifty-seven years have elapsed since she entered the hibernation of space travel, and she now learns of her daughter's recent death at age sixty-six. That she addresses her grief to the eight year old is evident in her dedication to the safety of the alien-invaded space colony's sole survivor. By the commitment to the traumatized girl, nicknamed Newt, Ripley brings the alien queen mother into focus as a total adversary against a backdrop of identification.

The creature in *Alien* embodies two trends of post-WWII science fiction. It belongs to the intermediary zone of animal behavior out of which the brain can be jumpstarted as an imitation or representation; in creature features, the re-release and mutation of prehistoric animals through nuclear testing advances this encounter. Regarding the coverage of Fukushima, a Japanese colleague living in Berlin argued that the notion of "catastrophe" was not available to her culture. The simple but subtle correction gives a clue to the intense beauty of the rolling destruction in Honda's original *Godzilla* (1954). The atom bombing happens to recur without end.

If crisis were not an opportunity for turning back and around, it wouldn't be such a rallying point for the Western mind. In the absence of repentance, however, even the perspective that builds on catastrophe cannot bestow a turning point to the spread of Godzilla's atomic breath/death.

The creature in *Alien* also gives staying power to a passing visualization of that uncanny force of imitation and effacement of human life visited upon Earth from Outer Space, which can be glimpsed in *Invasion of the Body Snatchers* (the book and films) and in John W. Campbell's 1938 novella "Who Goes There?" together with two of its film adaptations, both titled *The Thing* (1982, 2011). Before the perfect imitation is in place and the ruthlessly violent takeover is consummated, one can, during the brief span of metamorphosis, flash on what would be a more fully manifested monster in the creature features made in California and Japan. Even the film adaptation of *The Stepford Wives* (1975) offers a glimpse of the duplicate woman (prior to the merger with and murder of the original), another being with mirror-glow pupil-eyes who is not yet differentiated as human. The monstrous creature raging on Earth is the full projection of the transition or time of doubling.

Scheduling conflicts of life transmission in space travel also admit doubling. Science fiction may have traveled in time before traveling in Outer Space, but space transport would reintroduce the necessity of something like a jump forward (or back) coupled with the technical ability to stay there for the duration. Cryogenic storage during transportation through space leaves an astronaut as vulnerable as the vampire in his daytime crypt, the predicament exploited by the computer HAL in *2001: A Space Odyssey*. Some means of live transmission would be required to jump the spaceship and the perils of passage in deep freeze. If the jump in space travel must also be a jump in time, then it is also a jump to the side into doubling. The Doppelgänger in *The Student of Prague* (1913) already wielded its impact essentially by being ahead of the dual schedule, ahead of the student's second thoughts and resolutions, a forward movement emphasizing that, even at its most prosthetic, the double relationship is time-based.

In Michael Crichton's popular-science adventure novel *Timeline* (1999), time travel is the byproduct of the transmission that Norbert Wiener made into a kind of cybernetics credo: it should be possible to transmit a human being by phone. Crichton updates the analogue to facsimile transmission. However, the transmission of the amount of information that would equal a 3-D object requires computing resources that only the recent introduction of quantum computing can provide. Then the experimentally transmitted objects don't arrive as projected. When a recording device is transmitted, it keeps showing the desert surrounding the research facility under varying conditions. By transmitting yet another device aimed to record the sky, the evidence shows that the dispatched object entered another time (i.e., another universe).

For all the science and technology at the disposal of this research firm, the main goal is to provide vacation spots along the lines of Crichton's 1973 screenplay and film *Westworld*. It is not the aim of those involved in quantum transmission in *Timeline* to send the vacationers into the past via time travel. Time travel is set aside for the research going into the design of these resorts in order to attain the perfectibility of "authenticity." As a side effect of the live transmission of objects and bodies, time travel is limited by the inevitability of "transcription errors," which can skew the human form or even knock bodily systems out of alignment over time. The embodied life is not transmitted whole, as in a spaceship. When a person is transmitted as information (and memory), he or she is extinguished at one end yet rebuilt as the same, as still alive, at the other end. This process, represented here by sending and receiving, in fact transpires in no time, while skipping to another time. The bodies sent across time are therefore subject to the same parameters of doubling as the wives of Stepford. (In *Futureworld*, the 1976 sequel to *Westworld*, a mad scientist behind the technical-support scenes at history's last resort seeks to turn the VIP tourists into androids under his control in order to guarantee good publicity.)

The transport of the vacationers in *Westworld* simulates taking off across Outer Space. Upon landing, they take shuttles to one out of three historical time zones: Ancient Rome, Medieval Europe and the Wild West. The latter zone, what Disneyland demarcated as Frontierland, is the main attraction and model for the resort's SF-mediated staging of Western history. The TV series *Star Trek* was projected to be a series of Western-style adventures in Outer Space. This American genre or model of expansion across frontiers is contradicted already in the first season of *Star Trek* by the other fix on time basic to Harlan Ellison's time travel episode "The City on the Edge of Forever" (1967). Deranged by an accidental overdose of medication, McCoy jumps ship and, discovering the time portal on the planet below, jumps time. As in the scheduling of entropy within the allegory of commodities in Dick's *Ubik*, the limitlessness of new frontiers hits a bottom

line in the Cold War's repressed recent past. The search party looks for him and
the Enterprise suddenly vanishes—McCoy has already altered the past in such
a way that the Enterprise cannot exist. Survivors of the time paradox, Kirk and
Spock follow McCoy into the 1930s to set time aright. This becomes doubly
pressing when it is discovered that McCoy's alteration of the past led to delays
that made it possible for Nazi Germany to scoop the invention of the atom bomb
and win the war. In the meantime, the woman McCoy saved from death by traffic
accident—a pacifist who, given time, will defer US entry into the war—is the
love object of all the travelers in identification. That the men let her die in the
street to save the future from Nazi dominion still represents the kind of sacrificial
choice of one loss in lieu of another loss or other losses, doubling the prospect of
psychopathic violence.

In Thomas Disch's *Camp Concentration* (1968), just when everyone is in the
ready position to reverse time, a sacrificial switch between double and nothing
reduces the problem to fit the solution. The inmates have been infected with a brand
of syphilis that bestows a genius-award on each of them. They are test subjects in
the camp-administered experiment, which aims at thoroughgoing innovations in the
field of education. The problem, explains Dr. Busk, one of the administrators of the
camp experiment, is that the learning process is otherwise "sacrificed to the purpose
of socialization. . . . It is perhaps the chief mission of the science of psychology to
resolve this dilemma—to maximize intelligence without vitiating its social utility"
(24-25). The debate between Dr. Busk and the protagonist, Sacchetti, on the adaptive dilemma of genius in the culture of learning duplicates the quarrel between
Kantian and Hegelian positions within the original culture of *Bildung*.

> "The mind disintegrates, and the old, distinct categories are for a
> little while fluid and capable of re-formation."
>
> "But it's . . . the re-formation of the disrupted categories, in which
> the act of genius consists. It's not the breakdown that counts, but the new
> juxtapositions that follow." . . .
>
> "But doesn't that just beg the question? Education, memory itself, is
> but the recapitulation of all the moments of genius in that culture. Edu-
> cation is always breaking down old categories and recombining them
> in better ways. . . . Why if genius were a continuous process, instead of
> what it is—a fluke—it would be of no value to us whatsoever!" (58-59)

The title already says it. The US is Germany's continuity shot—for *Bildung* or wars. Sacchetti is incarcerated for being a conscientious objector to a new US total war before his recruitment for the experimental mobilization of the mind according to standards made in Germany. Mordecai steps out of Sacchetti's oversight of him in high school to welcome him to genius camp. Through the camp experiment, Mordecai is able to leave behind his lifelong invisibility as an African-American exception to the stereotype. Sacchetti, an author who accessorizes with an imaginary-friend double (Louis the Likewise), bears a cultural identification with Germany. Not Mordecai; he not only doesn't have rhythm, he also had a bad time when he was a GI stationed in Germany. Mordecai took his dose of Germanicity with the infection. Otherwise he denied himself the turn of integration's blender whereby West Germany, like the consummate grandparent who was a terrible parent, provided African Americans emotionally corrective experiences. Among the beer-soaked leaves of his senses, Mordecai felt that he had never left the United States. Rather, he had only been brought closer to the final atrocity.

Toward the end of the novel, the test subjects engage in an all-out search for a cure or postponement of the deadline to match its alternate-history setting. "We talked of: studies in mech. brain-wave duplication & storage; Yoga, & other methods of susp. animation, such as freeze-drying, until such time as a cure is developed; even, so help me, time travel—&, as an equiv., interstellar voyaging for a sim. purpose, i.e. returning to a world that would be (in an unrelativistic sense) in the future" (175). In keeping with the experimental administration of short cuts or flukes, the narrative spares itself the reversal of time and secures a cure through the violent usurpation, switching, or doubling of meat vehicles. Although Disch's narrative forecasts an updating of Mann's *Doctor Faustus* into an AIDS allegory, we instead discover (right up against the deadline) that we are already in an infernal body-switching fable, like Green's *If I Were You.*

Mordecai researches a way out of the experiment's fatal consequence under cover of the "crypt or code" of "'alchymic' twaddle" (182) derived from assorted "Troys of thought" (71). Haast, the camp commander, endorses the subterfuge. For the sake of the elixir of life, the advertised outcome of the occult experiments, Haast comes to prize alchemy for being an exploration of "Inner Space," which the scientific fixation on Outer Space has too long neglected (90). Mordecai updates the ceremony of initiation into extended life with wired helmet gadgets (like those transferring Maria's image to her robot in *Metropolis*), establishing an "homage to the cult of Cybernetick" (92). The test subject puts on the helmet to magnify or accelerate the otherwise slow-working effect of the elixir of life (98). But it's a put-on, another "crypt," which conceals the so-called mind reciprocator (182). The first body switch is effected at the staged ceremony between Mordecai and Haast. "It was a happy accident that Haast's mind, finding itself suddenly in Mordecai's exhausted frame, should panic so hectically as to produce an embolism. Mordecai maintains that it was the thought of being a Negro that undid him" (183).

At the Happy End, the dying bodies of the test subjects are handed over to assorted camp authorities and guards, an application of doubling that, as a projective identification, leaves the splitting (and hence the violence) unresolved. The switch is performed on Sacchetii without explanation, with only the mystery maintained, in order to circumvent his conscience. But he approvingly notes that, by his influence, three camp inmates who had the choice decided to forego the so-called resurrection: "Each chose to die his own death rather than condemn someone else to it" (183). Just the same, Sacchetti inherits his victim's flesh, a switch that belongs to the unsavory comedy under camp conditions that he writes about writing—but that is otherwise withheld (83).

Three years earlier Disch used a Camp title (*The Genocides*) for his version of a triffids-like invasion by the Plants from Outer Space, which are as tall as redwoods but hollow like dandelion stalks. Earth is seeded in 1972, then covered in green growth, and in no time forests of non-trees have grown tall. "It was like the speeded-up movies of plant growth he'd seen in Ag school years ago" (17). Another throwback to youth is on the audio track: "a strange, unwholesome solitude, a solitude more profound than adolescence, more unremitting than prison" (18). The deathly silence is resonant, in other words, with the impact of psychopathic violence.

The pastoralization of the planet, with the consequent extermination of life as the survivors know it, is carried out with the insouciance of aliens on a roadside picnic littering death and destruction in the path of unknown bystanders. The Strugatsky brothers give this explanation to account for the Outer Space deposit on Earth of a danger zone of toxic gifts. In his review of this work (before deploring the concluding epiphany of heroic trials, which yanks it all inside a fairy tale), Stanislaw Lem dismisses the projection of psychopathy upon aliens in science fiction, which shuts down the mystery of contact and says no more than it takes one to know one. However, this encirclement of the problem doesn't just repeat Wells, as Lem suggests, but squarely fits a postwar scenario of repression and return.

The Outer Space maintenance of the Plants includes the elimination of all "artefacts" (those still alive and their structures) by incendiary spheres reminiscent of "Volkswagens of the early Fifties" (42). The narrative takes place the year before the scheduled 1980 harvesting of the crop and scorching of Earth's surface. The Anderson family escapes the spheres and the winter season down the chutes inside the hollow alien stems.

Since the start of the invasion, survivors have had to deal with rival marauders. Since they posed a threat, the Anderson family chooses not only to kill this excess population, but to devour the kill in the form of sausages served at the Thanksgiving Day feast. Orville was adopted by the family because of his degree in mining engineering, but his partner Janet joined the ingredients of the sausages. The Donner dinner party and the raft of the Medusa would be justification enough if they had been starving (67). But the Anderson Family's celebration—on the day Lincoln declared a holiday during the Civil War—is less about rationing meat and more about mounting a totemic feast of mourning. "Beyond necessity, explanations grew elaborate and rather metaphysical. Thus, metaphysically, in this meal the community was united by a complex bond, the chief of whose elements was complicity in murder, but this complicity was achieved by a ritual as solemn and mysterious as the kiss by which Judas betrayed Christ: it was a sacrament. Mere horror was subsumed into tragedy, and the town's Thanksgiving dinner was the crime and the atonement, so to speak, in one blow" (ibid.).

Orville opted to be a sleeper awaiting the best, the coldest opportunity to exact revenge. He will marry the Anderson daughter, inherit the position of authority in the family, and then torment them all with his hatred. Sleeping on it, he discovers that he prefers the Anderson girl as a living substitute rather than a vengeful offering to a ghost. Like Clytemnestra's ghost, murdered Janet reproaches Orville for his delay (on the preceding page, he "Hamletlike" deliberately added delay to injury when he chanced upon Anderson like Claudius, defenseless but in prayer):

You've abandoned me for that child. You court an infant.
No! it was only that I might betray her. It was all for the sake of you.

Then betray her now. Betray her, and I will return to you. Then, only
then, will I kiss you. Then, when you touch me, your hand will feel flesh.
With those words she disappeared.

In the same instant he knew she had not been real, that this was,
quite possibly, the inception of madness. But he did not care. Though she
was not real, she was right. (137)

It was the first claim that proved right. The loss of Janet (which was the onset
of his love for her) and the hibernation of his revenge against the Anderson family
were steps in recovery from the mindset that locked into place after the invasion
of the Plants. "Like everyone else, Orville pretended to hate the invasion . . . but
secretly he relished it, he gloried in it, he wanted nothing else. . . . He (and anyone
else who survived) learned to be as unscrupulous as the heroes in the pulp adventure magazines he'd read as a boy—sometimes, as unscrupulous as the villains"
(46). Initially the government attempted to control the crisis through a kind of war
economy. It became an opportunity to direct slave labor. "At times he wondered
what difference there was between himself and, say, an Eichmann, but he didn't let
his speculations interfere with his work" (46).

2

In Jack Finney's *Invasion of the Body Snatchers*, the doubling prospect of transcription errors is as vast as the absence of empathy when the double is caught
in the image and act of transition not yet stamped with recognition value. Before
we can pry it loose and resituate it into an extra place within the protocols of
testing and mourning, the blank (as a stare or blanking of identification) does
time in adaptation to intolerance (which, for Dick, was the typical aspect of the
psychopathic norm). Time travel derives its starting position from the photo finish
it applies to the double's foregone conclusion—a state of blanking.

The only woman at the base in *The Thing from Another World* (1951) has
to excuse herself while the men continue to listen through stethoscopes to the
newborn sounds emanating from the blood-drenched plants. This adaptation of
Campbell's story faces the invasion of evolved plants from Outer Space that, by
pursuing their own replicational course, must, like Wells's Martians, eventually

destroy mankind. But the film leaves out the uncanny assault or insult of doubling. Shifting from hysteria to traumatic neurosis, the nausea in *Invasion of the Body Snatchers* is no longer restricted to the underbelly of the object of the male gaze.

> I hope I never again in my life see anything as frightful as those eyes. . . . They were almost, but not quite—not yet—as large as Becky's. They were not quite the same shape, or precisely the same shade—but getting there. . . . Watch an unconscious person come to, and at first the eyes show only the least dull beginnings of comprehension, the first faint flickers of returning intelligence. That is all that had yet happened to these eyes. The steady awareness, the quiet alertness of Becky Driscoll's eyes were horribly parodied and diluted here. Yet, washed out a dozen times over as they were, you could nevertheless see, in these blank blue eyes caught in the trembling beam of my light, the first faint hint of what—given time—would become Becky Driscoll's eyes. I moaned, and bent double, clutching my stomach tight under my folded arms. (60-61)

What is lacking in the fully formed double incites high anxiety. The one you know and love no longer looks back, doesn't return your gaze. "There's something *missing*. . . . That look, 'way in back of the eyes, is gone" (21). In other words: "There is no emotion—none—only the pretense of it. The words, the gestures, the tones of voice, everything else—but not the feeling" (ibid.). The dupe "looks, sounds, acts, and remembers exactly like" the original "[o]n the outside. But *inside* he's different. His responses . . . aren't *emotionally* right, if I can explain that" (ibid.).

It is hard to explain the horror evoked in the protagonist, Miles, when he overhears the dupes among themselves playing back the audio record of the words that they recently exchanged with the local humans. Before he can describe what shocks him, he is recalled to his college days and another scene of overhearing. "This is very hard to explain, but—when I was in college, a middle-aged black man had a shoeshine stand . . . and he was a town character. Everyone patronized Billy, because he was everyone's notion of what a 'character' should be. He had a title for each regular customer. . . . The flattery was obvious, and people always smiled to show they weren't taken in by it; but they liked it just the same" (133).

Then, sleeping off an all-nighter in his car parked in the run-down section of town, Miles is awakened by an exchange on the sidewalk next to the car window.

> "Man, just look at those shoes. You had them shoes—lemme see, now!—fifty-six years come Tuesday, and they still takes a lovely shine!" The voice was Billy's, the words and tone those the town knew with affection, but—parodied, and a shade off key. "Take it easy, Bill," the first voice murmured uneasily. . . . And then, for a full minute perhaps, standing there on a sidewalk of the slum he lived in, Billy went on with this quietly hysterical parody of himself. . . . Never before in my life had I heard such ugly, bitter, and vicious contempt in a voice, contempt for the people taken in by his daily antics, but even more for himself, the man who supplied the servility they bought from him. (134-5)

The character deformation of adaptation to racism, a corollary to Dick's understanding of the android, afflicts all parties to the underlying opposition, especially those occupying its safe shore. This affliction is brought home by the pod invasion of our identifications. As Miles says to the first person in town who tells him she is sure that those close to her are not the same inside, it is her problem and it lies inside her. The blank that you recognize is, most importantly, the wiping blank of the good object. The invasion from Outer Space not only doubles and usurps its victims but also breaks into the innocent bystander's psychic life-line to the good internal object.

The transmission underlying the doubling adaptation, however, misfires and errs. Emotion itself does not transmit in the duplication process. Only its memory does. The result, Miles wagers, reflects the absence of creativity in the alien copies, the lack of the industry of maintenance and repair. When the dupes take over any given community, they let it run down, then run it on empty, until it resembles an abandoned ghost town. The Moon and Mars were once living worlds that were wiped blank. "And now . . . it's the earth's turn. And when all of these planets are used up, it doesn't matter. The spores will move on, back into space again, to drift for—it doesn't matter for how long or to where" (184). After setting fire to a field of pods, Miles and Becky watch the remaining plants rise up from this inhospitable planet back into Outer Space. At this point, "a fragment of a wartime speech" crosses Miles's mind. Churchill calls to fight everywhere and never surrender to the Nazi German attack. The spores do the moving and living for the doubles, who are life transmissions to or into receivers but limited in time by transcription errors. "The duplication isn't perfect. . . . It's like the artificial compounds nuclear physicists are fooling with: unstable, unable to hold their form. . . . The last of us will be dead . . . in five years at the most" (183). The double lasts about as long as the memory of the dead under conditions of adaptation to psychopathy.

3

Among the analogues summoned to illustrate the blanking identification visible when the pod imitation is not yet complete, we also find the not yet fully developed photograph. "I've watched a man develop a photograph. . . . He dipped the sheet of blank sensitized paper into the solution, slowly swishing it back and forth, in the dim red light of the developing room. Then, underneath that colorless fluid, the image began to reveal itself—dimly and vaguely—yet unmistakably recognizable just the same. This thing, too . . . was an unfinished, underdeveloped, vague and indefinite Becky Driscoll" (59). In Finney's time travel novel *Time and Again* (1970), the historical medium of photography is a portal to cross into the late nineteenth century. Prior to his initiation into time travel, the protagonist, Si Morley, is characterized by his propensity for manipulating the inspiration and obstacle of photography to reach back into the past.

> Because I've always felt a wonder at old photographs not easy to explain. . . . I mean the sense of wonder, staring at the strange clothes and vanished backgrounds, at knowing that what you're seeing was once real. That light really did reflect into a lens from these lost faces and objects. That these people were *really there* once, smiling into a camera. You could have walked into the scene then, touched those people, and spoken to them. . . . Because now you really *see the arrested moment*, so actual it seems that if you watch intently, the life caught here must continue. . . . The feeling that the tantalizing reality of the vanished moment might somehow be seized— that if you watch long enough you might detect that first nearly imperceptible movement. (19)

But in this "illustrated novel," photographs alone cannot open up time travel. They must be tampered with and brought into association with mimetic drawing, as in late nineteenth-century newspapers, which rarely used photographs directly but instead printed illustrations based on them.

Out of this historical mix, Si's mentors train him in "translation" for the purpose of time travel. "We spent all that morning looking at, first, a drawing or photograph of the early eighties, then a 'translation'. . . Some of them worked, and I'd suddenly experience the thrill of glimpsing the actuality of a moment of the past" (82). Then he no longer needs the translation-drawing. "I, too, could look at an old cut or photograph and do the work of getting myself into and fully perceiving it until I found and touched the long-ago realness that had produced it" (ibid.). "I spent three days then, alone with the projector looking at scene after scene of the eighties, staring, working at finding the actuality that lay under the surface of each, gaining experience and speed as the time passed" (83).

In *The Man in the High Castle*, we enter the alternate era through Mr. Childan's shop, American Artistic Handcrafts, Inc. Mr. Tagomi is on the phone wanting to know the status of his order. "Did my Civil War recruiting poster, arrive yet, Sir?" (3). "The historic objects of American popular civilization" hold a special attraction for wealthy Japanese collectors (26). The TV Sensurround that, according to *Fahrenheit 451*, first spread with the fire/magnifier of photography out of burn'em wood around the time of the Civil War was destroyed decades ago, this time by Dick's alternate ending to WWII. The limited edition of Americana "debris" is further curtailed by the specific demand for Civil War memorabilia, which has led to the covert production of fakes on the occupied Coast. The forgery of Civil War pistols, for example, supplies workshops wherein, on the side, one woman can make contemporary silver jewelry (her husband is Jewish). When Tagomi goes to the handcrafts store to find another collectible in exchange for his Civil War pistol, Childan convinces him to give one of the new jewelry items a try. It is by its contemplation that Tagomi briefly time-trips upon the alternate setting of the present in which, decades ago, the Axis was defeated.

In "On Some Motifs in Baudelaire," Benjamin places photography at the forefront of the media calibration of technologization/massification's traumatic shocks. Quoting Paul Valéry, Benjamin avers that the psychoticizing impact finds relief through the "smooth functioning of the social mechanism" in crowds (328).

The comfort of this relief isolates subjects—but also brings those in the comfort zone closer to mechanization (328).

Sitting before consoles and manipulating the dials and switches, we are in the buffer zone of gadget love. Photography is best equipped to travel back into the past, but only in order to administer a "posthumous shock" (328). What is confusing about the photo finish is that it looks like melancholia but lasts like mourning. Every photo is a found photo, the detritus of unidentified forgetting. Properly parried and buffered by consciousness before a console of switches, pushbuttons and triggers, the shock of the new is not what you see but what you forget. Consciousness can register shocks by assigning the "character" of a date mark to the incident in question, which remains isolated in terms of what occurred at a certain hour in one's lifetime and has been lived through. On a schedule or calendar, memories can be contained and made disposable.

Benjamin defines aura succinctly in the contrast between painting and photography. When you look at a painting, your look is returned. The returned gaze is the aura of painting. A photograph cannot return the gaze except as "eyes that look at us with mirror-like blankness," eyes that "know nothing of distance" (340). This is the look that rises out of doubling in transit and is reflected in the eyes of the psychopath, which, without identification, peer through the mask of a certain android norm. Benjamin discovers in Baudelaire that the mirror-stare animates only at the sight of prey as a wary gleam in a carnivore's eye (ibid.).

Once given a chance to compare his time to the past, Si recognizes that the faces of our time are blanks. "*Today's faces are different*; they are much more alike and much less alive" (218). Today's faces come alive only in the crowd. "When alone they're blank, and closed in. I passed people in pairs or larger groups who were talking, sometimes laughing, occasionally more or less animated; but only as part of the group. They were shut off from the street around them, alien and separate from the city they lived in, suspicious of it, and that's not how New York was in the eighties" (219).

In the present, we are in the realtime of a novel published in 1970. There is little evidence binding this time to changes since the 1950s, the setting of *Invasion of the Body Snatchers*. A loner who observes but does not interact with groups, Si does issue an update when he rationalizes his avoidance of the group coming toward him. "[A] group of young Negroes was walking toward Lex, so I didn't hang around to encounter them and explain how fond I'd always been of Martin Luther King" (86).

Preliminary to entering into time travel is the metabolic shift from the blanking adaptation to intolerance toward the ambivalence of being in touch.

That we are in New York City and no longer in California (where the blanking identification from Outer Space had landed in the 1950s) is dictated by the time zone of preference. McLuhan diagnosed (Southern) California, like Germany, as bereft of the mass cultural influence of the late nineteenth century. Once a translation of photographic memorabilia has put him in the ready position, Si need only cross the street from the Dakota into and across Central Park to have entered the year 1882. He insists upon 1882 because there is a mystery in girl-friend Kate's family history to solve. In that year, the ancestor deposited in the mail what might have been a suicide note, but what has survived in Kate's posses-sion only as a torn fragment: "the destruction by fire of the entire world." When Si is recruited for time traveling, it has been two years since his divorce. Going back in time waylays what was supposed to come next, his marriage to Kate. Si breaks out of the divorce court of exogamous choosing, which, in *Invasion of the Body Snatchers*, was presided over by the stricken inner world of doubling and blanking. "'Becky, I heard about your divorce, of course; and I'm sorry.' She nodded. 'Thanks, Miles. And I've heard about yours. I'm sorry, too'" (10). In 1956, the first film adaptation placed this crisis squarely inside the mirror circle of doubling and division by projecting (and fictionalizing) the original setting, Mill Valley, as Santa Mira. What frames the crisis of uncanniness is the adult profile of doubling, the benign prospect of remarriage between the protagonists, Miles and Becky. In the second film adaptation (1978), the guru psychiatrist speculates that finding one's partner changed into an impersonation reflects the ease with which we apply the cure-all of divorce.

In Si's own time, Kate is the one he's serious about divorcing . . . I mean marrying. On one occasion, he crosses over with Kate into the past upon her insistence and against the protocols of the experiment. Together they recognize by contrast the blank stares in their present day. They are a proper couple. Around the bend in a past that is also Kate's family history, he finds another love interest, Julia, technically a dead woman. Like a loss in generation, an echo, this ghost, remote from the prospect of first or direct contact with loss, is Si's de-Oedipalized choice and ghost of a chance.

The sign of a change in the government project from benign authority to malignant imperialism becomes the new supervisor's rationalization of the atom bombings as a measure justified by saving lives in the longer run (389). The time technique is now to be used to change history according to US interests, beginning with the removal from time of the Cuban missile crisis. This is the reversal of the inventor's own approach, which he always coupled with work of caution not to alter the present via the past. After each sampling or "boring" that Si brought back, he was instructed to relate every fact of the present as he remembered it before his trip. By the boring recount, the scientists tested that no alteration had transpired—that the relationship to the future remained open. In the meantime, however, the government seeks to instrumentalize what Si is already willing to risk out of love.

> Observe, don't interfere: It was a rule easy to formulate and of obvious necessity at the project . . . where the people of this time were only ghosts long vanished from reality, nothing remaining of them but odd-looking sepia photographs lying in old albums or in nameless heaps shoved under antique-store counters in cardboard boxes. But where I was now, they were alive. Where I was now, Julia's life wasn't long since over and forgotten; it still lay ahead. *And was as valuable as any other.* (254)

In the end, he returns once and for all to Julia back in 1882 . . . and shuts the door. By making a change in the past, he erases the birth of the inventor of the technique that allowed him to go back and forth in time (398). He puts an end to the abuse of time travel as a kind of historical brainwashing. Si personalizes his advantage, which enabled him to circumvent responsibilities for the future, including the adult responsibility of divorce.

4

The alien imitations in *Invasion of the Body Snatchers* are based on wave prints in which an individual is contained intact. "Not only your brain, but your entire body, every cell of it emanates waves as individual as fingerprints" (175). Because wave identity is in flux, the individual to be replaced must be quiescent, in other words asleep. The aliens "murder sleep," the trajectory of the failed attempt by the Macbeth couple to double dead father upon dead child in a sole evacuation. The alien duplication procedure belongs to the future, which the media technologies invented in the course of the second industrial revolution already transmit. "'Do you believe that, Doctor?' He smiled. 'Well, do you believe that utterly invisible, unde-tectable waves can emanate from a room, move silently through space, be picked up, and then reproduce precisely every word, sound, and tone to be heard in that original room? . . . Your grandfather would never have believed such an impossi-bility, but you do—you believe in radio. You believe in television'" (175-76).

The identifying print of Finney's science fictional worlds is that, as in the span of belief above, the nineteenth-century era of media invention has been grandfathered—preserved outside the flow of time washing through it. It was not photography alone that compelled Si Morley to imagine the arresting of time as a station stop, but the collectible device of the stereoscope: "The wonder is even stronger with old stereoscopic views . . . Insert a view, slide it into focus, and the old scene leaps out at you, astonishingly three-dimensional. And then, for me, the awe becomes intense" (19). The 3D restaging of photography through stereoscopy is the address rehearsal of the past to which Si Morley subsequently travels—and the stage on which a whole fantasy complex of biding one's time in the prehistory of the new digital media is set. 3D, a throwback to stereoscopic representation, is the portal for revisiting the first mediations or transmissions. Once it's happening, mediation cannot be timed or limited.

Richard Matheson's *Bid Time Return* (1974) is set in 1971. The protagonist, Richard Collier, travels back in time to catch the moment in which a photograph that rivets him was taken. The support of government research attending Finney's fiction is no longer required. It suffices that an old photograph triggers the wish to cross the void of seventy-five years. Collier can fulfill his wish by self-helping himself to the literature on techniques for entering the past. In sum: "Using the principles of Psychocybernetics, I can 'reprogram' myself to believe that I exist, not in 1971, but in 1896" (74). Whereas Morley was so normal (or dissociative) that he was the government's test subject of choice, Collier fits the old neurotic norm. Consider the following recollection and a subsequent fantasy-match around his point of entry in 1896: "Obsession with my tricycle. Boo, Freud. . . . What if—Good God!—some married couple had just begun to experience 'nuptial conjuga-tion' as I suddenly appear in bed with them, most likely under or on top?" (18, 93).

As in *Time and Again*, the primal-scene impasse, the incestuous choosing between double or nothing, can be circumvented by contact with the ghosts that

photography hosts. In the close quarters of a terminal diagnosis, Collier decides
not to die in his brother's care and commences a road trip instead. First he visits the
Queen Mary, a time capsule saturated with the WWII era of his parents. Finding
its stranded loss of context oppressive, he moves on. Next stop is the hotel El
Coronado, which the author of teleplays manages not to recognize as the biggest
prop of Billy Wilder's *Some Like It Hot*. He has to be informed of the hotel's film
history, meaning it's not a memory that suffuses the site with its mediation. The
nineteenth-century hotel must frame the nineteenth-century photograph Collier
discovers among its encrypted memorabilia.

The kernel of separation of photographic and cinematic media from the televisual Sensurround, which underlies his oblivion of contact with the Wilder film as
seen on TV, is incorporated or "cocooned" (110) in Collier's sensation of "absorption" (106) at the point of entering the past. Absorption is piecemeal and secured
around one stage or dimension in the stereoscopic display, the pocket cinema, the
"shell" (110) of the past: "A physical sensation akin to sliding backward through a
film, I think. . . . The point is that the zone of conjunction, whether it may be—an
entryway, an opening, a film—is something very close and very thin" (107). And
again: "I was, in fact, in a *pocket* of 1896. . . . To travel in time, one begins at one's
core—one's mind, of course—and radiates the feeling outward, first affecting the
body, then making contact with immediate surroundings. The feeling of breaking
through a film might well be the moment when one has radiated the inner conviction
beyond the limits of the body" (110). Remaining in the past is the main problem in
time travel via absorption: "to reach another time is infinitely less demanding than
adapting to it" (130). Collier identifies on this score with specters. "Is this what
ghosts experience? I wondered. A dread of accosting people lest those people look
directly through them and they lose their fragile illusion of still being alive?" (125).

The credibility of Collier's document is compromised by the gathering
disease and the inevitable wish to escape it. Binding his narrative inside a loop
of possibilities, however, is his sudden recollection that he in fact met the actress
of the 1896 photograph when he was a young student (63). The old woman kept
looking at him as though she knew him, or because, as his date pointed out, she
liked what she saw. Then she muttered an enigmatic phrase of love. That night
she died. Now, since falling in love with her earlier incarnation in the photograph,
he has been reading up on her. An actress well-known in her day, she performed
at the hotel El Coronado in 1896. By all accounts, there is the mystery of what

happened there and then, which at once fulfilled and emptied her out to refill with sublimation for a better burn as an artist. Convinced it was the lost love she recalled upon seeing him in his youth, the Paul Newman lookalike wants to go back in time to deliver her from the trauma, a roundabout way of giving the old girl a mercy fuck.

Post-coitus, he finds a 1971 penny in the lining of his jacket—a penny for his thoughts, and his stay in 1896 is unstuck. He is the found and lost object who changes her for better and worse. In the 1980 film adaptation for which Matheson wrote the screenplay, the protagonist is an author suffering writer's block who falls for the woman in a picture taken in 1912 (squarely within the round of cinematic self-reflexivity). When he was a student he met her senior incarnation. Now he no longer looks like Newman but is in fact Christopher Reeves (a.k.a. Superman). He seeks out the professor who lectured on time travel at his college. The professor's name is a tribute: Dr. Finney. That Matheson subsequently retitled his novel after the film, *Somewhere in Time*, also follows Finney, who expanded the original title, *The Body Snatchers*, to echo the title of the first film adaptation. In the 1978 edition of *Invasion of the Body Snatchers*, the film Miles and Becky were watching when the local epidemic called them away was *Time and Again*. *Somewhere in Time* outbid (or already did) the adaptation of Finney's book. The hotel selected for the film—the Grand Hotel on Mackinac Island in Michigan—is a large Civil War era rectangle (doubled by the veranda) that subsumes a great many boxes and shots. The psychocybernetic focus of time travel requires a boxed-in setting oddly reminiscent of the contained quality of the England scenes in Dan Curtis's *Dracula*, the TV movie for which Matheson also wrote the screenplay. When the bad penny grabs Reeves, he is vacuum-sucked out of the box of their tryst into the other time, another boxed-in set where the TV set was left on while the crying out actress (Bond girl Jane Seymour) diminishes and warps within the filmy divide like a trace. In a week, Reeves dies in his hotel room and the boxes within boxes open upon a firmament in which, at the finish line, the lovers are reunited in suspended reanimation.

Finney responded to his fictional commemoration in *Somewhere in Time* in the mode of time travel. In 1995, he published *From Time to Time* in which the (family) history of the world wars displaces the centrality of love stories, and the government project in support of time travel spins its objectives of ambivalence into an allegory of the Manhattan Project. His second time travel novel was in fact a long deferred sequel; he picked up the story of Si Morley where it left off in *Time and Again*. Toward the end of the prequel, Si brought Julia over into his time to lose the police in the past. Catching up with the future, Julia discovered the world wars. She looked at a history book about the first one. But then she was devastated that there was another one. Si related the German bombings of cities, the Allied fire bombings of German cities, the genocide, and the atom bombings (377-78). Julia doesn't live here anymore. Morley followed her into the past and, by undoing the conditions for the invention of time travel and the subsequent application thereof for US revisionism, shut the portal behind him.

In the sequel, however, residual memories of the government project motivate one of its former agents to undo the undoing. Again the prospect of reanimating photos in the family album motivates Morley to agree to be enlisted, this time to travel in time to investigate and undo the disappearance of a secret US agent, identity unknown, together with the written agreements he obtained in negotiation with the European powers, which would have circumvented WWI. Once identification can be made, it turns out he went down with the *Titanic* the following year, 1912, the year of the revisited/reincarnated past in *Somewhere in Time*. But when one of the agents of the re-started project, the Jotta Girl, changes the course of the liner one jot, it turns out that only now is the hotel-ship set to sideswipe the iceberg. The dictum of the inventor of time travel—one must never interfere with the past—resounds like the destiny you perpetrate in the attempt to lose it. The time travelers struggle to be believed just like the Trojan princess Cassandra, who, according to Melanie Klein's interpretation of *The Oresteia*, represents the onset of the raising up of the superego from its unconscious part toward consciousness and conscience. The curse of a reception of disbelief expresses "the universal tendency towards denial. Denial is a potent defence against the persecutory anxiety and guilt which result from destructive impulses never being completely controlled. Denial, which is always bound up with persecutory anxiety, may . . . undermine sympathy and consideration both with the internal and external objects, and disturb the capacity for judgement and the sense of reality" (293).

Now that WWI is back on the horizon, Morley can at least try to avert the war casualty of his son, which he knows about. The open time trip that ends the novel parallels Sir Arthur Conan Doyle's response to and responsibility for his own son, a casualty of the Great War. He tried to locate the young man's erring spirit through the media technology of modern Spiritualism. The prospect of time travel entertained by Finney is not disseminated by alternate history or remembrance. Instead it is supported by the doubling or looping of the history we recognize through an alternative causation, one that is personalized. The time traveling intervention in traumatic history perpetrates the trauma that is no longer history.

5

In *Time and Again*, it is the historical fire of the World Building that binds Si and Julia even as it solves the mystery of the note passed down in Kate's family. It is also a point of crossover for the novel's discourse. The novel is the scrapbook of Si's time trips. One of his fellow boarders in 1882 has a new camera and gives Si some of the photographs. An illustrator by profession, Si is able to sketch likenesses of past scenes and people that also make it into the book. When the fire he and Julia survived makes it into the news, however, we enter an interlinear "translation" between the lines of the newspaper reports in the archive and in Si's experience. On the morning after the fire, he quotes the coverage from *The New York Times* and inserts between the lines: "I'll see that forever; the way they held out their hands" (304). And again, after quoting from his "copy of *The New York Times* for Wednesday, February 1, 1882," he inserts after a dash: "and now Julia and I stood in the silent crowd watching him" (308).

McLuhan considered newspaper literacy to be the nineteenth-century's civilizing inoculation against prehistory. For Benjamin, newspaper and photography belong to an advance guard of immunization that jettisoned Baudelaire into a last stand or understanding of poetry, which was otherwise in withdrawal within the neutralization of experience. To immerse himself in the process of translation, Si must enter the very inoculation or forget-together, as when he reads examples of 1880s B-literature in preparation for the time change (109-10). Einstein is called on briefly to motivate the conceivable availability of the past. Additionally, the habitats reconstructed for various projects of translation resemble film sets. But the project relies on photographs, or rather on their alteration (i.e., their alternation with reproductions and reconstructions of photographs in other media of representation) (45, 48).

Throughout his work, Benjamin waffles with regard to photography's relation to aura. This either/aura is photography's melancholic condition, which Roland

Barthes summarized at its summit in his reading of photography at the point of puncture. The melancholia is another name for the blank stare of the photograph that retains one's gaze. Benjamin cut loose from the photography impasse when he found in film the situation of testing and expertise that could turn the blank around.

Chris Marker's *La Jetée* (1962) is a time travel film consisting of photographs. There is one exception: the brief moving image of the woman in the past inserted like the consequence of reanimation at the end of a series of pictures. Marker approximates film with photographs, in other words, by tampering with *the* photograph. Where photographs are organized through inter-reference, we can no longer address the photograph as a vault of reference. Only in the singular is the photograph the souvenir of the past bearing a trace of its passing. The inscrutable melancholia of each photograph's "will have been" is open and shut. As Derrida argues in *Droit de regards*, when photographs communicate with one another—whether through the syntax of their interrelation and juxtaposition in a series, in the mix with other media, or even through retouching—the loosening from the referent summons ghosts. Valie Export's film *Invisible Adversaries* (1977), which she has called a remake of *Invasion of the Body Snatchers*, follows the process in reverse. The heroine-photographer suffers a Schreberesque breakdown and must forego the photographic syntax of her mixed media art. Henceforward she must take identifying photos of everyone she encounters, but in anticipation of the exposure of their doubles upon development.

When Marker's time traveler goes into the past, he makes contact with a woman who appears to be dead to him from the vantage point of the present time he inhabits. He goes back repeatedly—it is the *photo roman* that allows Marker's film to explore the deep space of haunting inside media. The couple visits a natural history museum. Supported by a defunct Gestell that was contemporary in the late nineteenth century, the museum is a Piranesi-like spatiality packed with niches of creaturely still-life. It holds the place of the museum that Wells's time traveler visits with Weena prior to losing her, mercifully not to Morlock consumerism but to cremation by the forest fire he accidentally sets.

The third world war drove the Paris survivors into an underworld that is also a test lab. Humanity will not survive under these postwar conditions. An emissary must be sent across time to seek aid. All scientists and technicians running the experiment speak German—German science fiction to the rescue. If it could spawn the rocket out of its Doppelgänger fabulations, then why not time transport, the ultimate double fantasy or science? As the research team crosses over into realization of its constructs, notably when the traveler brings back a small gadget-like energy source from the future, the German language group takes on an evil aspect. Like Germanic deities in a Wagner opera, the futuristic talking heads grant the hero his last request—that he return to the past rather than find safety in the future (of wish fulfilment). He doesn't choose fantasy and meets his doom by the consequence of what Wagner considered a contract. The law that no one can leave his own time behind must be enforced: the German-language contingent sends an assassin into the past to shoot the time traveler inside his souvenir.

"Warum?" ("Why?") can be found in West Berlin cemeteries as a popular benediction inscribed onto tombstones. But does the question belong to the deceased or the survivors? Why must Marker's film end with the time traveler's death? Why must the traveler die his proper death when the memory that he was fixated upon guarded him while guiding him to it in time?

The souvenir that destines him for time tripping belongs to the recent past, the post WWII era just before the third world war. It belongs to his childhood and is marked as traumatically memorable by his peripheral sense that a man was shot dead. As a wish or command, it would be his father's death that he recognizes but can't identify. The inner woman is at the airport in this memory picture, which means that he recognizes her from his childhood. It's not a stretch that she is his mother and that, in the final scene, he returns to her both as an adult lover and as her child. Does the assassin protect the time to come against the time paradox that the traveler is about to bring about through his double occupancy? Or is it the law of Oedipus that is being upheld? Does he die, then, like father like son?

The Terminator (1984) withdraws *La Jetée*'s terminal scene within a loop installed as a new beginning. In the future, technology jumps the gun of a final total war that mankind held in readiness. Liberated from the prosthetic relationship to humanity by its programmed recognition of human self-destructiveness, technology disposes of the leftover humans. Then a new leader rises up to carry an identification with the lost cause to victory. We see the machines sorting through the junkyard of human civilization. Time travel is the machine order's reading of the human psyche. On the terms and turf of psychic reality, the machine order sends a terminator, a humanoid double, back in time to eliminate the leader of the human survivors, John Connor, before he is born. But Connor launches the second time trip (or testament), sending his best friend as a delegate or double to protect his birth (with a photograph of his mother for a guide). Cameron's film never shows Connor, who, under the aegis of friendship, goes back to inseminate his mother with himself. The machine order of the first time trip or testament is undone through the loop that the new one opens wide by replacing the father with the son. *Terminator 2: Judgment Day* (1991) threads this loop through the near miss between the computer chip that Schwarzenegger's terminator destroys before he extinguishes himself and the hand he keeps leaving behind in the machine. The sequel's conclusion keeps the son-as-father going but also adds the affirmation of an unknown future. Loopy Christianity admits a secular-philosophical affirmation of the other as the time to come, a paradox that is a pop-cultural tendency more recently evident in the clone sermon in *Cloud Atlas* (2013). The assignment of a proper death of one's own is a philosophical perspective suitable for high culture, but B-culture questions it. This dialectic can always also be simulated inside the culture industry. As an item of mass market esoterica, *Donnie Darko* (2001) rides out the deregulation of a happening death in *Final Destination* (2000) unto the double finality that harbors one's proper death.

6

Telepathy is the psychic transmission that by its immediacy ushers in the prospect of double time, but in a milieu of deregulation that must be circumscribed. In Arthur C. Clarke's *Childhood's End*, alien overlords take control of human affairs to prepare mankind for the upcoming merger with the Overmind. To this end, the overlords must contain, cleanse, and sublate the ambiguous/ambivalent situation of telepathy in the human household. What lets the children come unto the union with the Overmind is their introductory free gift of real-time telepathic connection with all the other children. In no time, they begin to resemble one another. Then the mutational merger takes place.

In 1950, Alan Turing published an essay that was at the same time a science fiction. "Computing Machinery and Intelligence" first describes a test situation where an interrogator must discern by their answers which test subject is male and which is female. Then Turing proposes replacing the male subject with a machine and changing the distinction that the interrogator will evaluate to man vs. machine. The German science fiction of doubling between woman and machine thus makes a ghost appearance in computing's bid for the future of thinking.

In setting out the guidelines for his experiment, Turing admits that, if telepathy must be factored in, then his basic test conditions of sight unseen communication will require telepathy-proofing. But greater uncontainment appears to follow the acceptance of telepathy, which brings with it, Turing concludes, an acceptance of ghosts—the undoing of the proof of his experiment.

Before telepathy can be aligned exclusively with the unspoken communion going into the mutational merger with the Overmind in *Childhood's End*, the ghostly trajectory of telepathy, which is identified as a malignant cancer threatening the universe, must be contained. Telepathy is targeted to cut it adrift from contact with the dead and renders legible mankind's distinction as extinction. The mutation of mankind into another life form prior to the destruction of the Earth commences as the ending of childhood, i.e., the removal of mourning or unmourning from the horizon of human thought. The ambivalence of this end of childhood finds its caption in a recollection that doubles WWII back onto WWI as its Second Coming: "Somewhere long ago, I had seen a century-old newsreel of such an exodus. It must have been the beginning of the First World War—or the Second. There had been long lines of trains, crowded with children, pulling slowly out of the threatened cities" (186).

Let the children, including the pre-teens and the teens, come unto adventure in *Time for the Stars*—but on the double. Only twins (or rather, only telepathic twins) are admitted to the front of the line. The ghost connection is crowded out by all the other applications of telepathy to the problems of Outer Space transport at the border to time travel.

For his 1968 science fiction novel, Heinlein made telepathy the basis for a post-relativist universe. And yet its exceptional status as a communication or transport does not extend beyond the finitude of the correspondents. *Time for the Stars* is the ultimate postwar-science-fiction instrumentalization of the Doppelgänger and its milieu of occult relations. The instrumentalization is literalized among twins and triplets who communicate telepathically, but in realtime only. The name of the Outer Space project reaching to the stars addresses the literal or biological problem of overpopulation. In this future world, it is as neutral as Kindergarten: Project Lebensraum.

Interstellar travel at near light speed is hard to link by telecommunication with the Earth or with the other "torchships" traveling to other star systems in search of habitable planets. The working hypothesis—namely that telepathy is the exception to modern physics, since it doesn't transmit materially—gets those twins and triplets on board who thus maintain contact with their siblings on Earth or on other spacecraft.

The protagonist, Tom, thought he and his twin brother Pat were whispering to one another just below the threshold of overhearing others. But he was only uncanny-proofing a gift he and Pat were able to use directly through the lip-syncing ritual. Even if the lips need not be read, telepathy works best as a conversation, founders as a mind reading. The whispering ended up being Tom's best rehearsal for transmitting the words of a third person standing by. Letting one's "directed thoughts echo what someone else was saying," "a telepair acted almost like a microphone and a speaker" (62). Like the devices for broadcasting speech, however, visual media also don't really apply. It is possible to share photographs between Earth and the torchship only via a telepath's translation of them into drawings (89).

The expert who tests Tom at the recruitment center explains that it is almost unheard of that individuals who are not identically twinned can "tune in" telepathically. And only about ten percent of the identical twins can realize what must in theory be considered human potential. "It can't be the brain waves we detect with encephalograph equipment or we would have been selling commercial telepathic equipment long since" (27). When long-distance communication by radio telephony and telepathy can be measured side by side, telepathy comes in first. What's more, the signal strength continues unabated as though the twins are in adjoining rooms. "Telepathy doesn't pay the least bit of attention to the speed of light. . . . I don't know how you can be sure that telepathy is physical; we haven't been able to make it register on any instrument. . . . We don't even know how consciousness hooks into matter. Is consciousness physical?" (33).

The testing of the hypothesis that telepathy is not limited by the speed of light turns out to be the main (yet secret) mission of Project Lebensraum. Or, in the words of Dr. Babcock from Vienna, the telepaths are brought along "for research into the nature of time. . . . You might say that we are trying to find out what the word 'simultaneous' means" (80, 81).

Time aboard ship still proceeds within Einstein's physical universe. While Earth time passes in decades, then, those on board a torchship age only a few years, and the doubles back on Earth submit to a "geriatric" health regimen designed for extended longevity (49). The difficulty that interstellar travel poses for telepathic communication is that the speed of time on board the torchship is so out of synch with Earth time that the tele-words are speeded up or slowed down to the point of garbling. The Earthbound correspondent must be hypnotized (and if necessary drugged) while the traveling double tries to pace the articulation of his communication to compensate for the slippage (109). Tom turns out to be one of the few telepaths who, by a kind of contact high, can link with correspondents other than his twin brother. Around the time Tom discovers that he can tune in on a good friend's telepathic connection, he connects with Molly, his twin brother's daughter. New generations of telepaths are needed to give support during the trials of the Earthbound half of the tenuous connection across divergent velocities of time. Eventually his brother's granddaughter and great granddaughter inherit the position of Tom's tele-correspondent.

A catastrophic encounter on one planet with sea monsters or alien weapons reduces the population on board from 200 to 30. Thereafter the new captain prepares to continue the mission to the next star system rather than return to Earth. In the meantime, consultation with Earth reveals that they will be brought back after all—and by spaceships that will catch up with them not in six decades but in no time at all. "They've done it, they've done it, they've applied irrelevance. Dr. Babcock was right. . . . You telepaths were the reason the investigation started; you proved that "simultaneity" was an admissible concept . . . and the inevitable logical consequence was that time and space do not exist" (176-77). When Tom returns as the head of a household of generations and still a young man to his aged brother, his youngest correspondent immediately proposes that they stay connected, this time in marriage. Brother Pat never had a son and the patronymic was set to go with him. But then Tom comes back from Outer Space to secure for his brother (now a father) the Happy End as his brother's own son.

In Heinlein's "adult" time-travel novel *Farnham's Freehold* (1964), the trip to the future in the place you know already (but can never return to as it was) traverses a proximity to the notion of "parallel universes" (162) and their alternate histories. It is also Heinlein's opportunity to debunk and perform the ideological time trip of revisionism—the variation on double time that is his signature innovation in the Cold War science fictions *The Puppet Masters* and *Starship Troopers*. Heinlein loads the reversal prospects by the anachronism or contradiction that the Farnham household, in a Western state, occupies Joseph, a "houseboy" and "young Negro" (2), who advances without problem to "second-in-command" (23) when the extended family enters the fallout shelter during the escalation of the Cuban missile crisis. By the third nuclear blast the shelter is jettisoned 2,000 years into the future.

The new world order welcomes Joseph; in the meantime, the mutual destruction of East and West made room for the ascendancy of Africans. Why is Joseph so invested in the reversal? There were racist vibes in the Farnham household to be sure. But there is a historical reversal set up by Joseph's traumatic memories of Mississippi (227) that is supported by the history books of the future. "It says here that the United States, at the time of the war, held its black population as slaves. Somebody had chopped out a century" (211). The comparison-chopping protest is the saddest comment of all.

"The story maintained that the whites, with their evil ways, destroyed each other almost to the last man . . . leaving the innocent, charitable, merciful dark race—beloved by Uncle the Mighty—to inherit the Earth. The few white survivors, spared by Uncle's mercy, had been succored and cherished as children and now again were waxing numerous under the benevolent guidance of the Chosen. So it read" (212). The main lesson learned by Hugh, the head of the Farnham household, is that blacks are racist, too. Joseph reassured his former employer: "Hugh, I didn't make the rules. But I'm Chosen and you're not, and that's all there is to it. It's not my fault that you're white" (177-78). In consequence of the globalization of certain legacies of the American Civil War toward an African victory, to be Chosen is to be like poor white trash in Mississippi, only this time black. A white servant like Hugh is cared for like a pet (230). A male servant is neutered like a harem guard or pet, often after he served as "stud." The largest caste of women goes by the apparently value-free designation "sluts." While not as high up in the hierarchy as house servants, sluts can serve the masters as "bedwarmers" whose duties beyond the literal one are open to interpretation and need.

The society's avuncular order nevertheless reflects the centrality of a mother goddess. Men rule but inheritance is established through the sister's son, not the ruler's father or sons. "Under this system, marriage would never be important—bastardy might be a concept so abstract as to be unrecognized—but *family* would be more important than ever. Women (of the Chosen) could never be downgraded; they were more important than males even though they rule through their

brothers" (214). The problem with reversal is that something is preserved, in this case basic racism and sexism. The future African order is depicted as Egyptoid, (i.e., static, lacking in innovation or invention). Are blacks then better at living in the lap of luxury than white folks, who are more conscientious as servants, whether in housekeeping or engineering?

Hugh has benefitted from the nuclear strikes and resulting time trip by swapping his first miserable attempt at marriage and children for a fresh start with his new partner Barbara and their twin sons. He is motivated to escape servitude, however benign, to secure a future for the new family, even if only as members of the "runner" underground. He was too aware of "the oldest Law of the Conquered, that their women eventually submit—willingly" (246). While Barbara lives in sluts headquarters and Hugh is a house servant to the high official Their Charity (also known as Uncle), the partners must communicate their preparedness for flight in a code or "mishmash of German, Russian, colloquial English, beatnik jive, literary allusions, pig Latin, and special idioms" (255). They rest assured that no local scholar could translate it back into Language (as the high discourse of global Africa is called).

By his education, Hugh holds an upper hand in the court of Their Charity, which he deals through the introduction of long-extinct card games. He and Joseph can entice Their Charity to patent and market these games in what is otherwise a totalitarian communist economy (213), underscoring the basic Soviet identification behind every foe of Americans. But when Hugh shows his hand, the wild card he's holding—the idea of freedom—baffles Their Charity. "'Freedom!' . . . A concept without a referent, like 'ghosts'" (229). Time travelers might as well be ghosts; once the balancing act among parallel universes commences, the return to the time of their nuclear departure drops them off in time to see themselves and their others before the start of the war. "Maybe this is a different world. Or maybe it's the same one but just a tiny bit changed by—well, by us coming back, perhaps" (331). Hugh's daughter Karen, the one member of his first family he wasn't happy to lose, is still there. "Karen is alive right now, back there behind us—and yet we saw her die. So somehow, in some timeless sense, Karen is alive forever, somewhere" (322).

It was Their Charity who decided to send Hugh and his family back where they came from. Hugh's irrational "balky" (225) dissatisfaction would instill discontent among the other white servants. More to the point, it turns out Their Charity's

scientists have been studying the evidence of the shelter and have now succeeded in calculating the odds to secure the passage through time. "I understand it is not so much the amount of power—no atom-kernel bombs necessary—as the precise application of power" (308). Against the grain of Hugh's prejudice, they have sent a test mouse into the past and back. All along, in fact, Their Charity and his scholars were reading along in Hugh's encoded correspondence. The future order is capable of producing psy-fi items just like the Soviets in the recent past. When Hugh is back, he does not deposit any of the devices as instructed to loop his passage back through a black communist future.

7

The alien menace in Heinlein's novel *The Puppet Masters* (1951) or in William Cameron Menzies' science fiction classic *Invasion from Mars* (1953) can be resolutely plugged into the Cold War by dint of the brainwashing underlying the details of their administration of remote control. In *Invasion from Mars*, the brain plugs operate like post-hypnotic suggestions in the context of undercover assignments of assassination and destruction. The plug's ability to implode and snuff the agent calls attention to the fact that such assignments are suicidal. The wars against terror are throwbacks to the Cold War. But inasmuch as the destiny of Israel is now more than ever the issue, the intervening Cold era is at the same time realigned with hot traumatic histories.

The Puppet Masters effectively wipes out World War II from its horizon: following a hot world war between the US and the USSR, the future world has returned to the Cold War opposition. But there are details to the forecast that reflect a recent past before the Cold War. To their advantage, the alien slugs use the earthbound limitations of television transmission, which can be live only within a restricted orbit; beyond that, it must be forwarded without guarantee. "The reports from the contaminated areas were not materially different from the reports from other areas. Our stereocast and the follow-ups did not reach those areas. Back in the days of radio it could not have happened; the Washington station where the 'cast originated could have blanketed the country. But stereo-video rides wavelengths so short that horizon-to-horizon relay is necessary and local channels must be squirted out of local stations" (160). There are three space stations, a history

of exploration and colonization on Mars and Venus, but no satellites. A restricted relationship to television characterizes the alternate future world of Nazi victory according to Dick's *The Man in the High Castle*. Trying to figure out what exactly went down during one's former possession by an alien slug or master runs up against an acme of idealization. Only the human terms of a master race apply, "or perhaps I don't know what I am talking about; what does a bee know about Beethoven?" (85).

Menzies was a director who sought to control the entire look of a film. He was the acclaimed director of the burning of Atlanta sequence in *Gone with the Wind*, projected from a vantage point already documented in *Conquest of the Air* (1936), a propaganda film he contributed to on commission by the British air ministry. A frame of reference for his images is supported by the director's high-quality bi-cultural *Bildung*. He attended both his hometown college, Yale University, and the University of Edinburgh, back in his parents' country of origin. The horror films being made on other stages in the industry beginning in the 1930s adhered to art direction made in Germany, the other land of phantoms and inventions. Still in range of this influence would be his contact with Hitchcock: Menzies reshot the nightmare in *Spellbound*. Among the mementoes of German Expressionist film in *Invasion from Mars* would be the *Caligari*-like plot twist of a nightmare that recurs at the end either as insanity or as the real fulfilment of paranoid premonition. Oddly enough, the top secret plant commences in the backyard of the suburban home of the boy witness. It is even stranger that the boy looks out his window at the seaside set that Murnau derived from Caspar David Friedrich paintings for *Nosferatu*.

George Pal came to be best known for his association with three science fiction movies: the first two, *Destination Moon* (1950) and *The War of the Worlds* (1953), he produced, and the third, *The Time Machine* (1960), he directed and produced. Born in Hungary, he came to Hollywood in 1939 from Berlin via Britain. Together with David Duncan, who wrote the screenplay, Pal subtly skewers the time trip on a crypt of future warfare, a displaced and unacknowledged reference to WWII. In the future, the Eloi are 1960s flower children who aren't as devolved as in the narrative but lack concern for their neighbor just the same. George, the time traveler in the Duncan/Pal adaptation, concludes that Weena's move to intervene on his behalf without regard of risk proves that mankind still has a continuity shot at an open future. He identifies her empathy as self-sacrifice or suicide—a roundabout way (through philosophical narcissism) of circumventing the test. The Morlocks summon the Eloi cattle by a siren that induces them to enter the underworld in a trance state. The portal to the Morlock underworld is the fallout shelter, which we saw constructed in the fast-forwarding of history during the trip to the future. By 1966, the time traveler's home in London has been cleared away and the shelter installed nearby. Although this reference to shelters is lodged in a setting of nuclear warfare, it was during WWII that underground protection was sought by the London populace against air raids and V-2 rocket attacks. In the ruinscape of the future, the fallout shelter alone survives intact, still a functional structure albeit to another end as well as to another, equally displaced WWII reference. The Eloi are called not to gather for shelter against attack but, succumbing to benign tranquilization, to enter the facility of their extermination.

Whereas he couldn't cosign Heinlein's middlebrown politics, Dick singled the author out in his introduction to the *The Golden Man* (1980) as truly empathic, because he made nothing but exceptions on a personal and daily basis: "That is the best in humanity, there; that is who and what I love" (xix). But these exceptions or contradictions, which Dick noted in the interpersonal domain, can also shred the Cold War ideological envelope in *The Puppet Masters* or *Starship Troopers* (1959).

An ostensible disagreement between Heinlein in *Starship Troopers* and our spirit guide Philip K. Dick about the value of adolescence is contradicted (or rather circumvented) by the surprise doctrine that there is only adult delinquency. Before the current social order saved the day, which is based on citizenship secured through military service alone, "back in the XXth century" the "juvenile delinquent" was the poster boy of the social disorder that led to the "breakup of the North American republic" (112-13).

> These juvenile criminals hit a low level. Born with only the instinct for survival, the highest morality they achieved was a shaky loyalty to a peer group, a street gang. . . . "Juvenile delinquent" is a contradiction in terms. "Delinquent" means "failing in duty." But duty is an adult virtue—indeed a juvenile becomes an adult when (and only when) he acquires a knowledge of duty and embraces it as dearer than the self-love he was born with. There never was, there cannot be, a "juvenile delinquent." But for every juvenile criminal there are always one or more

adult delinquents—people of mature years who either do not know their
duty, or who, knowing it, fail. (118-20)

One implication is that the "shaky loyalty" to an in-group is a fundamental
part of the greater group in which duty is upheld. One's squadron is one's "gang"
(163). Otherwise the claim that revolution has been rendered impossible in a
society that equates authority with responsibility wouldn't make sense. "If you
separate out the aggressive ones and make them the sheep dogs, the sheep will
never give you trouble" (184).

Another unexpected exception or contradiction lies in Heinlein's championship
of the atomic era (which his science fiction leads out of the Cold War back into the
heat) by an evolutionary argument. Sanctuary is a planet that is Earth's apparently
benign double in so many features. That it even lacks radioactivity, however, turns out
to be a disadvantage. "With all these advantages it barely got away from the starting
gate. You see, it's short on mutations; it does not enjoy Earth's high level of natural
radiation" (155). In the long run, "evolutionary progress held down almost to zero
by lack of radiation and a consequent most unhealthily low mutation rate" cannot be
considered in a positive light. But will the colonists on this planet do the right thing
and set off a dirty-type nuclear explosion to secure their future in evolution by a proper
genetic heritage of mutation? No. "The human race is too individualistic, too self-
centered, to worry that much about future generations" (156).

In *The Puppet Masters*, the contradictions or contraindications that keep this
"controversial" work within the pale attend Heinlein's eroticization of the conflict. Mary is one special agent who can tell a "possessed" male "host" by the
absence of his sexual response to her presence: "Harem guards, if you know what
I mean" (21). But when she cites as evidence of an epidemic or invasion the non-
response she picked up from four men in a row, the President dismisses it as the
statistically possible coincidence of her meeting four Harem guards, if she knows
what he means. The slugs lodge themselves in the back of a host. The first line of
defense is therefore "Schedule Bare Back." What is ultimately guarded against by
compulsory beach attire are back-to-back "conferences" of the master slugs, also
identified as a form of conjugation. But is it really conjugal reproduction? No;
it's replicational sex at best. Already one slug alone can double and divide itself,
sending a second slug to crawl up the back available for riding bareback and thus
increase the network of hosts. In the 1994 film adaptation, a GI who is undercover

in occupied Des Moines is sorely tested when one zomboid host turns his back to him, indicating that he wants a back-to-back connection. Disgusted, without regard for the risk, he blasts the host.

Schedule Bare Back is replaced by Schedule Suntan, compulsory nudity, which is reinforced by vigilantes. Something more closely resembling full frontal heterosexuality (or is it sublimation?) takes over. Agent Mary's test by intuition no longer applies once the slugs, no doubt through the pressure of these schedules, discover the sex and violence in their hosts. Following out programmed scenarios, therefore, shows of sex and violence are directed by slugs on the backs of their performers for public broadcast within their closed-off television sections. A male and a female fight unto their near deaths. "There was a ring and a referee and two contestants pitted against each other. There were even fouls, i.e., doing anything which might damage the opponent's manager—I mean 'master,' the opponent's slug. Nothing else was a foul—nothing! It was a man versus a woman, both of them big and husky. She gouged out one of his eyes in the first clinch, but he broke her left wrist which kept the match on even enough terms to continue" (284). Before the slugs depart the used-up hosts, the triumphant male rapes his reward. "But the male slave had remained active a little longer than the female, slashed and damaged though he was, and he finished the match with a final act of triumph over her which I soon learned was customary. It seemed to be a signal to turn it into an 'audience participation show,' an orgy which would make a witches' Sabbat seem like a sewing circle. Oh, the slugs had discovered sex, all right!" (ibid.). The showdown of conjugal heterosexuality, a neurotic-to-normal primal scene, does not necessarily contradict the aliens' immediate pledge of a united, no-longer-lonely humanity, which captions the happiness they introduce from the rear. In the pre-Oedipus complex, anality is the source of happiness up front in carrying out one's duties, conjugal perhaps, but between father and son. Mary triangulates the father and son in-group that thus prevails in the end. In the words of the slug master ventriloquizing Sam, the son, both under interrogation by The Old Man, Sam's father (with Mary standing by): "'We come to bring you . . . peace . . . and contentment—and the joy of—of surrender.' I hesitated again; 'surrender' was not the right word. I struggled with it the way one struggles with a poorly grasped foreign language. 'The joy,' I repeated, 'the joy of . . . nirvana.' That was it; the word fitted. I felt like a dog being patted for fetching a stick; I wriggled with pleasure" (118).

The plugs and slugs from Outer Space in red-scare science fiction park in the back, a gesture that inspired Tobe Hooper's fleshing out of a fully anal alien underworld behind the suburban home in his 1986 remake of *Invaders from Mars*. It is to provide another such underworld that the 1994 film version of Heinlein's novel includes the clunky conceit that the slugs must convene regularly en masse in a "hive" that is transported with them as they progress through Iowa. During Mary's term of or turn at possession, she joins the group in communion among the tendrils and membranes hanging down. She alone, therefore, of the in-group of protagonists, each of whom experiences possession, has total knowledge of the invading group-of-one. She knows for sure that the slug removed from Sam's father was the last surviving one. She had a thousand voices in her head—Sam was there, too. But that's the preamble to the Happy End of coupification. She knows everything Sam tries to hide from himself. Since women on average are more open, they've already won the race against repression.

The slugs soon vary their approach by riding dogs to their proper host destinations. Mary was slugged through Sam's cat Pirate, who died of the hosting stint. "A hell of a world where you could not trust dogs! Apparently cats were hardly ever used because of their smaller size. Poor old Pirate was an exceptional case. In Zone Green dogs were almost never seen now, at least by day. They filtered out of Zone Red at night, traveled in the dark and hid out in the daytime. . . . It made one think of the werewolf legends" (282). That the future world is in a crisis from hell is illuminated by the withdrawal of dogs into instrumentalization, demonization, and slaughter.

The slugs invading Earth hail from Titan, one of Saturn's moons. Failing their mission on Venus, they arrive in flying saucers with their hosts, the Titan natives, "elfin" "androgynes" from the fantasy genre (311). In her repressed childhood, Mary was captive audience to the slug possession of all the adult colonizers on Venus, who no longer cared about her. This is the rehearsal, then, of her sexual-response test, the psychopathic disconnection that shattered something closer to unconditional mirroring. Out of her repressed memories, the fellow agents learn about one fever that is fatal to the slugs in a very short span of time. Like the reverse of the countdown to the spread of zombieism, Nine-Day Fever names a time difference between species into which the vaccine can be injected to twist survival off a poor prognosis. In the film version, Sam joins Mary, recently delivered of her slug, in exploring the hive laboratory where the aliens have also been running trials, specifically testing human responses to different diseases. The couple saves one other human for the pickup by helicopter, a prepubescent boy whose slug died of his illness. His illness, encephalitis, turns out to be fatal in no time for the aliens since they consist mostly of brain matter. Since they are all the parts of a single creature, the brain inflammation once administered spreads rapid fire. Live transmissions across a long distance are not interrupted when it's time for soldiers to take off their shirts and show their backs. They bare their backs to prove that the aliens are gone. Otherwise only Sam's studly body underwent showing to tell. When they go back into the hive, the interior décor now etiolated dried-out papier mâché, the sole-surviving slug skewers the back of Sam's father.

The film slugs have phallic probes which shoot out to enter a host's body below the brain. This is followed by the alignment of hooks on the slug's bulk form with the spinal cord. Thus the organ without a body overrides the host's nervous system. The probes are also elastic and allow the aliens to swing around like little Tarzans. When they hold conferences, little spindly ET hands shoot up. "You never told me how good it felt!" the father reproaches his son now that he too has been penetrated. The word that comes to the father's mind is "free." He also now has access to the alien intelligence of Oedipal constraints upon humans, which the slug in possession of Sam earlier on used against him. Now the tables are turned. "Are you capable of killing your father?"

Recruitment is the key term used to describe the alien efforts to extend their network of hosts. It is also an apt term for the covert operations of perversion that, in the absence of identified mutuality, must secure another's willingness to submit to an alien protocol (e.g., in the mode of dissociation). Recruitment can also stick. Even after he has been liberated, Sam, the first of the in-group to undergo possession, is wary of being near his slug. "I had a dark and certain thought that if I were alone with it, I would be able to do nothing, that I would freeze and wait while it crawled up me and settled again between my shoulder blades, searched out my spinal column, took possession of my brain and my very inner self" (106). The seduction-recruitment of perversion is aligned with a certain ideological offer. The plot line in *The Puppet Masters* catches up with the analogy that was already used over and again when we learn that the "masters" from Titan invaded the Soviet Union first and with complete and seamless success. The possession of the USSR has become evident in the meantime through reports of plague outbreaks.

As the survivor of the possession knows for sure, slugs neglect the hygiene of their hosts. In no time the human material is excrementalized, exhausted, and infected beyond repair.

8

The future of aeronautics in *The Puppet Masters* is monopolized by certain cars that can take off like rockets, almost always in violation of the law, as in speeding. In *The Dreams Our Stuff Is Made Of*, Thomas Disch identified the rocket as the hallmark of science fiction, but only to the extent that the rocket always covers for a car: "The image of the rocket—preferably a '50s model kind with Pontiac tail fins—remains the sci-fi image of preference" (57). While the German Autobahn system was conceived in the shadow of the cryptofetishism that attained its highpoint with the V-2 rocket, the US identification of *autos* or "self," as Friedrich Kittler pointed out in "Auto Bahnen," hitched its motility to the covered wagon. In Disch's history of science fiction, although ancestors like Wells are duly noted, the genre proper is seen to emerge in the Cold War as uniquely American. The subtitle of Disch's study, however, is written on the crypt left undisturbed: *How Science Fiction Conquered the World*. Only within the standard reception of American science fiction in the 1950s, as the red scare flashed forward, could Disch consider that Finney remade Heinlein's *The Puppet Masters* (85). The divergent frame of reference in *Invasion of the Body Snatchers* is signalled by the doubling that implements the alien control. The side effect of the doubling, diminished emotional capacity, is accordingly very subtle, indeed maddening.

Disch circles his wagons around the excluded introject of the Indian. He makes honorable mention of Mormonism, which included Native Americans as one of Israel's lost tribes. This, rather than the German reception of American history authored by Karl May, which also protects/projects the American Indian, would be responsible for the concluding empathy in mourning over the lost alien race in *Ender's Game* (written by a Card-carrying Mormon). The Lone Ranger and Tonto, however, were conceived and couplified in time to take account of an influence of childhood recollections among the German-language immigrants working in Hollywood.

Paul Verhoeven's 1997 adaptation of Heinlein's *Starship Troopers* picks up (accidentally or unconsciously on purpose) the dependency of *Ender's Game* on the novel it went about repairing. Verhoeven's formal conceit is the recurring layout of a computer screen that presents the news, each brief followed by the link: "Do you want to know more?" One item on the news screen concerns a Mormon colony established against all counsel in a territory claimed by the aliens. In no time, however, Port Joe Smith was for all good intentions wiped out. In a battle scene, an outpost under attack recalls the Western fort beset by Indians (or the Alamo by Mexicans).

Both *Starship Troopers* and *Ender's Game* largely chronicle the education of the marines of the future. In Heinlein's novel, the "ghost of Hitler" is summoned in the classroom to render a student's question whether violence ever settles anything absurd (26). In both works, "Hitler" belongs to knowledge embedded in the transference that schooling releases in the foreground. The logistics of the "final solution" resembled the train transport of cattle to central slaughterhouses, but the mass murder at close quarters was based on methods for the extermination of insect infestation. Does the homosexual panic inherent in the switch from Heinlein's Bugs to Card's Buggers bring about the ultimate proximity to the enemy on which the game change of public "mourning" turns?

Verhoeven drives home the High School teen setting, updating the future potentiation of the multi-ethnic introject of US military formation as coeducation on the football team and in the showers. The vigilance of control and self-control operates without a "restroom"—a place of respite from the stimulation of sexualization, which is nowhere off limits or no longer a pathogenic factor, neither an object nor a room to disown. In the military shower scene, a member of the group, who identifies himself as a budding journalist, interviews the others one by one, asking them why they enlisted. It's the rehearsal or repetition of the framed news, the desire to know more, to click to the next frame. The proximity of that cascade of frames offers respite, transition, stability in the absence of more recognizable forms of timeout from the social-sexual pressures of overstimulation.

Verhoeven's interactive Web of infotainment covers the war in all its items of interest and is an import foreign to the novel. The novel cultivates a sense of war as a series of discrete interventions in which one soldier at a time, contained in a "suit," is dropped from transport vessels (the small fast ones are called "corvette transports") upon a circumscribed terrain. Jumping, half flying from point to point of view of the destruction he spreads around, the suited soldier is "retrieved" following the brief tour of duty. Heinlein's version is less public broadcasting and more video game—closer to the simultaneous masking of live coverage during the second Gulf TV War. By their relative distance from steady conflict and conflagration, these drop and go troopers are "like aviators of the earlier mechanized wars" (147).

The "suit" is the key component of the technologization of war in this future scenario. It works by and subsumes negative feedback, the key innovation of the WWII era, which the V-2 rocket instrumentalized. In his history of science fiction, Disch quips that Superman is an embodied rocket: "Superman is nothing less than a rocket ship in human form, a man of steel able to fly by sheer willpower anywhere in the universe and equipped with X-ray vision and all kinds of internal *Star Wars* weaponry" (62). He is also the product of a crypt, picking up the rocket side effects as he enters history (i.e., the history of American adolescence) and secures in the environs of science fiction (together with all the other superheroes of the period) the ultimate victory over a master race won against cryptofetishism. The description of the "suit" suggests it could hang in Batman's cave:

> The "muscles," the pseudo-musculature, get all the publicity but it's the control of all that power which merits it. The real genius in the design is that you don't have to control the suit; you just wear it, like your clothes, like skin. . . . The secret lies in negative feedback and amplification. . . . The inside of the suit is a mass of pressure receptors, hundreds of them. . . . You jump, that heavy suit jumps, but higher than you can jump in your skin. Jump really hard and the suit's jets cut in, amplifying what the suit's leg "muscles" did, giving you a three-jet shove. (100-02)

In the classroom, the inner Hitler was the bugaboo of a war waged without limit; Hitler lost because he didn't know when to stop winning. The suit retrofits the psychotic sublime of techno-war to the comfort zone of gadget love. Without foregoing the body glove of primary narcissism, the new technology makes even the furthest horizon a body-proportional limit. The negative feedback that enhances bodily movement and harnesses it to the suit's habitat comes naturally to the adolescent (102). The suited adolescent personalizes the purposes of his actions in sync with the basics of the psychology or strategy of warfare: "War is not violence and killing, pure and simple; war is *controlled* violence, for a purpose. . . . The purpose is never to kill the enemy just to be killing him" (63).

To determine whether peace can be imposed by limited warfare, Bugs of the brain caste must be captured and studied. As whole "communal entities," the Bugs are organized like ants or termites (135). Higher functions belong to the brain caste and the queens. Either the soft spot of the human species or the unique strength that will win the war, it is a "racial conviction that when one human needs rescue, others should not count the price" (223). Heinlein thematizes this willingness as the paradox of survival. "Morals—all correct moral rules—derive from the instinct to survive; moral behavior is survival behavior above the individual level—as in a father who dies to save his children" (185).

The move toward identification with the enemy in *Starship Troopers* (the novel and film) is limited to psy-war objectives. After the Pearl-Harbor-like attack upon Buenos Aires, the movie screen of news briefs shows happy pupils, with their ecstatic schoolteacher standing by, stomping on garden variety insects. However, after the failure of the counterattack upon the home planet of the Bugs, all briefs point to a paradigm shift: humans need to learn how the Bugs think. Dead soldiers show evidence of their brains having been sucked out. The Bugs get into the minds they would control. But the brain draining is also performed to study how the humans think. "They're just like us." Indeed the Bugs onscreen attack with affect and show signs that they don't want to die. They can even run scared. These Bugs lack all recognizable technology. Large Bugs project highly destructive excremental substances out of their bodies. Other Bugs can fly. And they know how to direct asteroids like bombs. In the novel, resistance to alien intelligence flies in the face of the fact that the Bugs use spaceships and control a host of technologies.

The dissociation of surprise, like the big surprise that the Soviets were capable of launching a satellite, is basic to the reception of the aliens. "We were learning . . . just how efficient a total communism can be when used by a people actually adapted to it by evolution" (152). As the lessons pile up, the analogy with the Asian opponent is brought home. "Perhaps we could have figured this out about the Bugs by noting the grief the Chinese Hegemony gave the Russo-Anglo-American Alliance" (153). The film joins the book's alignment of a certain US experience in the Pacific theater of WWII with the subsequent wars against East-Asian communism. This is the hot war ember fanned in the future of Outer Space conflict but within a frame of history that works overtime to maintain a Cold War continuum.

ANTI-GONE

1

In John Wyndham's *Trouble with Lichen* (1960), Diana, a young lab researcher, and Francis, her boss at the facility (and husband-to-be), independently discover a true antigerone. It is a genus of lichen that, in Diana's estimation, produces not only an increase in life but "a kind of synthetic evolution—and the only evolutionary advance by man in a million years" (85). A recent widower, Francis responds by supplying himself and his children Biblical longevity via lichenin treatments, and Diana hitches the prospect for evolutionary advance to a techno-feminist movement that she cultivates in a chain of beauty spas opened for this purpose. By way of the "*resentment* of age and death" (154), which she perceives to be inevitably stronger in women, Diana builds up a "corps" of "living examples" (153) among her clients, who are in unwitting receipt of the antigerone. Once their treatment by this agent is revealed, their lobbying influence will rival that of the first patients of psychoanalysis, the high-society hysterics who promoted Freud.

Best known today from the *Village of the Damned* adaptations of his novel *The Midwich Cuckoos* (1957), Wyndham's science fiction carried the German science fiction of doubling into the postwar setting. In *Trouble with Lichen*, Wyndham varies the doubling phantasm in order to project (from marriage to education) the resolution of what Diana identifies as our precarious institutional life. Extended life will test our institutions, which "preserve continuity, and so dodge some of the difficulties which arise from the shortness of our individual lives . . . by continual replacement of worn-out parts" (87). The marriage standard will not "stand up at all well to the prospect of a hundred and fifty years to be spent with a partner grabbed in adolescence. . . . Or think of education. The sort of smattering that's been good enough to tide most of us over for fifty years isn't going to give us a full life for two hundred, or more" (ibid.). The issue of half-life versus full life takes us back to the bottom line skewering all the ages and genders of development: the life or death stakes of knowledge. Specifically, it is our relation to the mediation of knowledge that poses a problem of precarity and begs the Faustian solution. That "half-knowledge is precarious" (85) is our starting or end point. "We have only a precarious hold on the forces we do liberate—and problems that we ought to be trying to solve, we neglect. . . . We shall manage to postpone the worst one way and another, but postponement isn't solution. . . . That's why we *need* longer life, before it is too late" (89).

The halfway predicament of knowledge as our precarious hold reflects a divergence in perspectives between self and other over the issue of mortality. At the outset of her reflections on precarious life, Judith Butler identifies a script for performative transformation in the case of Freud's change in mind from mourning (the work that succeeds by substitution) to grief that fails to come to an end. For Freud, it is a melancholic identification at the foundation of two normative psychic institutions, the superego and sublimation. "Perhaps mourning has to do with agreeing to undergo a transformation (perhaps one should say *submitting* to a transformation) the full result of which one cannot know in advance" (*Precarious Life* 21). If mourning carries forward knowledge that we can only hope to catch up to, then it supplies the precarious condition of half knowledge.

In *Precarious Life*, Butler once again chose Sophocles' *Antigone* for her main literary intertext, the alternate to Sophocles' *Oedipus Rex* that's all in the family, but where the issue of mourning switches from background to foreground. Creon introduces crisis by his edict against mourning the dead enemy, albeit in a postwar period, otherwise the period of reparation set at the end of the sentencing of opposition. Antigone would set her time aright by burying the enemy of the state . . . He happens to be her brother; incest in the recent past links all members of the socius by slight degrees of separation. What holds for Thebes holds in the United States by degrees of migration. Identifiable local conflicts worldwide are included within the globalization of the socius at home. This fulfils one condition of Butler's plaint. In the US, there are going to be hybrid Americans who press for a recognition of their dead relations from both sides now at every point of conflict punctuating the globe.

As theorized by Klein, the inner world is not so much selective as it is highly vulnerable and in need of being re-established and re-secured incessantly even at its very foundations. First or direct contact with loss threatens to shatter the inner world. The work of mourning consists in the all-out effort to shore up this world: the first good objects to be internalized as lost and found must be re-incorporated. Klein supposes that the inner world is a hub of a relatedness approximated by the foundational incest in Thebes and the mix of the global and the local in the US reception of "The War against Terror." In her reading of *The Oresteia,* Klein can dismiss the edict of the Furies that matricide is the most grievous crime. It amounts to denial, she contends, also in the sense that love is thus denied the internal good object. She concludes that everyone who dies in our midst is the mother (292).

Antigone's claim that this brother is her one and only irreplaceable object is staked against and inside the madness that she enters to counter Creon, whose unmitigated hostility against the dead enemy, against his very remembrance, now puts the dead out with the trash, now entombs the mourners. The consequences of the encounter, which Antigone foresees and accepts, bring about her living death, or rather the realization that this undeath belongs to her case history as a melancholic going back to childhood. Antigone's melancholia introduces legibility—indeed, the tragedy itself—at the border to Creon's psycho behavior. In Freud's science, melancholia is the first borderline disorder, the first opening up of a zone of transferential legibility inside narcissistic illness. The deepest pockets of narcissistic derangement in the Ratman, Schreber and Wolfman cases are rendered accessible through the foreign body or caption of a melancholic narrative. In entering, accepting, containing, applying or (like Hamlet) feigning psychosis, a signature side effect appears to be psychopathic ruthlessness, as in Antigone's treatment of her sister Ismene or Hamlet's handling of Ophelia (the true psychotic). Antigone goes out to the border to meet Creon's derangement. Lacan sees this meeting as an instance of criminality or psychopathy that figures otherwise than psychosis proper as a limit concept of psychoanalysis.

Sometimes a B notion offers insight into the muddle of its transactions. "Psycho," an American nickname first applied to returning soldiers who counted among the psychological casualties of WWII, was appropriated by Robert Bloch and Alfred Hitchcock to fold out of a gap in understanding an overlap between psychotic and psychopathic disorders. Norman Bates and his heirs manifest the psychotic, but it is by dint of their ruthless violence that they hold mascot positions in mass culture that compel or admit doubling. In the setting of psycho-horror, the diagnosis of psychosis supplies a stopgap in the failure of the interpretation of psychopathic violence. But the psychopath remains our double at the close quarters of a near miss.

It is because everyone's adolescence is a time-based version of psychopathy that we come so close. Prior to a secondary gain of consolidation as criminality, there is the antisocial tendency, which Winnicott studied and treated in children and teens. The adolescent returns in fundamental ways to the starting block of infancy. What has changed is the teen's physical ability to act on the wish to kill his or her parents, who in the meantime bear the date mark of expiration. The teen must find room in psychic reality for this death. But first teenagers find themselves, "struggling to start again as if they had nothing they could take over from anyone" ("Struggling through the Doldrums" 152). They thus form group associations on the basis of cursory uniformities. Each adolescent association nevertheless coheres by means of the proxy or mascot service of one ill member in the group whose extreme symptom (often violence that includes a form or forum of suicidality) impinges on society, produces a social reaction, and makes the others feel real. And yet Winnicott concludes that "it is the individual relationships, one by one, that eventually lead to socialization" (147). What also starts over, then, is the delay of the ability to mourn. To catch up with the delay, the antisocial child or teen responds to a diffuse sense of deprivation and irreality by acts that call attention to the importance of the environment as a container and thereby signal hope. Hope refers to the ability to turn around impingement by balking, starting over, finding a new approach, carrying out reality testing. But hope also refers to the missing onset of the ability to mourn. That which is precarious literally means you have but a prayer and conveys this relationship of hope to mourning.

As his reflections on Antigone reach to the limit concepts, Lacan puts through the connection to Hamlet, although he, not unlike Carl Schmitt, proposes a mythic or structural reading in lieu of Freud's recourse to the Elizabethan protagonist/ patient in whom the tragedy of Oedipus is re-staged to include a representation or repression of motivation. Friedrich Kittler demonstrated that Freud's reading already had a shelf life in the culture of *Bildung* as Goethe's *Wilhelm Meister's*

Apprenticeship. Lacan returns to this shelf when he reads *Antigone* with Hegel. Without Hamlet, the Oedipus complex is a mythic or psychotic enactment. The psychoanalytic discourse on *Bildung* grounds Antigone for/via the suicide in which two or three others join, a family pact the chorus comments on and extends as a group sentiment. Winnicott implies that the individual relationships work toward the ability to mourn. With the free pass that accompanies group membership, we skip the work toward mourning and go directly to the simulation of mourning (e.g., public mourning, which affords a controlled affective bonding that admits suicide is its group structure or plan).

At the point of Antigone's suicide, Lacan lodges his notion of second death. It is a point of honor to underscore that this excess is inherent in desire, perhaps as the little death, which, for Lacan, defies and reconstitutes the symbolic itself. On the schedule of the big death, however, the second death exceeds by coming after the concluded transactions of substitution. Slavoi Žižek reads into opera this distinction between a biological death and the second death that the subject dies in freedom once all accounts have been rendered and guilt no longer haunts remembrance. But it is in the seminar on *Hamlet* that the immunological significance of secondary death is made explicit by Lacan. The first death is our initiation into loss and the containment of loss through castration. Subsequent losses are mediated by the buffer zone of this accomplishment.

2

In his eulogy-review of Thomas Disch's final publication (and suicide note), Norman Spinrad finds motivation for Dick's paranoid denunciation of Disch as a communist agent in the division of their labor. In *Camp Concentration*, Disch's appropriation of Dick's conceit of an alternate fascist future underwent an updating of the "communist type." (Spinrad's *The Iron Dream*, his own communist-type story, frames a revisionist version of the alternate historicization of WWII.) In his afterword to *The Penultimate Truth*, Disch argues that each of Dick's future worlds "simply denies that the Cold War is happening" ("In the Mold of 1964" 163), a reflection about Dick's focus on (or Disch's disavowal of) the traumatic history of WWII as the secret that the Cold War opposition carried forward.

Lem was a suspect in Dick's season of political acting out. This was another type of typecasting. A self-conscious mourner, Dick's political response was set off by the import of a second death in *Solaris*. Like *La Jetée*, *Solaris* is another instance of a genre of philosophical fiction that sets a proper death of one's own above and beyond the other's passing.

Inscribed within the novel's internal simulacrum over and again is the archive of study of the planet Solaris. In *Solaris,* we are up against the limits of knowledge. For example: "All things considered . . . it was not simply a question of penetrating Solarist civilization, it was essentially a test of ourselves, of the limitations of human knowledge" (23).

The object of scientific study, the surface organism of Solaris, is regularly called "ocean," fitting its appearance from a distance. It is not, however, the primal soup from which we construe life's origin on Earth. It is instead a "homeostatic ocean" (18) that has projected (or dreamed up) its own time/space continuum (19); otherwise life could not be sustained in the orbit around and between two suns. The postulation of the active but unknown surface as the inscrutable exterior of the brain, the alien's as our own, is entered in the archive of Solarist studies. "For some time there was a widely held notion . . . to the effect that the 'thinking ocean' of Solaris was a gigantic brain" (24).

In Tarkovsky's adaptation, the injection of films and images approximates the archive of Solaris Studies. By tampering with its shell, the movie also works to shake itself loose from the melancholic blank of our first glimpse of Kelvin's visitor in the photograph that he sorts out from the rest of his mementoes, which he burns before leaving for Outer Space. In the novel, the visitors undergo a period of creaturely transition unto duplication, like the body snatchers: "When it arrives, the visitor is almost blank—only a ghost made up of memories and vague images dredged out of its . . . source. The longer it stays with you, the more human it becomes" (150). Contact with the planet organism is consistently denied, but the story of Kelvin's sojourn at Solaris Station with colleagues Snow and Sartorius is one of the encounters with doubles of souvenirs that the planet-organism scanned in and projected out of their minds.

The first visitor we get a close look at is a giant "Negress" (47). Kelvin finds her under the shroud with the corpse of her host, Gibrarian. As in Klein's study of the painter Ruth Kjär, this double without a personalized model suggests the image of the internal mother. The cyberneticist Snow confirms the pre-Oedipal provenance of the visitors.

Who hasn't had, at some moment in his life, a crazy daydream, an obsession? . . . Imagine a fetishist who becomes infatuated with . . . a grubby piece of cloth, and who threatens and entreats and defies every risk in order to acquire this beloved bit of rag. . . . So, in the same way, there are things, situations, that no one has dared to externalize, but which the mind has produced by accident in a moment of aberration, of madness, call it what you will. At the next stage, the idea becomes flesh and blood. (71)

As it probed the brains of the scientists, the ocean sorted through "isolated psychic processes, enclosed, stifled, encysted—foci smoldering under the ashes of memory" (73). Only in Kelvin's case did the ghost that the ocean summoned embody an object relation suggestive of mourning or unmourning.

Looking forward to a reunion with Gibrarian, his former advisor, Kelvin arrives at Solaris Station to find that he must do the aftermath of his doctor-father's suicide. Gibrarian left behind notes and a journal on tape, not as a continuation of or testament to their studies of Solaris, but as an emergency broadcast of the perils of imminent doubling. With the commencement of his own ghostly visitation, Kelvin finds that the hard shell of mournability is beset by the unmournables.

The hosts of visitation ultimately respond by inventing methods for the annihilation of the doubles. Every attempt to make contact with the alien intelligence of the planet becomes the scientist's failure to uncover anything other than his own mirror and describes the arc of the visitors' doom. In Lem's test for humanity, empathy, the hallmark of the other, does not have the significance it has in Dick's test situation. Dick spells out their difference in *The Exegesis*:

(1) The other exists.
(2) We can experience it.
(3) It is found everywhere.
(4) Therefore since it exists, since we can experience it, and since it can be found everywhere, we can encounter it here. The opportunity exists now. Lem is wrong in all respects. (44)

With the exception of a comparison of one planetary phenomenon with an "ancient zeppelin" (201), there appears to be no reference to German science fiction in *Solaris*. And yet one of the early scientist-explorers of Solaris—the first to die on the planet, and under mysterious circumstances—is named Fechner (like Gustav Theodor Fechner). The historical Fechner's development of a psychological science based on Kant and empiricism was the subject of a monograph by Kurd Laßwitz. Laßwitz's admission of Fechner's tolerant consideration of Spiritualism was his own concession to the greater Spiritualist context of the new global discourse of science fiction (60-64).

In a language reminiscent of Fechner's psychology, there is the theory in the archive of theories concerning Solaris that the "source" of all phenomena observed is "Fechner's brain, subjected to an unimaginable 'psychic dissection' for the purposes of a sort of re-creation, an experimental reconstruction, based on impressions (undoubtedly the most durable ones) engraved on his memory" (87). In the copy of the Little Apocrypha that Gibrarian left him, Kelvin finds a facsimile of a request for information that offers hints to the unmourning underlying these phenomena, including the hallucination or manifestation of a young boy. (A child's footsteps can be heard behind the closed door of Sartorius's laboratory.)

> I should be grateful if you could send me the following information by return post:
>
> i)   Fechner's biography, in particular details about his childhood.
> ii) Everything you know about his family, facts and dates—he probably lost his parents while still a child.
> iii) The topography of the place where he was brought up. (86-87)

Snow remarks that the doubles usher in a test situation lying outside our morality in which they can be experimented upon to the point of extinction (another otherwise unidentified reference to German history). In an interview with Stanislaw Beres, Lem says the protocols of the Nazi death camps were only conceivable as the last stand or understanding of life split off from one's own death. Throughout his work, Lem tries to convey this significance of the camps. In *Solaris*, then, Lem could be seen to sentence the Nazi German realization of the science fiction of the Doppelgänger in the court of one's own death.

To induce the response of contact, the scientists introduce experimentally a ruthless radiation probe whereupon the ocean begins sending out contact-doubles.

Interpersonalized, the violence of the research for a reaction results in Kelvin revisiting his murderous relationship with Rheya, the woman the planet sent him on the double. Kelvin's ex marks the spot she put him in by killing herself and thus booking her returns. Bearing the mark of the fatal injection, the visitor doubles her incarnation in his serial dreams at the moment he discovers her "already growing cold." "It was as though, in my sleep, I tried to relive what she had gone through; as though I hoped to turn back the clock and ask her forgiveness, or keep her company during those final minutes when she was feeling the effects of the injection and was overcome by terror" (55).

At first contact, his ambivalence is kept under control, as in the dream. "I thought of throwing something at her, but, even in a dream, I could not bring myself to harm a dead person" (53). A few more pages into the encounter with Rheya's ghost, who now looks at him attentively as though she didn't know that he killed her, he finds the resolve to admit his selfish death wish. "I no longer told myself: 'It's a dream.' I had ceased to believe that. Now I was thinking: 'I must be ready to defend myself!'" (57). In spite of the ghost's extreme separation anxiety, Kelvin tricks her into entering a space capsule that he subsequently locks up and launches into oblivion. Like the internal burial of Rheya whereby he tried to lose the evidence of murder, however, the external solution also doesn't last. Once there are two Rheyas, there can be an infinite number more. Now, for better or worse, he enters into the relationship.

In his manifesto "Metafantasia," Lem addresses the failure of science fiction authors to recognize the changes in the literary field and explore new formal frontiers by dint of new contents. We are led into the scene of a crime for which Rheya and her love story can be seen to stand.

> In the first place, we consider the primary unsolved problem of SF: the lack of a theoretical typology of its paradigmatic structures. Since writers of SF do not even recognize the existence of this problem, the structures they use most frequently are neither aesthetically nor epistemologically adequate for their chosen themes. An example of aesthetic inadequacy is the practice of authors who attempt mimetic (pseudorealistic) works, and yet model such phenomena as "contact with another civilization" or an invasion from Outer Space after the relationship between detective and criminal. (67)

The sorting out of ambivalence that Rheya's return compels is the crime scene (or love story) that diverted the film adaptations from addressing the impossibility of contact as the form of its possibility. Kelvin is both the culprit and the agent of outside chance or change.

Lem argues that throughout literature the barrier reefs of tradition and transcendence are no longer available for dialectical breaching and support. The only boundary left cannot be crossed. Since art cannot transgress the body of physical laws without undergoing a reduction to nothingness, it is doomed to be a replica or shadow of science (63). For Lem, empiricism is the culprit responsible for the global clearing of opportunities for creative breaching.

> It was empiricism that proved to be culture's Trojan horse, since its principal criteria are those of ultility, which naturally raise questions of comfort and convenience. For empiricism, the only inviolable barrier is the totality of the attributes of nature it calls the body of physical laws. Thus, observing the human world from an empirical standpoint necessarily leads to the complete relativization of cultural norms everywhere where they impose "unfounded" imperatives and restraints. (62)

Differing from A-list literature in its following of completely new scientific content, science fiction is a Trojan horse, at once the double of the body of physical laws and the means of transmitting this content to outer (or inner) limits.

Tarkovsky's adaptation realizes Lem's allegory. Kelvin is the extreme case of an empirical scientist, a mismatch from the get-go with his mission to evaluate the conditions that beset Solaris station. But then Kelvin ends up in Outer Space encountering and entering his inner world. Although the spousal relationship of mourning that occupies the foreground undergoes complication (but confirmation) by the visitor's undecidable status as an android or human, Tarkovsky's film also fully projects the separate peace Lem assigned Kelvin in the novel. In the inverted inner world at the end of the film, he is back home where the film began and all the while on an island that the ocean has simulated. Kelvin reunites with his father, whose mortality was the measure of his sojourn at Solaris Station. He would not be back in time to bury his father. Like tears in the rain, when it rains it pours inside the house his father built from the memory of his own grandfather's home. Returning to the home of fathers is

Tarkovsky's inner-cinematic representation of Kelvin's arrival at the prospect of his proper death.

The visitor arrives while the host sleeps or is at the liminal moment of awakening. To update the dream-based data that the ocean first scanned by introducing the host's whole brain, Kelvin's conscious thoughts are to be recorded as an encephalogram, which will be irradiated into the ocean. Sartorius has devised an experiment in two parts to find a way to bring the ocean's recycling of a given ghost to a full stop. Kelvin goes along with the first part of the experiment (the update given the ocean on the full psychological significance of the host's encounter with visitation). But he refuses to consider the second step. Sartorius and Snow stand by with the newly developed neutrino-destroyer that can annihilate any visitor. It is hoped that a communication of the first part will have convinced the ocean no longer to respond with more of the same.

For the recording of Kelvin's consciousness sent to the ocean, Sartorius encourages Kelvin to focus on the theme of contact, the long tradition of scientists grappling with the outside chance of communicating with the ocean's alien intelligence. Kelvin opens or empties his conscious mind as a seat of judgment: His "mind was an empty grey arena ringed by a crowd of invisible onlookers . . . emanating in their silence an ironic contempt for . . . the Mission" (161). Although encouraged to keep out the intrusion of individual personalities, Kelvin's first thought turns to Rheya, "alive inside" him, but then, "as if imprinted on that despairing presence," he can make out Giese, the "father" of the study of Solaris (161). Giese's portrait from the frontispiece of one of his books begins to merge with Kelvin's souvenir of his father's head. "I was finally no longer able to tell which of them was looking at me, my father or Giese" (162). The double father is revealed in passing to be unburied. "They were dead, and neither of them buried, but then deaths without burial are not uncommon in our time" (ibid.). We know that Giese was lost during an eruption of the ocean. The final thought, which Kelvin consigns to transmission to the ocean, displaces the Station, the experiment, Rheya, and the ocean. "Recent memories were obliterated by the overwhelming conviction that these two men, my father and Giese, nothing but ashes now, had once faced up to the totality of their existence, and this conviction afforded a profound calm which annihilated the formless assembly clustered around the grey arena in the expectation of my defeat" (ibid.). He remains on this honor roll until he enters the site of his ending.

After Rheya's second death, a change comes over him in the test situation. When Kelvin visits the ocean, he engages in a kind of handshake. "The main body of the wave remained motionless on the shore . . . like some strange beast patiently waiting for the experiment to finish" (203). Although it is a well-known experiment, Kelvin feels "changed" by his experience of the exchange (ibid.). He is on the beach of a mimoid, the ectoplasmic extrusion of the ocean, decked out with the degradable semblance of ruinscapes of terran architectural history. Scholars of Solaris have analogized the mimoid as the ocean brain's computer. Kelvin adheres to a view of the whole brain that the creature contact initiated when he identifies with the ocean itself. "[I]t was as if I had forgiven it everything, without the slightest effort of word or thought" (203-04).

Now Kelvin accepts that Rheya cannot return. "We all know that we are material creatures, subject to the laws of physiology and physics, and not even the power of all our feelings combined can defeat those laws" (204). Consequent to the concluded season of phantasmagoric visitation, this non-sequitur falls into place like an ironclad credo. Kelvin hopes for nothing and indeed knows nothing. He now foregoes the plan of returning to Earth that Rheya's ultimate suicide was supposed to secure unto the prospect of substitution. He steps out of the milieu of the other's two deaths into the arena of the expectation of his own death.

Tarkovsky drives home that "at the same time" Kelvin mourns or unmourns his corporeal father, beginning with the embodiment provided by the ghost of woman past who awaits him in the place removed from the father's funeral. As in the case of Haitzmann, the painter in Freud's "A Seventeenth-Century Demono-logical Neurosis," the hallucinatory mix of gender traits in the painter's apparition (like Kelvin's double feature of souvenirs of the father and ex) signals that the mournful recollection of the father has reached back into pre-Oedipal precincts where the father is embodied by close association with the pre-Oedipal mother, his body witch or switch.

3

However it is staged, the Lacanian notion of the second death takes the self as POV. If mortality is my big problem, though, one that is not addressed in the first place to or through the other, then mourning is hardly a consequence. The basis of Freud's reflections on mourning—relocated by Klein at the foundation of the inner world—is that there is no relationship to one's own death and, to that extent, no self-relation. Only the death of the other counts; in going first, the other sets the place inside us, now of mourning and unmourning, now of manic defense and suicidality. And yet the resistance to Freud's view is as pervasive as the popular idiom in which we tend to render the death wish one can have. After I corrected and recorrected this use as a symptom in various B works of film and literature (and in the words of my students), I discovered that "to have a death wish" in fact signifies one's own contemplation of suicide in the Anglo-American language.

For Freud, the death wish backfires upon the self only when a loved one on the target range dies. That's when the acknowledgment of death-wishing ambivalence (the therapeutic bottom line of analytic understanding) becomes impossible at close quarters and must be projected instead onto the deceased who enters the phantasmagoria of undeath that is out to get us. The unacknowledgment of the death wish is stowed away in the idiomatic fantasy that to have a death wish means to contemplate or work toward one's own end. By viewing suicide as a pact with and against internal others, Freudian analysis treats this so-called self-relation as the test case of the impossibility of conceiving a death of one's own. Even Klein's view of suicide as the definitive effort made to protect the lifeline to the good object against contamination by the bad object (= oneself) only *seems* contrary. In fact, it fulfils terms of commitment to the inner world writ large.

The *Bildungs*-notion of Faustian striving, which passes through magic and technology, offers a related option: deferral of the suicide that tempted Faust to end it all in the mood-swinging opening of Goethe's tragedy. Critical of gullible colleagues, Winnicott quipped that many patients enter analysis not to be recognized and treated but to defer suicide until mortality's claim renders the voluntary option overkill ("The Use of an Object" 87). For Goethe's Faust, however, the deferral extends to and through the very end; Faust does not so much die as commence divesting himself of the debt of his identifications. A free subject in second death, this tutelage is possible only because his lost objects have returned. First they did the dying for him, now they do the mourning. One man's Heaven is another man's schooling in the mourning he lost, reassigned as perspectives on loss that he reversed yet preserved.

Within a perspective of "self storage," the prospect of mourning is secretly inscribed in the frame of one's own death suspended between suicide and finite life's affirmation or acceptance. In his reading of E. T. A. Hoffmann's story, Freud recognized the ever-returning Sandman in the temporal application of doubling. It is an objective relation that Goethe's Faust reclaims on the upbeat, both from the compulsion that yields the death drive and from the infernal investment in finite quality time secured by the Devil's compact. Faust obtains one more lifetime in which the deferral of suicide gives way to living beyond the terms of decision between modes of murder. The prospect of extending the finite time of remembrance must be pried loose from the old comfort—the double and nothing that replication on the spot advertises. Thus Faustian striving appears to relate to uncanny doubling as a counter-intuition that is also within the endopsychic setting of science fiction.

In *Trouble with Lichen*, Wyndham applied Faustian staggering to doubling in your face in space. It was his first temptation and dangerous alliance. *The Day of the Triffids* meets the standards of techno-evolutionary fantasy in a setting split off from the identifiable recent past. While composing the novel, Wyndham took a break and explored the continuity shot otherwise disowned in his own science fiction. Published decades after his death, *Plan for Chaos* projects the inimical Nazi conspiracy of a new and improved mass psychology of human replication out of the protagonist's somewhat controversial plan to wed his cousin. Wyndham pitched all his works to an American audience, and this one was populated by Americans. Only the American melting pot could extend mere degrees of separation on a global scale. The cousins knew they were of mixed European descent (including stopovers in England, Germany, and Sweden). They discover that they are directly related to a new German melting plot for world domination using divisions of doubles. Scenes of murder featuring victims who strangely resemble them give them the lead they follow. It turns out that these doubles, searching for an escape into the world of exogamous choice, were executed by the guardians of conspiratorial purity.

Because the leader of the plot and the mother of all doubles is their own aunt, they come in for their resemblance without the same taboo of the blood tie separating the mobilized doubles. The doubles are siblings who cannot mate. The couple of cousins are spectacularly exogamous in this context and are soon to be enlisted as the reproductive genitals to be shared in group. If the conspiracy succeeds in releasing total suicidal conflict by secretly introducing technical difficulties into the stalemate of the Cold War (which can only be mistaken at their source in the terms of the opposition), then the clan of doubles can repopulate the earth with their American cousins.

In the world of James Bond, SPECTRE's more enigmatic emergency out of the Cold War's recent past succeeded as a secret agency. Wyndham's figment coupling the incestuous bond with the realization of German science fiction could not be admitted. But the psychopathic violence on both sides now could get across. In *The Midwich Cuckoos*, Wyndham was able to see the doubling theme through to publication; deploying an Outer Space provenance, he separated it both from WWII and the incestuous proximity to blood ties. The lookalike alien children use telepathy to communicate among themselves and to keep outsiders under internal surveillance. They represent an evolutionary advance (the mass mind), but they also exhibit a decline into psychopathy. The alien kids deal ruthlessly with any inadvertent or deliberate threat that the humans might pose. In the end, there is only one human that the children will allow in their proximity. He shores up his defences against telepathy in order to protect the inner world that he leaves out against the double threat of annihilation. He includes the aliens in his suicide-bombing before they can divine its ideation in his thoughts.

An alternative to the strain of doubling in Wyndham's oeuvre, *Trouble with Lichen* also circumvents the science fictional prospect of living on with or as our extrinsic technologies, which would then be doing the evolving for us. In his first science fiction novel, *The Secret People* (1935), Wyndham included a lasting reflection on prosthetic relations that doubly obscured our recognition of what we want in ourselves. It is a view presented in contrast to the prevailing one of our relationship to technology as the success story of prosthetic substitution. Does humanity's ability to broadcast, for example, include an acceptance of our own limitation? "I doubt it. I should say that we recognised it as a limitation of the system we have evolved, not of ourselves. We put up an inferior substitute called telegraph and radio, and forget our limitations—but they are still there. How many men, do you suppose, realise the limitations of using words to convey our meanings? They may find that there are inconvenient misunderstandings, and blame language, but how many admit that the words are just a substitute for the thing they really lack—mental communication?" (59).

In "Early Stages of the Oedipus Complex," Klein says that psychopathic violence irrupts at the outset of the desire to know the ins and outs of mother's creativity, her body. The young child presses two inquiries against the limits: Where do the dead go? Where do babies come from? "One of the most bitter grievances we come upon in the unconscious is that these . . . overwhelming questions . . . remain unanswered. Another reproach follows hard upon this, namely, that the child could not understand words and speech" (188). In Klein's understanding of the sense of loneliness, the prosthetic substitutes that aid our half-knowledge fall short of integration and pull up short before the prospect of irreversible loss. For Klein, the irreversible loss is not what castration binds but what is laid bare by the withdrawal of a telepathic unity with mother ("On the Sense of Loneliness" 301). Back in the "Early Stages," "[t]he early feeling of not knowing has manifold connections. It unites with the feeling of being incapable, impotent, which soon results from the Oedipus situation. . . . In analysis . . . these grievances give rise to an extraordinary amount of hate. Singly or in conjunction they are the cause of numerous inhibitions of the epistemophilic impulse: for instance, the incapacity to learn foreign languages, and, further, hatred of those who speak a different tongue" (188).

During the early years of WWI, Freud contemplated the delay in primal man's discovery of the need to be able to mourn. In contrast to the philosophical view that the mystery of death was the starting-point of all speculation, Freud distinguished two or three relations not so much to death as to the dead, which, conjugated by imbrications between self and other, resulted in the new relationship to knowledge.

> In my view, primaeval man must have triumphed beside the body of his slain enemy, without being led to rack his brains about the enigma of life and death. What released the spirit of enquiry in man was not the intellectual enigma, and not every death, but the conflict of feeling at the death of loved yet alien and hated persons. . . . Man could no longer keep death at a distance, for he had tasted it in his pain about the dead; but he was nevertheless unwilling to acknowledge it, for he could not conceive of himself as dead. So he devised a compromise: he conceded the fact of his own death as well, but denied it the significance of annihilation—a significance which he had had no motive for denying where the death of his enemy was concerned. . . . His persisting memory of the dead became the basis for assuming other forms of existence and gave him the conception of a life continuing after apparent death. (SE 14: 293-94)

The immediate ability to kill ruthlessly accompanies the onset of brooding upon a divergence of perspectives on mortality between self and other. The death wish—the representative in every individual psyche of the primal killer—guarantees that our relationship to what's worth knowing is introduced and fragmented by the need to be able to mourn. It is our halfway condition of relating and knowing that mourning addresses—much as half-knowledge (*Halbbildung*), according to Adorno, remains for *Bildung* its condition of mourning, the only topic of knowledge.

CONCLUSION

In the film version of Carl Sagan's *Contact* (1985), it was Nazi TV that alerted alien intelligence to television as the medium to watch. The composite picture of Earthling civilization was thus assembled via the sum total of TV broadcasts between 1936 and 1974. They have it all on tape. The contact that begins on TV, however, must withdraw into conspiracy theories and belief systems.

Television isn't image—it is only tape. It allowed Jean Baudrillard to tape together the stowaway of the return of repressed German science fiction. In *Simulacra and Simulation*, Baudrillard submitted that the 1978 TV miniseries *The Holocaust* was evidence of simulation. "The medium itself of this supposed exorcism" is the form whereby the cold case of the Holocaust can be found "currently reproducing itself" (49). The chill factory of forgetting extermination is part of the process of extermination. "This forgetting is as essential as the event, in any case unlocatable by us, inaccessible to us in its truth. This forgetting is still too dangerous, it must be effaced by an artificial memory . . . This artificial memory will be the restaging of extermination . . . One no longer makes the Jews pass through the crematorium of the gas chamber, but through the sound track and image track, through the universal screen and the microprocessor" (49). None of this, however, contradicts the general sense that, by the 1980s, a global reception of the Holocaust was on the rise. Through the very medium of its annihilation or forgetting, this reception touched us at the threshold to the universal screen of digital mediation and transmission.

Baudrillard's dismissal of truth-TV is belied in that simulation's yield takes on attributes of inoculation and integration in a mass setting. He projects the on or off purpose of Holocaust-TV "to rekindle this cold event through a cold medium, television, and for the masses who are themselves cold, who will only have the opportunity for a tactile thrill and a posthumous emotion" (50). Our digital connectivity's response to touch is a surprisingly new phenomenon. Pulled or pressed, the earlier gadget connections were prosthetic doubles of the touch itself, which only now alone activates the sensorium. Literal digits are the allegory of digitalization. At the literal end, the surprise touch was identified by Elias Canetti as the individual's greatest fear. Only a member of a crowd can reclaim the uncanny touch and carry it forward as a binding pleasure. McLuhan absorbed Canetti's understanding of touch, referring to it as the taboo that dissolves in the crowd within the haptic relationship to numbers. "The pleasure of being among the masses is the sense of the joy in the multiplication of numbers" (104). In the psychoanalytic lexicon, a crowded feeling inclusive of touch approximates narcissism (for which group psychology is the syndication and outside chance). By knowing that its number was up, the touch taboo could be separated upon its dispersion from mere "skin contact with things" and reclaimed as "the very life of things in the mind" (105). While Theodor Adorno found a dangerous immediacy in numbers themselves, McLuhan did the math or aftermath of new mediation, projecting the model of TV reception. The "glass teat" (Harlan Ellison) or soporific service that Adorno, among others, considered to be an enforcing adaptation to a delusional system (the culture industry, which found its completion in or on TV) was for McLuhan a mosaic mode of keeping in touch that lies beyond and goes deeper than the post-*Titanic* injunction to stay tuned. "The TV image requires each instant that we 'close' the spaces in the mesh by a convulsive sensuous participation that is profoundly kinetic and tactile, because tactility is the interplay of the senses, rather than the isolated contact of skin and object" (273).

Walter Benjamin introduced the test situation, the positive attribute of the film medium and its culture or reception, as the overriding frame for an evaluation of innovation in mass media. The dampening Adorno added to his friend's optimism was that television was the proof in the plotting of new test subjects. While Martin Heidegger identified the opening season of an industrialization of corpses, Adorno looked forward to the fixation on the psychopath in the TV culture of post-WWII America, not only as the boogie man, but as the mascot of group adaptation to ruthlessness, the enabling limit of a new norm.

In "Prologue to Television," Adorno argues that the image language of the culture industry "awakens" that which "slumbers pre-conceptually" in the TV viewer, who is thus open to receive owner's manual instruction in how to adapt to an imposed adaptation (514). The TV viewer is manipulated to fit in with the status quo via startled stops and starts. By identifying this manipulation as a whittling down to size or "zurechtstutzen"—the very term, *Stutzen*, signifies the startle response so central, for example, to Gustav Bally's psychoanalytic study of the test situation—Adorno underscores the hope withdrawn. Through the images buried inside us, we accept as the spirit of the times that a controlling interest benefits from our manipulated adaptation. As seen on TV, the mind warp that concludes the culture industry's promotion of the acceptance of our manipulation as psychic reality is that "not the murderer, but rather the murder victim, is guilty" (514-15). The victim transgressed against the norm of adaptive survival. The criminal, not the victim, tests for this will to fit in and survive.

In his follow-up reflections in "Television as Ideology," Adorno identifies the adaptation on TV as proceeding via an ambivalent normalization of criminality. Defense mechanisms are valorized and individuality and autonomy discounted in deference to a higher power (528). By the manipulation of the signifier appeal of psychoanalysis, old patriarchal ideas are promoted to new therapy fictions (525). In one TV show, Adorno analyzes the conceit of a therapeutic relationship like the one organizing Jensen's or Freud's *Gradiva*, which leads a narcissistic actress to a dramatist who directs her to take the cure of marrying him. This instrumentalization of the Freudian understanding of transference represents psychoanalysis in reverse, the formulaic diagnosis he applied earlier to the conflation of psychological warfare and mass psychology in Nazi Germany.

The 1950s date mark of Adorno's reading of TV appears displaced against the grain of the postwar era. However, Adorno's vigilance against premature reconciliation with the traumatic histories lying in the recent past, which he saw as a most pernicious form of adaptation, is the point he again brings home in his analysis of television. It would be wrong, just the same, to throw out the test situation with the bathos of false deliverance from the recent past.

In Philip K. Dick's revalorization of the test situation, the possible impossible distinction between the human and the android, what he terms "balking" introduces the contraband of empathy into the psychopathic setting of the norm. A hesitating pause, a pang of conscience, interrupts one's adaptation to the system and potentially rethinks it as protest (i.e., pro-test). For McLuhan, it is TV's own Mosaic medium nature that makes it a testing forum. He diagnosed the excess of involvement with the cool TV medium in terms Benjamin already applied to the progressive reaction to film, characterizing it as informed by the direct, intimate fusion of visual and emotional enjoyment with the orientation of the expert.

In "The Work of Art in the Age of Mechanical Reproduction," Benjamin cites newspaper boys discussing a bicycle race in which they are implicated by their own bikes and the lottery that could involve them in the event of its coverage. They become evidence of the interactivity that the expanded press was already beginning to offer and that the newsreel facilitated: "the newsreel offers everyone the opportunity to rise from passer-by to movie extra" (231). The structure in which anyone can theoretically double as an extra (but only to the extent that he or she is already an expert) is cinematic. Our identification with film passes through the apparatus, including the camera and the test situation before the camera. Expertise tests and can be tested. "It is inherent in the technique of the film as well as that of sports that everybody who witnesses its accomplishments is somewhat of an expert" (ibid.).

In the TV viewing rooms set up throughout Nazi Berlin at the time of the 1936 Olympic Games, the programming that continued beyond the sports coverage included spots on crime that called on the audience to view the evidence in close-up and help find the perpetrator. During this primal time, TV was also already pressed into the service of surveillance and placed within the network of testing. Television was used to watch test results at a distance (e.g., during the testing of weapons, in particular the V-1 and V-2 rockets) after the experimental video phone connection between Nürnberg and Berlin was withdrawn from public service.

The typical dream Jacques Lacan presents on the "mirror stage"—a stadium flanked by the fantasy architecture of castles (94)—is a souvenir of the trip he took to Berlin following his premier presentation of the mirror theory that year in Marienbad. His intent was to witness the live transmission of *Sport ist Mord*, as German children like to rhyme their gym resistance. Television is the mascot medium to which Lacan would return (in *Télévision*) for the group psychology he otherwise splits (e.g., to watch the moon landing, which is all about doing the math, the plain text of technologization). Mass psychologization mediates and staggers our technologization and massification in essential ways and tends to be downplayed by Lacan and Heidegger, Frankfurt School truants.

In television, one can see and record from a distance or from some secret place. The medium is indispensable to research with subjects, including psychological and parapsychological tests, experiments, and sessions. The conceit Fritz Lang exploited for his final film and testament, *The 1000 Eyes of Dr. Mabuse* (1960), concerning a hotel under TV surveillance, was cited from the archives of the Third Reich. In the film, the hotel surveillance attends the outcome of test situations in which traumatic incidents are staged to see if they trigger certain responses in targeted guests. It is admitted into the foreground in the form of sessions with the in-house Spiritualist medium, who benefits from the surveillance, however ambiguously.

McLuhan's reading of TV determines his genealogy of media. It renders *Understanding Media* another exhibit in wonder rooms dedicated to projections of a future that never happened—alongside LA's layout of endless automobility, for example, found footage that recycles through early science fiction films as the setting prior to the end of the world. Baudrillard's view of the forget-together of TV is another case for an exhibition of the phantasmagoria of projected futures.

Jean François Lyotard addressed the impact of the Holocaust not via the TV miniseries but just the same in California. To counter the tendentiousness of topical application, Lyotard always turned to the archive of German Romanticism to unsay it, too. In *Pacific Wall*, Lyotard presents a relay of self-cancelling reflections folding out of and around a text that the protagonist or editor found in the library of UC-San Diego. It was composed by a certain "Vachez," who is hard to identify. The finder shares the text and his commentary with his correspondent in France, the unidentified author's "namesake," Vachey.

The Pacific wall is first thrown-up as a genealogical marker in the background of discussions around an installation by US artist Edward Kienholz. Exhibited in 1972 as part of Documenta 5 in Kassel, West Germany, *Five Car Stud* stages a black man's castration by white vigilantes who appear to have intervened in his sexual liaison with a white woman. The integration at issue unleashes turbulence across boundaries of identification. In the alphabet soup of the oil pan on the victim's chest, which spells out the N-word, two American-Jewish visitors to the Documenta (one a Holocaust survivor) saw instead the other word: "Jude" (14-15). The German visitors are "monsters" (15). At the same time: "In their minds, whoever approached was guilty" (14).

Two psy-fi time tracks emerge out of this mix of testimony to the racism and integration in *Five Car Stud*. One belongs to the internal text, the other to the editorial commentary. Vachez addresses a leitmotif of French thought: the pathogenic entrapment of "Germany" throughout modernity gave rise to German inventions of ways out of historical spacetime. "If a people can't succeed in satisfying its demands for territorial unity, . . . this people will seek out and will find an identity in some spacetime other than that of the political history of occupations of the soil" (49). The rocket's takeoff is an advance preview of space travel that goes unmentioned here. But it parallels (and in theory outflies) what is thematized instead—the deterritorialization in which Germans and Jews are doubles. Their showdown was the Holocaust, the murderous expulsion of the adherents to a prior claim to election that bars the way for a German establishment of territory in another spacetime.

The editor of the internal text ultimately decodes Vachez's repeated evocation of the imperial racism of white skin. The endless permutations of violation skewer the western or West Coast woman and the greasy foreigner (i.e., teenager and midlifer) as the prospect of a new spacetime of digital mediation and doubling. (Everything but the rocket is folded into this saving trace.) It is the limit or wall of the Pacific coast that reverses all tendencies up to this point and communicates the change, like the blank plinth in *2001: A Space Odyssey*. Up against the Pacific wall, our question can no longer hinge on the occupation of lands or resources. "The issue is conquest of this or that kind of knowledge, committing it to memory, making it available, and the usefulness of this knowledge in creating new plans or developments" (57). The affirmation of the Web as a new identification setting transmits from the Pacific wall to the world as globalization or integration.

For Nietzsche, democracy was a diagnosis. Likewise for Freud and Wittgenstein—the literalization of equality represented a kind of psychotic breakdown of distinction itself, and thus of thought or language. Derrida was flown in to the Soviet Union to cosign that glasnost (the opening of a new era of integration in the Eastern Block) was indeed deconstruction. In *Specters of Marx*, he summarized the setting of the end of the Cold War in terms of haunting, the return that returns, but without the spooking of repression. No longer an outsider specialization, a scratch in the record of the media, ghostly return became all-pervasive, integrating the very stance of opposition as another return. In the US news, an African American president and an insurgent Christian Right could count among the many parts that seemed together again in a crowd of return engagements. Barack Obama's election was not so much the realization of the Civil Rights struggle—the resolution at the end of the opposition—as the return of that era in the midst of all the other returns.

The timeline of a career has intervened since the Holocaust went global and the return of German science fiction entered our screening of everyday life. (Is it possible to reverse its focus on forgiveness and extract from Derrida's reading that the psychotherapy of integration cannot amount to forgiveness? These returns belong to that psychotherapy, after all.) The Cold War opposition kept the recent past, the traumatic histories of the twentieth century, in cold pack. There was one defective cornerstone: the Middle East conflict. This protracted crisis counted as the post-Cold War world's continuity shot and open wound. It brought us closer to the truth.

In 1991, Ulrike Ottinger's *Countdown* summoned the event or advent of traumatic realization in the absence of the rocket's mention but in the midst of the admission of the grief that is otherwise withheld from science fiction. Already the title cites the formal conceit that Lang devised for the fictional takeoff of his rocket, although it was adopted for the subsequent practice, rocket by rocket, of the so-called conquest of space. Albert Einstein's attendance at the celebrated Berlin premiere of Lang's rocket film is caught in another commemoration. As *Countdown* explores Erich Mendelssohn's Einstein Tower in Potsdam, another kind of upsurge accompanies the performance of a dirge for the victims of the Nazi era. At the same time, the film is the document of the ten days leading up to a unification of the German currencies in 1990. This introduces a layering of untenably paralleled histories—what we are calling the ambivalent introject, a crucial phase in the metabolization of traumatic histories whereby the heirs to psychopathic violence approach the onset of the ability to mourn, now by reparation, now by integration.

Bramkamp's *Test Stand 7* reassembles the film history of the rocket by pulling the realized rocket back through Pynchon's *Gravity's Rainbow*. What the streamlining of science faction had deferred for German history (although all of us participate in this deferral) underwent an ambivalent introjection in the course of Pynchon's fabulation of the rocket. A score of pages following the disclosure in Gravity's Rainbow that the air war "modified, precisely, deliberately, by bombing" sites for conversion "only waiting for the right connections to be set up to be switched on" (520), Katje asks: "Is there room here for the dead?" (544). She has to correct the guilty assumption of a proper response twice over for the shame of it. Those now getting through the recent past and making it to the postwar period at the end of the sentencing recognize that "the worst part's the shame" (541). "I meant, would I be allowed to bring my dead in with me. . . . They are my credentials, after all" (545). Nor does she mean to summon her dead ancestors. "I mean the ones who owe their deadness directly to me" (ibid.). Her roundabout way of circumscribing and addressing, as she admits, the genocide—"think of the things you've done. Think of all your 'credentials,' and all mine" (546)—is suddenly recognized by her interlocutor as the medium of postwar recovery, the industry of reparation. "That's the only medium we've got now . . . our gift for bad faith. We'll have to build everything with it . . . deal it, as the prosecutors deal you your freedom" (ibid.). The closing reference to a shame that cannot be left behind, which hangs on as a corporeal connection with dead bodies, connects "building everything" to the advertised and internalized prospect of making the object of repair good again.

Daughter, love object, and object of mourning, Bianca searches in Bram-kamp's film for her origin in the rocket, but she keeps running up against the so-called oven inside it, sparking the eternal flame in a place gone without mention. The eternal or internal feminine of mourning, however, cannot draw us onward by so direct a hit. Hence the film enters the blind alley of the figure of the severed and thrown hand to mediate Bianca's search for the traumatic history internal to the rocket. The severed and thrown hand touches on the mythic signifi-cance of Antwerp, even in name, as a target of the V-2 rocket attacks. It also joins in the mystery of a photograph of Wernher von Braun, his arm in a cast, taken at the moment he was crossing the threshold to his postwar assimilation, the mystery Kubrick perhaps revalorized as the reflex salute otherwise so hard to contain in *Dr. Strangelove* (1964). From Ernst Kapp through Freud and McLuhan, the detachable hand waves through the prosthetic understanding of our relationship to technologization. In Pynchon's novel, the rocket (as in Friedrich Kittler's gene-alogy of media) opens up a technological horizon of auto-development before which the prosthetic or humanist reach of our following falls short. And yet, to the extent that technologization cannot be separated from the European culture of death diagnosed in the novel, the prosthetic relation comes to be reinserted in our effort to understand and make amends for violence that we cannot but consider as externalized in our technological relation. To make reparation, commence inte-gration, and aim for the onset of the ability to mourn, we reclaim our prosthetic responsibility for the automatic course of technologization, auto-accelerating by velocities or computations that our intellect cannot overtake.

In *Test Stand 7*, a relay of direct hits on the repressed past alternates with blind alleys of allegorization. We move closer to mourning's admission of a collective or global work. Otherwise mourning would be the prerogative of individuals or couples and group commemoration would be solely a forum of denial. Judith Butler's reconsideration of mournability and unmournability (no longer from the glamorous perspective of undeath, but from the point of view of the living) was not, then, a late arrival of the study of repressed mourning. Instead it was a timely reflection of a chance or change for the new in our setting of digitalization. In *Countdown*, the document of the first gay rights demonstration and celebration on Alexander Platz in the span of German reunification is not just a strong sign of Ottinger's basic reversal of traumatic exclusion and the affirmative embarkation upon the adventure of an encounter with the margins where reality begins. It is also another instance of the film's double take: after the opening commemoration, it doubles back to stagger and layer mourning's release within the ongoing work of integration that makes history contemporary. To address problems and processes that are, as we say, bigger than the two of us, Bramkamp brings us closer to his goal, collective narration, which must be extended to mourning. We will catch up with deferred individual mourning only if the possibility of collective mourning can be reclaimed from the denial.

BIBLIOGRAPHY

BIBLIOGRAPHY

Adorno, Theodor W. "Fernsehen als Ideologie." *Gesammelte Schriften*. Ed. Rolf Tiedemann. Vol. 10.2. Frankfurt a/M: Suhrkamp Verlag, 2003. 518-35.

————. *Negative Dialektik: Gesammelte Schriften*. Ed. Rolf Tiedemann. Vol. 6. Frankfurt a/M: Suhrkamp Verlag, 2003.

————. "Prolog zum Fernsehen." *Gesammelte Schriften*. Ed. Rolf Tiedemann. Vol. 10.2. Frankfurt a/M: Suhrkamp Verlag, 2003. 507-17.

————. "Theorie der Halbbildung." *Gesammelte Schriften*. Ed. Rolf Tiedemann. Vol. 8. Soziologische Schriften I. Frankfurt a/M: Suhrkamp Verlag, 2003. 93-121.

————. "Was bedeutet: Aufarbeitung der Vergangenheit." *Gesammelte Schriften*. Hrsg. v. Rolf Tiedemann. Band 10.2 (Kulturkritik und Gesellschaft II). Frankfurt a/M: Suhrkamp Verlag, 2003.

Anonymous. "Werner Erhard." *People* 29 (Dec. 1975): 60.

Arendt, Hannah. "The Conquest of Space and the Stature of Man." *Between Past and Future: Eight Exercises in Political Thought*. New York: Penguin Classics, 2006. 260-74.

Bachelard, Gaston. *Psychoanalyse des Feuers*. 1949. Trans. Simon Werle. Munich: Carl Hanser Verlag, 1985.

Bally, Gustav. *Vom Spielraum der Freiheit: Die Bedeutung des Spiels bei Tier und Mensch*. Basel: Schwabe, 1945.

Benjamin, Walter. "Bücher von Geisteskranken: Aus meiner Sammlung." 1928. *Gesammelte Schriften*. Ed. Rolf Tiedemann and Hermann Schweppenhäuser. Vol. 4. Frankfurt a/M: Suhrkamp Verlag, 1972. 615-16.

————. "On Some Motifs in Baudelaire." 1940. Trans. Edmund Jephcott and Others. *Selected Writings*. Ed. Howard Eiland and Michael W. Jennings. Vol. 4. Cambridge: Harvard University Press, 2003. 313-55.

————. "The Storyteller: Observations on the Works of Nicolai Leskov." 1936. Trans. Harry Zohn. *Selected Writings*. Ed. Howard Eiland and Michael W. Jennings. Vol. 3. Cambridge: Harvard University Press, 2002. 143-66.

————. "The Work of Art in the Age of Mechanical Reproduction." 1936. Trans. Harry Zohn. *Illuminations*. Ed. Hannah Arendt. New York: Schocken Books, 1969. 217-51.

————. *Ursprung des deutschen Trauerspiels: Gesammelte Schriften*. 1928. Ed. Rolf Tiedemann and Hermann Schweppenhäuser. Vol. 1, Part 1. Frankfurt a/M: Suhrkamp Verlag, 1974.

Beres, Stanislaw. *Tako rzecze Lem*. Cracow: Wyndawnictwo Literackie, 2002.

Bernays, Edward. *Propaganda*. 1928. Brooklyn: Ig Publishing, 2004.

Binswanger, Ludwig. "Der Fall Ellen West."*Ausgewählte Werke*. Vol. 4. Ed. Alice Holzhey-Kunz. Heidelberg: Roland Asanger Verlag, 1994. 73-209.

Bradbury, Ray. *Fahrenheit 451*. 1953. New York: Ballantine Books, 1991.

Bramkamp, Robert and Olga Fedianina, eds. *Project Mars: A Technical Tale*. Burlington: Collector's Guide Publishing, 2006.

Braun, Wernher von. *First Men to the Moon*. New York: Holt, Rinehart and Winston, 1960.

————. *Prüfstand 7: Das Buch zum Film*. Berlin: Maas Verlag, 2002.

————. *The Mars Project*. 1952. Urbana: University of Illinois Press, 1991.

Burgess, Anthony. *A Clockwork Orange*. 1962. New York: W. W. Norton & Company, Inc., 1995.

Butler, Judith. *Precarious Life: The Powers of Mourning and Violence*. London: Verso, 2004.

Canetti, Elias. *Masse und Macht*. 1960. Frankfurt a/M: Fischer, 1980.

Clarke, Arthur C. *Childhood's End*. 1953. New York: Ballantine Books, 1990.

————. "The Sentinel." *The Avon Science Fiction Reader*. New York: Avon, 1951.

————. "The Space-Station: Its Radio Applications." 1945. *Spaceflight* 10.3 (Mar. 1968): 85-88.

————. *2001: A Space Odyssey*. London: Hutchinson, 1968.

Cobet, Justus. *Heinrich Schliemann: Archäologe und Abenteurer*. Munich: C. H. Beck, 2007.

Crichton, Michael. *Timeline*. 1999. London: Arrow Books, 2000.

Damm, Steffan and Klaus Siebenhaar. *Ernst Liftaß und sein Erbe: Eine kulturgeschichte der Litfaßsäule*. Berlin: B & S Siebenhaar, 2005.

Danto, Arthur C. "All about Eva." *The Nation*. 17 July 2006. 30-34.

de Man, Paul. "The Rhetoric of Temporality." 1969. *Blindness and Insight: Essays in the Rhetoric of Contemporary Criticism*. Minneapolis: University of Minnesota Press, 1983. 187-228.

Derrida, Jacques. *Droit de regards*. Paris: Minuit, 1985.

———. *On Cosmopolitanism and Forgiveness*. Trans. Mark Dooley and Michael Hughes. London: Routledge, 2003.

———. *Specters of Marx: The State of the Debt, the Work of Mourning, and the New International*. 1993. Trans. Peggy Kamuf. London: Routledge, 2006.

Dick, Philip K. "Afterword." 1972. *Dr Adder*. London: Grafton Books, 1987. 248-52.

———. *Do Androids Dream of Electric Sheep?* 1968. New York: Ballantine, 1996.

———. "Introduction." *The Golden Man*. Ed. Mark Hurst. New York: Berkley Books, 1980. xv-xxviii.

———. "Man, Android, and Machine." 1976. *The Shifting Realities of Philip K. Dick: Selected Literary and Philosophical Writings*. New York: Vintage Books, 1995. 211-32.

———. *Simulacra*. Trans. Uwe Anton. Munich: Heyne, 1978.

———. "The Android and the Human." 1972. *The Shifting Realities of Philip K. Dick: Selected Literary and Philosophical Writings*. Ed. Lawrence Sutin. New York: Vintage Books, 1995. 183-210.

———. *The Exegesis of Philip K. Dick*. Ed. Pamela Jackson and Jonathan Lethem. Boston: Houghton Mifflin Harcourt, 2011.

———. *The Man in the High Castle*. 1962. New York: Vintage Books, 1992.

———. *The Man Who Japed*. 1956. New York: Vintage Books, 2002.

———. *The Selected Letters of Philip K. Dick: 1974*. Ed. Paul Williams. Novato: Underwood-Miller, 1991.

———. *The Selected Letters of Philip K. Dick: 1977-1979*. Ed. Don Herron. Novato: Underwood-Miller, 1993.

———. *The Simulacra*. 1964. New York: Vintage Books, 2002.

———. *The Transmigration of Timothy Archer*. 1982. New York: Vintage Books, 1991.

————. *Time out of Joint*. 1959. New York: Vintage Books, 2002.

————. *We Can Build You*. 1972. New York: Vintage Books, 1994.

Disch, Thomas M. *Camp Concentration*. 1969. New York: Vintage Books, 1999.

————. *Echo Round His Bones*. 1969. London: Panther, 1970.

————. "In the Mold of 1964: An Afterword." *On SF*. Ann Arbor: University of Michigan Press, 2005. 160-68.

————. *The Dreams Our Stuff Is Made Of: How Science Fiction Conquered the World*. New York: Simon & Schuster, 2000.

————. *The Genocides*. London: Pantheon Books, 1970.

Ellison, Harlan. *The Glass Teat*. New York: Ace Paperback, 1970.

Federman, Raymond. "An Interview with Stanislaw Lem." *Science Fiction Studies* 10:1 (March 1983): 2-14.

Finney, Jack. *From Time to Time*. New York: Scribner, 1996.

————. *Invasion of the Body Snatchers*. 1978. New York: Scribner Paperbacks, 1998.

————. *Time and Again*. 1970. New York: Touchstone, 1995.

Foulkes, S. H. "Observation on the Significance of the Name in a Schizophrenic." *Selected Papers: Psychoanalysis and Group Analysis*. Ed. Elizabeth Foulkes. London: Karnac Books, 2004.

Freud, Sigmund. "Creative Writers and Day-Dreaming." *The Standard Edition of the Complete Psychological Works*. Ed. and trans. James Strachey. Vol. 9. London: The Hogarth Press, 1961. 143-53.

————. "Fetishism." 1927. *The Standard Edition of the Complete Psychological Works*. Ed. and trans. James Strachey. Vol. 21. London: The Hogarth Press, 1961. 152-57.

————. *Group Psychology and the Analysis of the Ego*. 1921. *The Standard Edition of the Complete Psychological Works*. Ed. and trans. James Strachey. Vol. 18. London: The Hogarth Press, 1955. 69-143.

————. "Introduction to *Psychoanalysis and the War Neuroses*." 1919. *The Standard Edition of the Complete Psychological Works of Sigmund Freud*. Ed. and trans. James Strachey. Vol. 17. London: The Hogarth Press, 1961. 207-10.

————. "Mourning and Melancholia." 1917. *The Standard Edition of the Complete Psychological Works*. Ed. and trans. James Strachey. Vol. 14. London: The Hogarth Press, 1957. 243-58.

————. "Notes upon a Case of Obsessional Neurosis." 1909. *The Standard Edition of the Complete Psychological Works*. Ed. and trans. James Strachey. Vol. 10. London: The Hogarth Press, 1955. 155-249.

————. "Psychoanalytic Notes on an Autobiographical Account of a Case of Paranoia (Dementia Paranoides)." 1911. *The Standard Edition of the Complete Psychological Works*. Ed. and trans. James Strachey. Vol. 12. London: The Hogarth Press, 1958. 9-82.

————. "Some Character-Types Met with in Psychoanalytic Work." 1916. *The Standard Edition of the Complete Psychological Works*. Ed. and trans. James Strachey. Vol. 14. London: The Hogarth Press, 1957. 311-33.

————. "The 'Uncanny.'" 1919. *The Standard Edition of the Complete Psychological Works*. Ed. and trans. James Strachey. Vol. 17. London: The Hogarth Press, 1955. 219-52.

————. "Thoughts for the Times on War and Death." 1919. *The Standard Edition of the Complete Psychological Works*. Ed. and trans. James Strachey. Vol. 14. London: The Hogarth Press, 1957. 275-300.

————. *Totem and Taboo*. 1913. *The Standard Edition of the Complete Psychological Works*. Ed. and trans. James Strachey. Vol. 13. London: The Hogarth Press, 1955. 1-162.

Galouye, Daniel. *Simulacron 3*. New York: Bantam, 1964.

Godfrey, Mark. "A String of Nots: Eva Hesse's Hanging Sculpture." *Eva Hesse: Sculpture*. Ed. Elisabeth Sussman and Fred Wasserman. New Haven: Yale University Press, 2006. 29-52.

Goethe, Johann Wolfgang von. *Faust*. In *Werke*. Ed. Paul Stapf. Vol. 3. Berlin: Deutsche Buch-Gemeinschaft, 1963.

Gould, Stephen Jay. "A Biological Homage to Mickey Mouse." *The Panda's Thumb: More Reflections in Natural History*. New York: W. W. Norton & Company, Inc., 1980. 93-107.

Green, Julian. *If I Were You*. Trans. J. H. P. McEwen. London: Eyre and Spottiswoode, 1950.

————. *Memories of Happy Days*. New York: Harper & Brothers, 1942.

————. *The Apprentice Writer: Essays*. London: Marion Boyars, 1993.

Günther, Gotthard. "Achilles and the Tortoise." 1954. Günther Electronic Archive. 1997. Web.

————. *Das Bewusstsein der Maschinen: Eine Metaphysik der Kybernetik*.

Baden-Baden: Agis, 2002.

———. "Die Entdeckung Amerikas und die Sache mit der Weltraumliteratur." *Weltraum-Bücher*. Ed. Gotthard Günther. Düsseldorf: Verlag von Karl Rauch, 1952.

———. "The SEETEE Mind." 1954. Günther Electronic Archive. 2010. Web.

Heidegger, Martin. "Bauen Wohnen Denken." *Vorträge und Aufsätze*. Pfullingen: Verlag Günther Neske, 1954. 139-56.

———. "Building Dwelling Thinking." *Poetry, Language, Thought*. Trans. Albert Hofstadter. New York: Harper, 2001. 143-59.

Heinlein, Robert. *Farnham's Freehold*. Riverdale: Baen Publishing Enterprises, 2011.

———. *Rocketship Galileo*. 1947. London: New English Library, 1971.

———. *Starship Troopers*. 1959. New York: Ace, 1987.

———. *The Puppet Masters*. 1951. Riverdale: Baen Publishing Enterprises, 2010.

———. *Time for the Stars*. 1956. London: Pan Books, 1968.

Huxley, Aldous. *Brave New World*. 1932. New York: Harper Collins, 1989.

Jeter, K. W. *Dr. Adder*. London: Grafton Books, 1987.

Jones, Ernest. *On the Nightmare*. London: The Hogarth Press, 1949.

Jones, Raymond F. *This Island Earth*. 1952. London: Grafton Books, 1991.

Jung, C. G. "America Facing Its Most Tragic Moment." 1912. Trans. R. F. C. Hull. *C. G. Jung Speaking: Interviews and Encounters*. Ed. William McGuire and R. F. C. Hull. Princeton: Princeton University Press, 1977. 11-24.

———. *Analytical Psychology: Its Theory & Practice*. Trans. R. F. C. Hull. New York: Vintage Books, 1970.

———. *The Psychology of Dementia Praecox*. Trans. R. F. C. Hull. Princeton: Princeton University Press, 1974.

Kapp, Ernst. *Grundlinien einer Philosophie der Technik*. Braunschweig: Verlag George Westermann, 1877.

Kerouac, Jack. *On the Road*. 1957. London: Penguin Books, 2000.

Kittler, Friedrich. "Auto Bahnen." *KultuRRevolution: Zeitschrift für angewandte diskurstheorie* 5 (Feb. 1984): 44-47.

———. "Flechsig/Schreber/Freud: An Informations Network of 1910." *Qui Parle* 2.1 (Spring 1988): 1-17.

———. *Grammophon Film Typewriter*. Berlin: Brinkmann & Bose, 1986.

———. "Medien und Drogen in Pynchons Zweitem Weltkrieg." *Prüfstand 7:*

Das Buch zum Film. Ed. Robert Bramkamp and Olga Fedianina. Berlin: Maas Verlag, 2002. 51-64.

———. "Romantik—Psychoanalyse—Film: eine Doppelgängergeschichte." *Draculas Vermächtnis*: *Technische Schriften*. Leipzig: Reclam Verlag, 1993. 81-104.

Kittler, Friedrich and Gerhard Kaiser. *Dichtung als Sozialisationsspiel*. Göttingen: Vandenhoeck & Ruprecht: 1978.

Klein, Melanie. "A Contribution to the Psychogenesis of Manic-Depressive States." 1940. *Love, Guilt and Reparation and Other Works: 1921-1945*. New York: The Free Press, 1984. 262-89.

———. "Early Stages of the Oedipus Complex." 1940. *Love, Guilt and Reparation and Other Works: 1921-1945*. New York: The Free Press, 1984. 186-98.

———. "Envy and Gratitude." *Envy and Gratitude and Other Works: 1946-1963*. New York: The Free Press, 1984: 176-235.

———. "On Identification." 1955. *Envy and Gratitude and Other Works: 1946-1963*. New York: The Free Press, 1984. 141-75.

———. "Mourning and Its Relation to Manic-Depressive States." 1940. *Love, Guilt and Reparation and Other Works: 1921-1945*. New York: The Free Press, 1984. 344-69.

———. *Narrative of a Child Analysis: The Conduct of the Psychoanalysis of Children as Seen in the Treatment of a Ten-Year-Old Boy*. 1961. New York: The Free Press, 1984.

———. "On the Sense of Loneliness." 1963. *Envy and Gratitude and Other Works: 1946-1963*. New York: The Free Press, 1984. 300-13.

———. "Some Reflections on *The Oresteia*." 1963. *Envy and Gratitude and Other Works: 1946-1963*. New York: The Free Press, 1984. 275-99.

———. "The Importance of Symbol Formation in the Development of the Ego." 1930. *Love, Guilt and Reparation and Other Works: 1921-1945*. New York: The Free Press, 1984. 219-32.

Kohner, Frederick. *Gidget*. 1957. New York: Berkley Books, 2001.

———. *The Magician of Sunset Boulevard: The Improbable Life of Paul Kohner, Hollywood Agent*. Palos Verdes: Morgan Press, 1977.

Krystal, Henry, ed. *Massive Psychic Trauma*. New York: International Universities Press, 1968.

Kuhn, Roland. "Mordversuch eines depressiven Fetischisten und Sodomisten an einer Dirne." *Monatsschrift für Psychiatrie und Neurologie.* Vol. 116. Basel: Karger, 1948. 66-155.

———. "The Attempted Murder of a Prostitute." Trans. Ernest Angel. *Existence: A New Dimension in Psychiatry and Psychology.* Ed. Rollo May, Ernest Angel, and Henri F. Ellenberger. New York: Basic Books, 1958. 365-425.

Lacan, Jacques. "Desire and the Interpretation of Desire in *Hamlet.*" 1977. Trans. James Hulbert. *Literature and Psychoanalysis: The Question of Reading: Otherwise.* Ed. Shoshana Felman. Baltimore: The Johns Hopkins University Press, 1982. 11-52.

———. *Le Seminaire, Livre VII: L'ethique de la psychanalyse (1959-1960).* Paris: Éditions du Seuil, 1986.

———. "Le stade du miroir comme formateur de la fonction du Je." *Écrits.* Paris: Éditions du Seuil, 1966: 93-100.

———. *Télévision.* Paris: Éditions du Seuil, 1974.

Langelaan, George. "The Fly." *Playboy* 4.6 (June 1957): 17-18, 22, 36, 38, 46, 64-68.

———. *The Masks of War.* Garden City: Doubleday & Company, 1959.

Laßwitz, Kurd. *Auf zwei Planeten.* 1897. Munich: Wilhelm Heyne Verlag, 1998.

———. *Gustav Theodor Fechner.* Stuttgart: Fr. Frommanns Verlag, 1902.

———. *Two Planets.* Trans. Hans H. Rudnick. Carbondale: Southern Illinois University Press, 1971.

Le Guin, Ursula K. "On Norman Spinrad's *The Iron Dream.*" *Science Fiction Studies* 1.1 (Spring 1973): 41-44.

———. *The Lathe of Heaven.* London: Grafton, 1974.

Lem, Stanislaw. "Metafantasia: The Possibilities of Science Fiction." Trans. Etelka de Laczay and Istvan Csicsery-Ronay, Jr. *Science-Fiction Studies* 8.1 (March 1981): 54-71.

———. *Solaris.* 1961. Trans. (from the French) Joanna Kilmartin and Steve Cox. Boston: Mariner Books, 2002.

Levin, Ira. *The Stepford Wives.* New York: Random House, 1972.

Lorenz, Konrad. *Studies in Animal and Human Behavior.* Cambridge: Harvard University Press, 1971.

Lyotard, Jean-François. *Pacific Wall.* 1979. Trans. Bruce Boone. Venice: The Lapis Press, 1990.

Matheson, Richard. *Somewhere in Time.* 1975. New York: Tor, 2008.

McKinnon, E. Luanne. "Preface." *Eva Hesse Spectres 1960*. New Haven: Yale University Press, 2010.

McLuhan, Marshall. *Understanding Media: The Extensions of Man*. New York: Signet, 1964.

Moore, Ward. *Bring the Jubilee*. 1953. London: Gollancz, 2001.

Morgenthau, Henry. *Germany is Our Problem*. New York: Harper & Brothers, 1945.

Murphy, Pat. "Rachel in Love." *Asimov's Science Fiction* 11.4 (April 1987): 70-95.

Nolan, William F. and George Clayton. *Logan's Run*. 1967. New York: Bantam, 1976.

Orwell, George. *Nineteen Eighty-Four*. 1949. Orlando: Harcourt Brace, 2003.

Pavlov, Ivan P. *Psychopathology and Psychiatry*. Trans. D. Myshne and S. Belsky. New Brunswick: Transaction, 1994.

Penley, Constance. "Time Travel, Primal Scene, and the Critical Dystopia." *Close Encounters: Film, Feminism, and Science Fiction*. Ed. Constance Penley, Elisabeth Lyon, Lynn Spigel, and Janet Bergstrom. Minneapolis: University of Minnesota Press, 1991. 63-80.

Pynchon, Thomas. "Foreword." George Orwell. *Nineteen Eighty-Four*. Orlando: Harcourt Brace, 2003. vii-xxvi.

———. *Gravity's Rainbow*. New York: The Viking Press, 1973.

———. *V.* 1963. London: Vintage Books, 2000.

Rank, Otto. *The Myth of the Birth of the Hero: A Psychological Interpretation of Mythology*. 1909. Trans. F. Robbins and Smith Ely Jelliffe. In *The Myth of the Birth of the Hero and Other Writings*. Ed. Philip Freund. New York: Vintage Books, 1959. 1-96.

Rickels, Laurence A. *I Think I Am: Philip K. Dick*. Minneapolis: University of Minnesota Press, 2010.

———. *Nazi Psychoanalysis*. Minneapolis: University of Minnesota Press, 2002.

———. *SPECTRE*. Fort Wayne: Anti Oedipus Press, 2013.

———. "Spooky Electricity: An Interview with Friedrich Kittler." *Artforum International* 31:4 (Dec. 1992): 66-70.

———. *The Devil Notebooks*. Minneapolis: University of Minnesota Press, 2008.

Ronell, Avital. *Loser Sons: Politics and Authority*. Urbana: University of Illinois Press, 2012.

————. *The Test Drive*. Urbana: University of Illinois Press, 2005.

Sachs, Hanns. "The Delay of the Machine Age." 1933. *The Creative Unconscious: Studies in the Psychoanalysis of Art*. Cambridge: Sci-Art Publishers, 1942. 100-31.

Sagan, Carl. *Contact*. New York: Simon & Schuster, 1986.

Schmitt, Carl. *Hamlet oder Hekuba: Der Einbruch der Zeit in das Spiel*. Stuttgart: Kletta-Cotta, 1985.

Shakespeare, William. *The Tragedy of Macbeth*. 1606. Ed. Eugene M. Waith. New Haven: Yale University Press, 1954.

Sontag, Susan. "Syberberg's Hitler." 1980. *Under the Sign of Saturn*. New York: Picador, 2002. 137-65.

————. "The Imagination of Disaster." 1965. *Against Interpretation and Other Essays*. London: Penguin Classics, 2009. 209-25.

Spinrad, Norman. "On Books: *The Word of God* by Thomas M. Disch."*Asimov's Science Fiction* April-May 1974: Web.

Stapledon, Olaf. *Sirius: A Fantasy of Love and Discord*. 1944. London: Penguin Books, 1979.

Stein, Gertrude. *Everybody's Autobiography*. 1937. New York: Cooper's Square, 1971.

Sternfeld, Felicia H. "Scholz, Walter Hans *Georg* Curt." *Neue Deutsche Biographie* 23 (2007): 457-58.

Sussman, Elisabeth. "Eva Hesse: Sculpture 1968." *Eva Hesse: Sculpture*. Ed. Elisabeth Sussman and Fred Wasserman. New Haven: Yale University Press, 2006.

Tausk, Viktor. "On the Origin of the 'Influencing Machine' in Schizophrenia." 1919. Trans. Dorian Feigenbaum. *Sexuality, War and Schizophrenia: Collected Psychoanalytic Papers*. Ed. Paul Roazen. New Brunswick: Transaction, 1991. 185-220.

Tevis, Walter. *The Man Who Fell to Earth*. 1963. New York: Del Rey, 1991.

Theweleit, Klaus. *Männerphantasien*. 1977. Munich: Piper Taschenbuch, 2000.

Thompson, James. "Should I Sacrifice to Live 'Half-American?'" *Pittsburgh Courier* 7 Feb. 1942: 5.

Turing, Alan. "Computing Machinery and Intelligence." *Mind: A Quarterly Review of Psychology* 59.236 (October 1950): 433-60.

Verne, Jules. *From the Earth to the Moon; and, Round the Moon*. 1865; 1870.

Charleston: Bibliobazaar, 2007.

Vonnegut, Kurt. *Slaughterhouse-Five*. New York: Random House, 1969.

Walter, W. Grey. *The Living Brain*. 1953. New York: The Norton Library, 1963.

Warburg, Aby. *Schlangenritual: Ein Reisebericht.* Berlin: Verlag Klaus Wagenbach, 1988.

Wells, H. G. *Experiment in Autobiography: Discoveries and Conclusions of a Very Ordinary Brain (since 1866)*. New York: Macmillan, 1934.

———. *The First Men in the Moon*. 1901. In *Seven Famous Novels by H. G. Wells*. Minneapolis: Amaranth Press, 1979. 391-528.

———. *The Invisible Man*. 1897. New York: Dover Publications, 1992.

———. *The Island of Dr. Moreau*. 1896. New York: Dover Publications, 1996.

———. *The Time Machine*. 1895. Garden City: Dolphin/Doubleday, 1961.

———. *The War of the Worlds*. 1897. In *Seven Famous Novels by H. G. Wells*. New York: Alfred A. Knopf, 1979. 265-388.

Werfel, Franz. *Star of the Unborn*. Trans. Gustave O. Arlt. New York: The Viking Press, 1946.

Wiener, Norbert. *Cybernetics: Or Control and Communication in the Animal and the Machine*. 1948. Cambridge: The MIT Press, 1965.

———. *The Human Use of Human Beings: Cybernetics and Society*. Garden City: Doubleday, 1954.

Winnicott, D. W. "Contemporary Concepts of Adolescent Development." 1968. *Playing and Reality*. Hove: Brunner-Routledge, 2002. 138-50.

———. "Deductions Drawn from a Psychotherapeutic Interview with an Adolescent." 1964. *Psychoanalytic Explorations*. Ed. Clare Winnicott, Ray Shepherd and Madeleine Davis. Cambridge: Harvard University Press, 1992. 325-40.

———. "Delinquency as a Sign of Hope." *Home Is Where We Start From: Essays by a Psychoanalyst*. New York: W. W. Norton & Company, 1990. 90-100.

———. *Human Nature*. 1988. London: Free Association Books, 1999.

———. "Struggling through the Doldrums." 1963. *Deprivation and Delinquency*. Ed. Clare Winnicott, Ray Shepherd and Madeleine Davis. London and New York: Routledge, 2000. 145-55.

———. "The Antisocial Tendency." 1956. *Deprivation and Delinquency*. Ed. Clare Winnicott, Ray Shepherd and Madeleine Davis. London: Routledge, 2000. 120-31.

———. "The Psychology of Separation." 1958. *Deprivation and Delinquency*.

Ed. Clare Winnicott, Ray Shepherd and Madeleine Davis. London: Routledge, 2000. 132-35.

———. "The Use of an Object and Relating through Identifications." 1968. *Playing and Reality*. Hove: Brunner-Routledge, 2002. 86-94.

———. "Transitional Objects and Transitional Phenomena." 1951. *Playing and Reality*. Hove: Brunner-Routledge, 2002. 1-25.

Wyndham, John. *Plan for Chaos*. Ed. David Ketterer and Andy Sawyer. London: Penguin Books, 2010.

———. *The Day of the Triffids*. 1951. New York: The Modern Library, 2003.

———. *The Midwich Cuckoos*. 1957. London: Penguin Books, 2008.

———. *The Secret People*. 1935. New York: Lancer Books, 1964.

———. *Trouble with Lichen*. 1960. London: Penguin Books, 2008.

Ziegler, Thomas. *Die Stimmen der Nacht*. Frankfurt a/M: Ullstein, 1984.

———. *Stimmen der Nacht*. Munich: Wilhelm Heyne Verlag, 1993.

Žižek, Savoj and Mladen Dolar. *Opera's Second Death*. London: Routledge, 2002.

IMAGES

Eva Hesse, *Untitled*, 1960. Double Bride of Undeath. (The Estate of Eva Hesse.)

Eva Hesse, *Untitled*, Rope Piece, 1970. Remaking an earlier piece more properly Hesse-lich. (The Estate of Eva Hesse.)

Georg Scholz, *Selbstbildnis vor der Litfaßsäule*, 1926. Wrapping a place for absence. (Staatliche Kunsthalle Karlsruhe.)

Robert Bramkamp, *Prüfstand 7*, Still, 2002. The ghost of Friedrich A. Kittler. (Robert Bramkamp.)

Stephen G. Rhodes, *Interregnum Repetition Restoration: Lincoln*, Still, 2008. Nothing to lose but your whips. (Stephen G. Rhodes.)

Stephen G. Rhodes, *The Law of the Unknown Neighbor*, Still, 2013. The underworld's standard of exchange. (Stephen G. Rhodes.)

Robert Bramkamp, *Prüfstand 7*, Still, 2002. Bianca contemplates the "oven." (Robert Bramkamp.)

Ken Weaver, "On the 2nd of December," 2014.

LAURENCE A. RICKELS moved to the Coast in 1981 after completing his graduate training in German philology at Princeton University. In California, he earned a psychotherapy license. He has published numerous studies of the phenomenon he calls "unmourning," a term that became the title of his trilogy *Aberrations of Mourning*, *The Case of California*, and *Nazi Psychoanalysis*. He has also written two "course books," *The Vampire Lectures* and *The Devil Notebooks*, as well as *I Think I Am: Philip K. Dick*, a schizoanalysis of the science fiction author's life and work, and *SPECTRE*, a psychoanalytic study of the James Bond oeuvre. Rickels is Emeritus Professor of German and Comparative Literature at the University of California-Santa Barbara. Currently he is Professor of Art and Theory at the Academy of Fine Arts-Karlsruhe and Sigmund Freud Professor of Media and Philosophy at the European Graduate School. Visit him online at LARickels.com.

GERMANY